Economic Complexity and Evolution

Research on the dynamics and evolution of economies and their subsystems has increasingly attracted attention during the past three decades. Micro-level activities related to innovation, imitation, adoption and adaptation are sources of often important impulses for abrupt as well as continuous, local as well as generic, systemic as well as modular changes in mesoeconomic and macroeconomic structures. These changes driven by selection and co-evolution, by path-dependencies and lock-ins as well as by transitions and jumps in turn feedback to the system's microeconomic units. Out of this a highly interconnected system of interaction between agents, subsystems and levels of aggregation emerges and confronts researchers with the challenges to grasp, reduce and understand the complexity and her dynamics involved. The series "Economic Complexity and Evolution" addresses this wide field of economic and social phenomena and attempts to publish work which comprehensively discusses special topics therein allowing for a broad spectrum of different methodological viewpoints and approaches.

All titles in this series are peer-reviewed.

This book series is indexed in Scopus.

Ulrich Wilke

Towards Sustainable Innovations

Knowledge Processes and the Role of Proximity

Springer

Ulrich Wilke
Dissertation University of Hohenheim,
D100
Reutlingen University
Reutlingen, Baden-Württemberg, Germany

ISSN 2199-3173 ISSN 2199-3181 (electronic)
Economic Complexity and Evolution
ISBN 978-3-032-31023-1 ISBN 978-3-032-31024-8 (eBook)
https://doi.org/10.1007/978-3-032-31024-8

This Springer imprint is published by the registered company Springer Nature Switzerland AG
The registered company address is: Gewerbestrasse 11, 6330 Cham, Switzerland

To
Janine, Lotta and Frida

Preface and Acknowledgments

The following book addresses a subject that matters now more than ever: How can we live more sustainable and preserve earth for the generations to come. Despite the grim outlook painted by numerous current developments, I am optimistic. We can achieve sustainability and one pivotal element is knowledge-based innovation. That is what I focused on during my doctorate, and the result is this book. It took me more than five years. Years which were at times frustrating, at times very exciting, always demanding and never boring.

I owe deep gratitude to my supervisors, who made this book possible. Prof. Dr. Andreas Pyka, who has guided me in my academic and intellectual development. And my second advisor Prof. Dr. Stephan Seiter, who constantly supported and encouraged me. I'd also like to thank Prof. Dr. Andreas Kuckertz in his role as chair of the examination committee.

During the years of my doctorate, I worked with many smart people. I would like to especially mention Dr. Matthias Müller, Dr. Sophie Urmetzer and Dr. Michael Schlaile, from whom I learned quite a bit.

I am deeply grateful to my parents, Gertrud Wilke and Prof. Dr. Kay-Michael Wilke, and my brothers, Bernhard Wilke and Christian Wilke, who have always been there for me. I could always count on them, no matter what.

Finally: I can hardly put into words how grateful I am to my wife Janine and my daughters Lotta and Frida. Your love and patience carried me through the years of my doctorate. And more important: You reminded me there's life beyond the thesis. You are the reasons I remain optimistic.

Pfullingen, Germany
March 2026

Ulrich Wilke

Competing Interests The author has no competing interests to declare that are relevant to the content of this manuscript.

Contents

List of Figures

List of Tables

Chapter 1
Introduction

1.1 Humanity and the Path toward Sustainability

Humanity's current production and consumption patterns are unsustainable. Our economic system is for most parts based on technology-led industrial mass production which requires the extraction of enormous quantities of fossil, mineral, and renewable resources, consumes tremendous amounts of energy, and produces vast amounts of waste and greenhouse gases, leading to biodiversity loss, environmental degradation, and global warming. While technological advancements and economic progress have brought social benefits and material prosperity for many, there are still hundreds of millions of people living in poverty. At the same time, there are rising inequality and persistent threats of economic crisis and uncertainty. The existing sociotechnical systems designed to fulfill humanity's fundamental requirements regarding food, drinking water, housing, energy, transportation, materials, and so on, appear as socially, environmentally, and economically unsustainable (Schot & Steinmueller, 2018).

History knows numerous examples of human civilizations declining as a result of mutually reinforcing environmental, social, and economic problems that caused disasters with catastrophic consequences (see for example ProClim, 1997, Diamond, 2005). Unlike the historic examples, humanity today is interconnected on a global scale, through trade in goods and services, capital flows, the exchange of ideas and knowledge, but also through the existence of global environmental threats such as global warming. The question about a sustainable economic system today is linked to keeping planet Earth in a stable state that makes humanity's survival likely while promising prosperity and social security to the majority of people (compare Dixson-Declève et al., 2022; Rockström et al., 2009). It is about the need to get away from a system that is depleting the world's natural resources at an alarming rate, causing environmental pollution and climate change, while producing severe inequalities regarding wealth, opportunities, and security, and keeping a bottom billion in extreme

U. Wilke, *Towards Sustainable Innovations*, Economic Complexity and Evolution,
https://doi.org/10.1007/978-3-032-31024-8_1

poverty (Collier, 2008), where they are left extremely vulnerable to global crises such as the COVID-19 Pandemic (see World Bank, 2020).

Although there is widespread awareness of this grand challenge (see Schlaile et al., 2017), with some authors claiming that the need for drastic changes toward sustainability has already reached the political mainstream (Steward, 2012), we are far away from seeing a significant turn toward sustainability on a global scale (see for example Richardson et al., 2023; United Nations - Department of Economic and Social Affairs (DESA), 2023). The reasons are manifold and elucidate the difficulty of mastering the necessary transformation toward sustainability on a comprehensive, global scale.

Delving into possible strategies for achieving a change of the prevailing socioeconomic and technological paradigm that steers the global economy (confer Dosi, 1982), innovations move into the focus of attention. Innovations as drivers of economic progress and societal change have a prominent place on economists' research agenda, not least since Schumpeter's seminal works shed light on the role of novel technologies, processes, and approaches for economic development.[1] However, innovations are not per se conducive to a transformation toward sustainability. On the contrary, much of the current environmental problems stem from processes induced by industrial innovations. It is thus necessary to distinguish between different kinds of innovations and take a detailed look at so-called sustainable innovations, which are innovations that bear positive impacts on the different aspects of sustainability, including its social and environmental dimensions. Such sustainable innovations seem to be powerful instruments to trigger radical, systemic change toward more sustainable modes of production and consumption.

1.2 Research Design

1.2.1 Aim and Scope

Based on the understanding that the transformation toward sustainability is one of the grand challenges of our time, this study aims to analyze the occurrence of sustainable innovations by examining the underlying knowledge and the corresponding processes of knowledge creation and transfer. Knowledge in this regard is considered to be the foundation of every innovation (Acs et al., 2017; Arbo & Benneworth, 2007; Lundvall, 2016). However, knowledge is no easy object of research. It is highly dynamic, and defining or capturing the stock of knowledge at a certain point in time of a specific actor is a cumbersome issue with questionable relevance. It thus appears fruitful to concentrate on knowledge processes and the factors that shape and influence them.

[1] See Schumpeter (1997), which was originally published in 1911/1912, and Schumpeter (1994), which was originally published in 1942.

In the context of sustainable innovations, these processes involve a wide range of different stakeholders, who interact, exchange knowledge, create and co-create new knowledge together, engage in interactive learning, and thereby lay the ground for the emergence of novel technologies, practices, frameworks, or institutions that diffuse and are being applied, and thus become innovations with positive economic, social, and environmental impacts. This study examines the knowledge-related interactions of stakeholders of varying types for the purpose of getting a better understanding of the occurrence of sustainable innovations. By understanding the factors that are relevant regarding the collaboration of different partners, it seems plausible to be able to better explain why knowledge (co-) creation and knowledge transfer for sustainable innovations work better in some cases than in others.

For analyzing the processes of knowledge creation and transfer in multi-actor constellations, the concept of proximity is a powerful analytical tool.[2] It can be used to analyze and describe various aspects of inter-agent relations that are relevant for knowledge-based collaboration and joint innovation projects. Covering various dimensions, it serves to examine geographical, cognitive, institutional, organizational, and social features of different actor constellations and the relationships between specific actors. A main focus of this study is thus the utilization of proximity as an analytical framework to gain insights into the knowledge processes that lead to sustainable innovations.

1.2.2 Research Questions

The study deals with a complex and multifaceted topic. Based on the aim and topic of the study, the investigation was guided by several different research questions, which are listed in the following:

Is there a specific knowledge base considered necessary for sustainable innovations?

Are there specific knowledge types that are deemed particularly relevant for sustainable innovations?

Do the knowledge processes connected to sustainable innovations show any idiosyncrasies or particular features?

Which proximity dimensions are deemed relevant for knowledge processes related to sustainable innovations?

What are the working mechanisms and effects of the different proximity dimensions?

What are common combinations regarding the levels of the different proximity dimensions?

Are there connections between the specific features of the sustainability-related knowledge processes and the different proximity dimensions?

[2] See for example Boschma (2005), Balland et al. (2015), Knoben and Oerlemans (2006), as well as Chapter 7 for more details.

The answers to these questions shall provide novel insights into the factors and processes that shape and influence knowledge processes relevant for the occurrence of sustainable innovations. The approach and methodology for answering these questions are outlined in the next chapter.

1.2.3 Methodology

The methodology for answering the above-listed research questions is based on the theoretical foundation laid by the innovation system approach, which was widely introduced into economic theory by seminal works of authors such as Lundvall (1992), Nelson (1993), and Cooke (1992). The innovation system approach emphasizes the interplay of various elements, actors, and institutions, that shape the creation and diffusion of new knowledge and subsequently the occurrence of innovations. Rooted in the field of evolutionary economics, this approach is particularly suitable for analyzing dynamic processes of change within complex systems.

The study furthermore draws extensively from findings of sustainability science.[3] Being a comparably young scientific discipline, with a considerable level of epistemological and methodological variety, sustainability science seeks to integrate findings and methods from various other fields of research including economics, humanities, and natural science, to explain the complex challenges related to sustainability (Wiek et al., 2012).

Several different steps were conducted in this study to answer the research questions (Fig. 1.1). The starting point was the conceptual clarification of key terms such as sustainability, sustainable innovations, knowledge, knowledge creation, and knowledge transfer. This implies theoretical considerations about the corresponding innovation systems and the involved actors, the relevant knowledge types for sustainability-oriented innovations, and the specific features of the corresponding knowledge processes. Based on an analysis of the pertinent literature, the key aspects and central relations were identified.

A systematic literature review with an exploratory character was the next step. For identifying relevant elements, working mechanisms, and interdependencies for answering the research questions, relevant publications were searched via an approach informed by Palmatier et al. (2018) and Tranfield et al. (2003). The search was conducted in the databases Web of Science and Scopus, covering the terms knowledge, innovation, and sustainability.[4] The analysis and subsequent findings of

[3] A detailed description of this branch of research is provided by Kates et al. (2001).

[4] The exact search terms were "TS=((universit* OR "Higher education institution" OR HEI) AND sustainab* AND innovatio* AND knowledge)" for Web of Science, and "TITLE-ABS-KEY((universit* OR "Higher education institution" OR HEI) AND sustainab* AND innovatio* AND knowledge)" for Scopus. The search yielded 684 journal articles (exclusion of conference papers, book chapters and other publications), of which 96 articles were deemed relevant and read in detail.

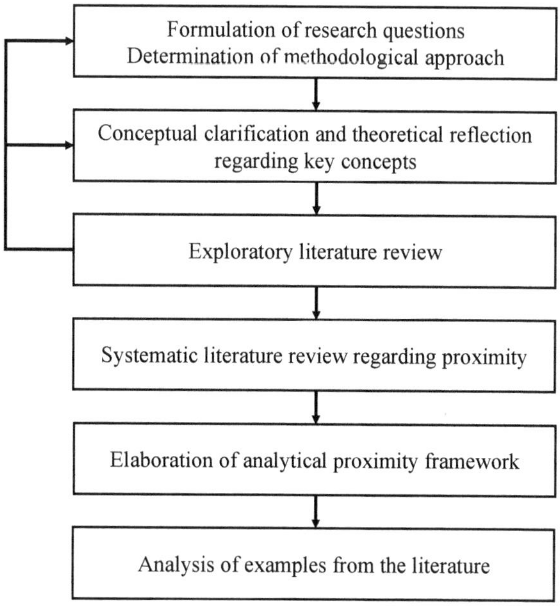

Fig. 1.1 Research design

this review helped in refining the conceptual clarifications of key issues and the identification of their central aspects. It furthermore provided valuable conclusions for identifying research gaps and thus contributed to formulating the research questions more precisely and informed the succeeding methodological approach for answering them.

The next step for analyzing the multi-actor knowledge processes was to utilize the concept of proximity, which is rooted in the field of economic geography. Based upon the presentation of the theoretical foundation of the concept, a systematic literature review was done to gain a comprehensive overview of the concept's use in the literature dealing with sustainable innovations. The methodology and detailed findings of this literature review are presented in Chapter 7.

Based upon the findings of the literature review and taking into account the findings of the conceptual and theoretical considerations, a refined analytical proximity framework was elaborated. This framework incorporates insights from the literature on knowledge and knowledge processes relevant in the context of sustainability, as well as insights from innovation systems theory about the knowledge-based interactions in multi-actor innovation networks. The analytical proximity framework was then used for an in-depth analysis of examples from publications examining sustainable innovations, thus providing further insight into the knowledge processes leading to sustainable innovations.

1.2.4 Outline

The rest of the study is outlined as follows. Chapter 2 deals with the concept of sustainability, which is widely applied but lacks a coherent definition or operationalization. However, due to its multidimensionality, it appears cumbersome if not futile to seek a definite, clear-cut conceptualization of the term sustainability. Based on the pertinent literature, the various aspects of the concept are elucidated and the core features relevant for this study are presented.

Chapter 3 is concerned with innovations in general, and sustainable innovations in specific. It starts with introductory considerations about the concept of innovations on a more general level and provides then an overview of different definitions of sustainable innovations, as well as a presentation of key aspects of the different approaches.

The following Chapter 4 provides an introduction to innovation systems theory by discussing key definitions, assumptions, and theoretical constructs. It gives an overview of different existing types of innovation systems and levels of analysis, namely national, regional, and technological or sectoral innovation systems. It then provides insights into the specific features of innovation systems that bear sustainable innovations and finally presents considerations regarding the actors in such sustainable innovation systems.

Knowledge is the central topic of Chapters 5 and 6. Chapter 5 gives an introduction, covering central theoretical and epistemological aspects and presenting different approaches for elaborating knowledge typologies. It furthermore deals with the economic perspective of treating knowledge as a commodity with all its implications and the resulting difficulties. Chapter 5 closes by presenting findings regarding knowledge types that are deemed especially relevant for investigations in the context of sustainability.

Chapter 6 sheds light on the processes of knowledge creation and transfer. The first part of this chapter gives an overview of more general considerations regarding these processes. The second part concentrates on the findings regarding processes that are supposed to generate and transfer sustainability-related knowledge and associated peculiarities. It provides a detailed analysis of different aspects and approaches that are deemed especially relevant for (co-)creating and transferring sustainability-related knowledge.

Chapter 7 deals with the concept of proximity. It starts with an introduction to the concept and its theoretical underpinnings, detailing the five dimensions of proximity. Next comes the systematic literature analysis, which sheds light on the concept's role in analyzing sustainable innovations, the corresponding knowledge processes, and the associated multi-actor networks. The chapter proceeds with the elaboration of a refined analytical proximity framework, based upon the findings presented in the preceding chapters. The framework is then applied to several examples from the literature. This analysis provides further insights regarding the flows of knowledge between actors in networks bearing sustainable innovations.

In Chapter 8, the findings of this study are summarized, and conclusions are drawn. Furthermore, some implications of these findings and conclusions are presented. Lastly, the shortcomings of this study are shown and avenues for further research are outlined.

References

Acs, Z. J., Audretsch, D. B., Lehmann, E. E., & Licht, G. (2017). National systems of innovation. *The Journal of Technology Transfer, 42*(5), 997–1008.

Arbo, P., & Benneworth, P. (2007). Understanding the regional contribution of higher education institutions: A literature review. OECD Education Working Papers, 9, 0–78.

Balland, P.-A., Boschma, R., & Frenken, K. (2015). Proximity and innovation: From statics to dynamics. *Regional Studies, 49*(6), 907–920.

Boschma, R. (2005). Proximity and innovation: A critical assessment. *Regional Studies, 39*(1), 61–74.

Collier, P. (2008). *The bottom billion: Why the poorest countries are failing and what can be done about it* (1. OUP paperback). Univ. Press.

Cooke, P. (1992). Regional innovation systems: Competitive regulation in the new Europe. *Geoforum, 23*(3), 365–382.

Diamond, J. M. (2005). *Collapse: How societies choose to fail or succeed*. Penguin Books.

Dixson-Declève, S., Gaffney, O., Ghosh, J., Randers, J., Rockström, J., & Stoknes, P. E. (2022). *Earth for all: A survival guide for humanity: A report to the Club of Rome (2022), fifty years after the limits of growth (1972)*. New Society Publishers.

Dosi, G. (1982). Technological paradigms and technological trajectories. *Research Policy, 11*(3), 147–162.

Kates, R. W., Clark, W. C., Corell, R., Hall, J. M., Jaeger, C. C., Lowe, I., et al. (2001). Sustainability science. *Science,* 292(5517), 641–642.

Knoben, J., & Oerlemans, L. (2006). Proximity and inter-organizational collaboration: A literature review. *International Journal of Management Reviews, 8*(2), 71–89.

Lundvall, B.-Å. (Ed.) (1992). National systems of innovation: Towards a theory of innovation and interactive learning (Paperback ed., 1. publ). Pinter.

Lundvall, B.-Å. (2016). The learning economy and the economics of *Hope:* Anthem Press.

Nelson, R. R. (Ed.). (1993). *National innovation systems: A comparative analysis*. Oxford Univ. Press.

Palmatier, R. W., Houston, M. B., & Hulland, J. (2018). Review articles: Purpose, process, and structure. *Journal of the Academy of Marketing Science, 46*(1), 1–5.

ProClim (1997). *ProClim - Research on Sustainability: ProClim - Schweizerische Akademie der Naturwissenschaften SANW.*

Richardson, K., Steffen, W., Lucht, W., Bendtsen, J., Cornell, S. E., Donges, J. F., et al. (2023). Earth beyond six of nine planetary boundaries. *Science Advances, 9*(37), eadh2458.

Rockström, J., Steffen, W., Noone, K., Persson, A., Chapin, F. S., Lambin, E. F., et al. (2009). A safe operating space for humanity. *Nature, 461*(7263), 472–475.

Schlaile, M., Urmetzer, S., Blok, V., Andersen, A., Timmermans, J., Mueller, M., et al. (2017). Innovation Systems for Transformations towards sustainability?: Taking the normative dimension seriously. *Sustainability, 9*(12, 2253), 1–20.

Schot, J., & Steinmueller, W. E. (2018). Three frames for innovation policy: R&D, systems of innovation and transformative change. *Research Policy, 47*(9), 1554–1567.

Schumpeter, J. A. (1994). *Capitalism, socialism, and democracy*. Routledge.

Schumpeter, J. A. (1997). *Theorie der wirtschaftlichen Entwicklung: Eine Untersuchung über Unternehmergewinn, Kapital, Kredit, Zins und den Konjunkturzyklus (Neunte Auflage, unveränderter Nachdruck der 1934 erschienen vierten Auflage). ProQuest Ebook Central.* Duncker & Humblot.

Steward, F. (2012). Transformative innovation policy to meet the challenge of climate change: Sociotechnical networks aligned with consumption and end-use as new transition arenas for a low-carbon society or green economy. *Technology Analysis & Strategic Management, 24*(4), 331–343.

Tranfield, D., Denyer, D., & Smart, P. (2003). Towards a methodology for developing evidence-informed management knowledge by means of systematic review. *British Journal of Management, 14*(3), 207–222.

United Nations - Department of Economic and Social Affairs (DESA) (2023). *The Sustainable Development Goals Report 2023: Special edition.*: United Nations Publications.

Wiek, A., Ness, B., Schweizer-Ries, P., Brand, F. S., & Farioli, F. (2012). From complex systems analysis to transformational change: A comparative appraisal of sustainability science projects. *Sustainability Science, 7*(S1), 5–24.

World Bank. (2020). *Poverty and shared prosperity 2020: Reversing reversals of fortune. Poverty and shared prosperity ser.* World Bank Publications.

Chapter 2
The Concept of Sustainability

2.1 Approaching a Definition of Sustainability

The basic idea that unbridled growth might lead to catastrophic consequences was introduced early in the history of classical economics. In his book *An Essay on the Principle of Population*, published in 1798, Thomas Robert Malthus (1798) argues that the needs of an exponentially growing population cannot be met in the long run by linearly growing agricultural production. He states that technological advancements increase the supply of resources, leading to higher living standards. At the same time, the surpluses induce population growth, eventually outweighing the increased supply of resources, leading to food shortages and conflicts, and consequently lower per capita endowments than initially. Today, we know that Malthus (1798) underestimated human ingenuity. So far, technological progress has outpaced population growth by far, leading to unprecedented standards of living, at least when looking at humanity on a global scale. The Industrial Revolution (and later the Green Revolution) prevented the Malthusian catastrophe from materializing. However, the underlying idea that humanity's prosperity might face constraints inherent to the land we live on is still highly relevant, maybe today more than ever.

In the middle of the twentieth century, a new concern gained widespread attention. Seminal works such as *A Sand County Almanac* by Aldo Leopold (1949) or *Silent Spring* by Rachel Carson (1962) illustrated that the Industrial Revolution, which led to widespread prosperity, might also lead to severe environmental degradation, which will then, in turn, harm humanity. The destruction of ecosystems and the spread of hazardous wastes pose serious risks to the human population. Together with a series of environmental disasters, such books stimulated public awareness about the fragility of ecosystems and the importance of their conservation as they form the basis for humanity's survival. Thus, the main concern was no longer that humanity might not be able to extract enough resources from planet Earth but rather that the processes of resource extraction and the subsequent industrial production, consumption, and the

U. Wilke, *Towards Sustainable Innovations*, Economic Complexity and Evolution,
https://doi.org/10.1007/978-3-032-31024-8_2

resulting pollutants and wastes might actively destroy the planet that we are living on, depriving humanity and most other species of the livelihoods we depend on.

During the nineteen seventies, scholarly discussion about whether constant economic growth might be feasible on a finite planet with limited resources and limited regenerative capacity gained momentum. The report *The Limits of Growth* (Meadows, Meadows, Randers, & Behrens, 1972), commissioned by the Club of Rome, received particularly high attention. But also other works such as Nicholas Georgescu-Roegen's *The Entropy Law and the Economic Process* (1971) or Ernst Friedrich Schuhmacher's *Small is Beautiful* (1973) received attention for critically examining the global economic system, its foundation based on resource extraction, its implication for the natural environment and its long-term viability. Meadows et al. (1972) argue that the interplay of population growth, agricultural and industrial production, environmental pollution, and resource depletion will lead to a situation in which the natural limits of the planet Earth are reached, potentially causing a severe economic downturn. The report was criticized for its methods and conclusions immediately after publication. However, the report's core message that the prevailing economic system is unsustainable, is not questioned today.

While the concepts of sustainability and sustainable development have been vividly discussed since the seventies, it was the so-called *Brundtland Report* (WCED, 1987) that gave a widely recognized definition of sustainable development and subsequently induced political discussions on a global scale, which resulted in a series of international high-level summits such as the *Earth Summit* in 1992, and pioneering political papers and declarations such as United Nations' *Agenda 21* (UNCED, 1992), the *Rio Declaration* (United Nations, 1992), and the formulation of *Millennium Development Goals* at the *Millennium Summit* in 2000 and eventually the *Sustainable Development Goals*, created by the United Nations General Assembly in 2015.

The *Brundtland Report* (WCED, 1987) recognizes that the natural environment limits the possibilities of economic growth, at least in the prevailing logic of growth based on ever more resource consumption. It addresses the need to simultaneously look at issues of wealth distribution and poverty reduction together with ecological concerns. The authors argue that it would not be feasible to approach one issue without the other as they are closely interlinked. They furthermore introduce an intergenerational component, stating that the needs of future generations have to be considered as well. Consequently, the report defines sustainable development as "Development that meets the needs of the present without compromising the ability of future generations to meet their own needs" (WCED, 1987, p. 16). Following this logic, Anderson et al. (2016) provide a more detailed yet still concise catalog of criteria for defining sustainability, stating that a societal course of action should feature four attributes to be called sustainable: "Meets the needs of people in the present; Meets the needs of people in the future; Reduces poverty; Conserves the planet's life support systems" (Anderson et al. 2016, p. 374). This is very much in line with the principles laid down in the *Brundtland Report* (WCED, 1987), but also explicitly addresses the natural environment.

The broad attention that the report received, and the subsequent political action should not hide the fact that today, we are far from a universally accepted definition of sustainability or sustainable development. There is no agreement regarding the scope of the concept, its specific features, or particular indicators. There are countless definitions of sustainability, which can differ considerably, depending on the context for which the definition was drafted.

At the same time, even popular definitions such as the one from the *Brundtland Report* (WCED, 1987) leave ample room for different interpretations, especially when it comes to concrete goals or recommendations for action. Looking at the report's definition, it is far from clear what people need now and what they will need in the future, as this is not a clearly defined, objective target dimension (Littig & Griessler, 2005). Even the seemingly unambiguous issue of poverty reduction, which is usually associated with sustainability, is neither easy to define nor easy to measure (Bourguignon, 2003). When it comes to the environmental aspect of sustainability, addressed as conserving planetary life support systems, it is even less clear, what is meant, in particular as we still have a limited understanding of the myriad of interdependencies characterizing Earth's biosphere (confer Redpath et al., 2013). Furthermore, the inherent tensions of the concept become obvious, as the concept of sustainability is about finding a balance between the goals and conditions of different entities, namely the people living now, the people living in the future, and the environment. And the people living now are already engaged in countless conflicts about formulating and fulfilling their needs and wants, too often at the expense of others.

Hence, it is no surprise that today, the understanding of what sustainability is and what it entails spans a broad spectrum of different meanings. It becomes evident that sustainability must be understood as a primarily normative assertion (confer Abson et al., 2014; Blättel-Mink & Kastenholz, 2005; Grunwald, 2007). Values and norms are a critical component of the concept of sustainability, as they provide the ground for formulating the needs of people now, the needs of future people, the needs of the environment, and the relation between them. In other words, sustainability can be seen as a profoundly ethical concept that connects questions about nature's value with questions about social justice and the current generations' responsibility for future generations (Miller et al., 2014). This however raises questions about whose values should be included and how they should be weighted (Anderson, Teisl, & Noblet, 2016). It is thus to be expected that the discussions about the exact scope and meaning of sustainability will continue, and hence it is questionable whether a single, precise definition of sustainability can be reached at all (Amaral et al., 2015).

2.2 Sustainability as a Normative Concept with Three Pillars

Sustainability is a highly complex, normative concept covering different, potentially conflicting, or even contradictory economic, environmental, and social objectives, based on norms, values, and ethical considerations. It has a time dimension

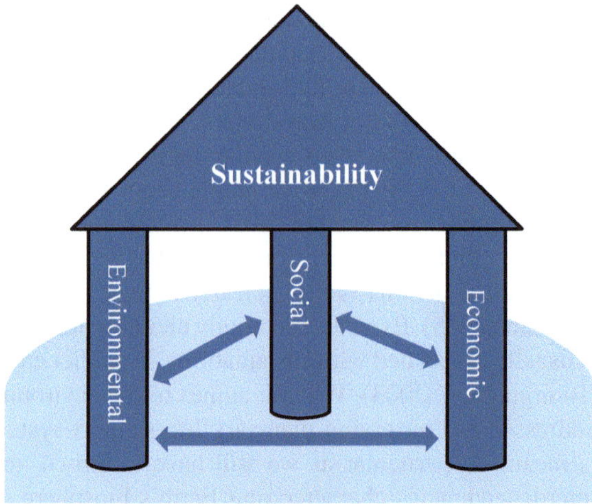

Fig. 2.1 The three pillars of sustainability

which extends into the future until an uncertain point in time, covers issues of social justice on an intra-generational and an inter-generational level (Grunwald, 2007), and refers to cause and effect relations on a global scale. These characteristics have led numerous authors to call sustainability a wicked problem (Batie, 2008; Haas et al., 2016; Wiek et al., 2012) or even a super-wicked problem (Levin et al., 2012; Wehrden et al., 2017).[1] Figure 2.1 depicts the three thematic aspects of sustainability as three interdependent pillars.

2.2.1 Economic Sustainability

The economic dimension or pillar of sustainability refers to an appropriate amount of wealth, a steady income over a continuous period, or other means that allow a certain standard of living or well-being for present and future generations. It is connected to the provision of a permanent income based on non-declining capital stocks, incorporating human, manufactured, social, and natural capital (in line with a Hicksian income, confer Goodland, 1995; Spangenberg, 2005), or put differently, the capacities of humanity to create a certain amount of welfare for all, now and in the future (Anand & Sen, 2000). The economic dimension of sustainability is

[1] The concept of wicked problems goes back to Rittel & Webber (1973), who refer to social problems that bear no easy solution. They list ten properties of a wicked problem: there is no single correct definition; there is no stopping mechanism; potential solutions are not correct or incorrect but rather good fits or bad fits; the solutions cannot be tested; it is unlikely that different solutions can be applied as the problems are 'one-shot operations'; it is not possible to formulate a set of all potential solutions; each wicked problem has its own unsurpassed characteristics; each wicked problem is closely connected to another one; the underlying discrepancies of wicked problems can be explained in different ways which impacts on the possible solutions; an authority approaching the solution of a wicked problem has no right to be wrong.

closely associated with economic growth in the sense of a rising gross domestic product (GDP) or gross national product (GNP), but also with resilient, diversified economic systems that can withstand shocks and uncertainties, promoting long-term stability by applying appropriate policies and practices that consider the long-term consequences of economic decisions.

The basic idea behind a rising GDP or GNP is that it benefits people with low incomes and increases the means for promoting human development (Anand & Sen, 2000). However, this implies that additional income is actually used for these purposes. It furthermore implies that the same goals could be reached by different means. The second implication (which of course is not a fundamentally new idea as criticisms about uncontrolled or exponential growth are very old), has gained momentum in recent years under the label of (sustainable) degrowth (see e. g. Schneider et al., 2010 or Alexander, 2012), postulating an equitable downscaling of economic activity or planned economic contraction for the sake of the natural environment, but also for improving human development and well-being.

Nonetheless, economic growth is still a universally accepted goal of policy around the globe, whereby universally accepted means that the majority within a society supports this goal. The aim is to raise the standard of living for most of a country's inhabitants. Looking at economic sustainability on a global level, the focus quickly falls on the "bottom billion" of the earth's population (Collier, 2008). Those people living in poverty or extreme poverty are left behind regarding economic development and well-being and seem to have little chance of catching up. The economic dimension of sustainability is of utmost importance for these parts of humanity. Put differently, the economies of low-income countries need to grow (economic sustainability), ideally while at the same time reducing inequality (social sustainability), avoiding environmental degradation (environmental sustainability), and thus following a comprehensively sustainable path (Dixson-Declève et al., 2022).

The situation of the low-income countries illustrates the interdependencies of the different sustainability dimensions[2] as well as the difficulties of strictly separating them. The notion of poverty reduction, or pro-poor economic growth, could also be attributed to the social dimension of sustainability. An example of a comprehensive approach from the literature in this regard is the theoretical framework developed by Arrow et al. (2012), which focuses on wealth as an indicator of the capacity to create intergenerational well-being. In this framework, wealth covers not only the conventional stocks of capital (human, natural, and reproducible) but also health capital and technological improvements, and thus a combination of economic and social aspects is seen as a vehicle for achieving sustainability.

[2] This topic is further detailed in chap. 2.4.4.

2.2.2 *Environmental Sustainability*

The environmental or ecological dimension refers to the impact of human activity on the natural environment and the biophysical systems of our planet. It covers aspects such as biodiversity loss, environmental pollution, climate change, acidification of oceans, and soil and water degradation (Arora et al., 2018; Sachs, 2008; Schot & Steinmueller, 2018; Stephens et al., 2008). More generally, the ecological dimension concerns the earth system, which is the basis for life on Earth.[3] It is about the ability of the global natural capital to provide the inputs needed by humanity and to absorb the wastes produced by humanity (Goodland, 1995). Natural resources are used as raw materials for various purposes, such as food, energy, construction, or input in industrial production processes. The rate of harvesting natural resources must be kept within the limits of their regenerative capacities to achieve environmental sustainability. At the same time, the capacity of the natural and biophysical environments and all its parts (such as the ozone shield of the atmosphere) to assimilate the wastes and pollution produced by humanity is limited. Thus, environmental sustainability implies the need for humanity to adjust emission rates adequately (Goodland, 1995). Morelli (2011) emphasizes environmentally sustainable human behavior "as a condition of balance, resilience, and interconnectedness" (Morelli, 2011, p. 6) that keeps the capacity of the ecosystems intact to provide the resources and services needed by current and future generations to satisfy their needs, while at the same time preserving biological diversity.

Favorable conditions of the earth system are pivotal for the prosperity and more fundamentally for the survival of humanity. In a much-acclaimed work, Rockström et al. (2009b, 2009a) argue for the existence of so-called planetary boundaries, which define a "safe operating space" for humanity. Those nine interlinked boundaries are, in an updated version of the concept by Steffen et al. (2015), climate change, introduction of novel entities (being new substances, new forms of existing substances and modified life forms), ocean acidification, stratospheric ozone depletion, atmospheric aerosol loading, biochemical flows (consisting of global nitrogen cycle and global phosphorus cycle), global freshwater use, biosphere integrity (consisting of functional diversity and genetic diversity), and land-system change. Those boundaries constitute thresholds that, if exceeded, could have potentially disastrous consequences for humanity by bringing the earth system into a new state, which is likely not as favorable for contemporary human societies as the current Holocene epoch (Steffen et al., 2015). In a current update, Richardson et al. (2023) see six of the nine boundaries transgressed, suggesting that "Earth is now well outside of the safe operating space for humanity" (Richardson et al. (2023), p. 1).

---

[3] Reflecting the exact definition of such a system is far beyond the scope of this thesis. The difficulty of such an definition however is easy to imagine, considering the multitude and complexity of geophysical processes and the vast variety of different forms of life on this planet, including extraordinary forms such as extremophile bacteria living under extreme conditions like deep-sea hydrothermal vents or sulfate-reducing bacteria living kilometers below the surface of the earth (see Lollar et al., 2019 for this astonishing example of life on, or rather within earth).

2.2.3 Social Sustainability

The existence of a social dimension of sustainability is widely accepted. However, there is no agreement on what precisely this dimension entails or how it is defined (Boström, 2012; Dempsey, Bramley, Power, & Brown, 2011; Vallance, Perkins, & Dixon, 2011). On the contrary, the social pillar is presumably the one that holds the most potential for controversy, as this dimension concerns the distribution of wealth, rights, and obligations, and is often associated with notions of justice and social inclusion. For example, Vallance et al. (2011) elaborate a threefold scheme of social sustainability, with one aspect being "development social sustainability", which concerns poverty and inequality and covers aspects such as basic needs (access to drinking water, food, housing, and basic health care) but also access to education, jobs, as well as concerns regarding equity and justice. The second aspect is "bridge social sustainability", which refers to changes in individual behavior to achieve environmental sustainability goals. The third aspect is "maintenance social sustainability", which refers to the maintenance of socio-cultural preferences, practices, and traditions in the process of economic and social transformation. Vallance et al. (2011) state that many disputes and misunderstandings regarding social sustainability stem from tensions between these different aspects of social sustainability.

Boström (2012) distinguishes between substantive and procedural aspects of social sustainability. The substantive aspects concern social sustainability goals, entailing aspects such as basic needs, equal rights such as human rights, access to social infrastructure, employment, social inclusion, cultural diversity and traditions, and quality of life, including happiness and well-being. The procedural aspects refer to the process of achieving sustainable development and are about access to information, participation in decision-making, empowerment, social monitoring, and accountable governance (Boström, 2012).

For Dempsey et al. (2011), social sustainability entails two dimensions. One is the goal of social equity, and the other dimension concerns the long-term functioning and viability of society itself. This second dimension refers to society as being a community of individuals that is based on norms and institutions. Littig and Griessler (2005) put social sustainability in relation to the natural environment and refer to an extended set of human needs, which also covers normative notions such as social justice considerations, political participation, and human dignity. They see employment and the related institutional arrangements as pivotal for achieving social sustainability. To give a last example, Cuthill (2010) elaborates on a framework for social sustainability that entails social infrastructure, social capital, governance, and social justice and equity.

These different approaches to the social pillar of sustainability depict the strong normative, multilayered, and potentially ambiguous and controversial nature of this dimension, showing the multitude of different aspects that can be associated with this pillar. Even though there are reoccurring themes like social well-being, inclusivity, fair labor practices, health, safety, equal rights and opportunities, cultural diversity, non-discrimination, and justice, the exact meanings and implications of these issues are highly subjective. Within different cultural contexts, questions about political participation and civil rights will evoke different, if not opposing answers. And even within relatively homogenous societies, questions about public welfare policy and the redistribution of income and wealth are discussed vividly. In general, there are various approaches to assessing the fairness of a particular distribution (of benefits or burdens) and its implications.[4] Depending on the answers to those fundamental considerations about the justness of different distributive mechanisms, the concrete meaning of social sustainability will differ considerably.

2.2.4 *Interdependencies of the Three Pillars*

The interdependencies between economic, social, and environmental aspects of sustainability are crucial to understanding the holistic nature of sustainable development. Their interconnections highlight the need for an integrated approach to addressing global challenges. For example, environmental conditions, such as air and water quality, directly impact public health. Poor environmental quality can lead to health issues, disproportionately affecting vulnerable communities. Another example can be found in Indigenous cultures, which often have deep connections to their environments. Environmental degradation in this regard can have profound social and cultural consequences. Economic decline, as a third example, can lead to unemployment and have severe impacts on social cohesion, health, and public safety.

On the other hand, the economic, social, and environmental aspects of sustainability are in tension (Anderson et al., 2016) and can stand in strong contrast to each other, meaning that reaching a desired new state in one of these dimensions can have strong negative effects on aspects of another dimension. Such negative interdependencies often involve externalities and broader impacts of economic activities, such as the environmental costs of production or the social consequences of certain business practices.

The conflict between economic growth and environmentally sustainable development is a key issue in this regard (Pyka, 2017). Most economic activities still rely heavily on the use of natural resources, such as water, energy, and raw materials. Sustainable economic practices involve managing these resources efficiently to minimize environmental impact. Statistics such as the global material footprint (see Fig. 2.2) show the close link between resource consumption and global GDP growth. Both still go together, meaning that a rise in GDP comes along with increasing resource extraction, associated with additional waste generation, and increasing pressure on natural resources. A similar link can be seen regarding primary energy consumption, which has been continuously rising for decades together with growing global GDP. The economic recovery after the COVID-19 downturn has led to a new high in total primary energy consumption (see Fig. 2.3), which exceeds the pre-COVID-19 level of 2019 by 3% in 2022, with a steady share of fossil fuel consumption

[4] Konow (2003) gives an excellent overview on different justice theories in economics.

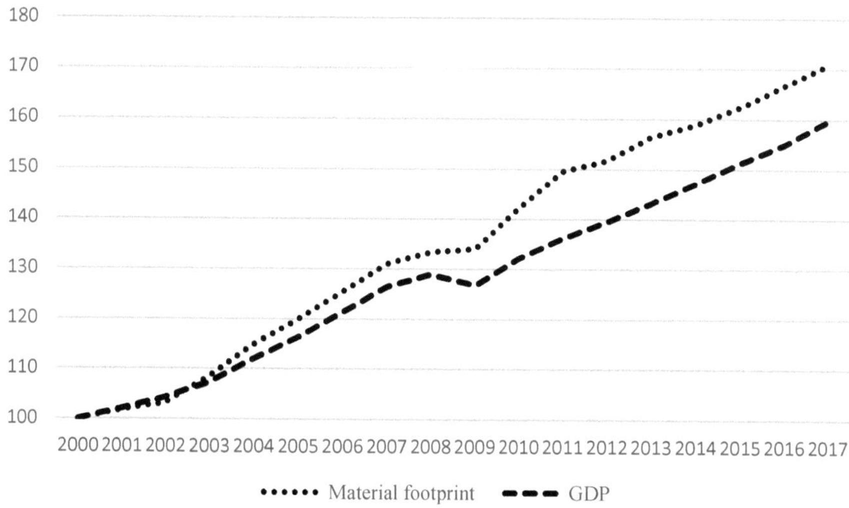

Fig. 2.2 Material footprint and global GDP growth. *Note* GDP growth index with year 2000 as baseline year (value = 100). Data extracted on 26 June 2023 from https://unstats.un.org/sdgs/report/2019/goal-12/. Copyright 2023 by United Nations

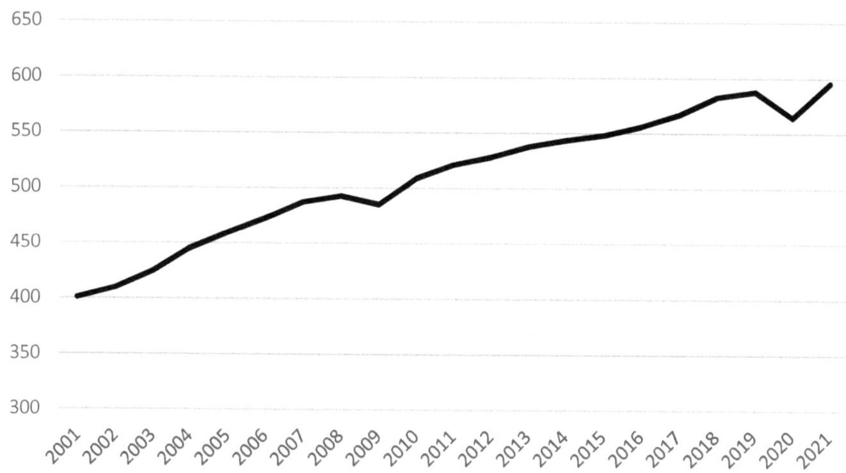

Fig. 2.3 Global primary energy consumption in exajoules. *Note* Data extracted on 02 July 2023 from https://www.energyinst.org/statistical-review/resources-and-data-downloads. Copyright 2023 by Energy Institute

at 82% and a new record high of carbon dioxide emissions in 2022 (Energy Institute, 2023).[5]

[5] Carbon dioxide emissions from energy consumption constituted a share of 87% of total global emissions (Energy Institute, 2023).

Apart from the obvious conflicts between the different sustainability dimensions, there is furthermore the risk of unintended consequences of specific policy measures or initiatives, meaning that a measure intended for improving a certain aspect of sustainability can have a negative impact on another aspect, which was not anticipated (Luederitz et al., 2017). An example is the use of biomass as a substitute for fossil resources in the production of energy and materials, which led to strong tensions due to unintended negative effects on food security (OECD, 2018). Other examples are so-called green-green dilemmas, in which two objectives within the same sustainability dimension stand in conflict with each other. One example is green energy production with wind turbines which can have detrimental effects on biodiversity preservation, as windmills can potentially kill large amounts of airborne wildlife (see e. g. Straka et al., 2020). Another example is the negative implications of hydropower on the ecosystems of lakes and rivers. More generally in social planning processes, it is rather common that the actual outcome state of an intervention differs from the planned or predicted state (Rydin, 2007). This applies to an even greater extent when dealing with a wicked problem (Waddell, 2016).

On the other hand, there are various positive links and interdependencies between the different dimensions of sustainability. Healthy ecosystems provide essential services, such as pollination, water purification, and climate regulation, which directly and indirectly contribute to economic activities. Economic development generates employment opportunities and income, influencing social well-being. However, the nature of employment (e.g. working conditions, wages) can impact social equity and inclusivity. Another connection exists between a reduction of inequality (social dimension), which is likely to positively influence economic sustainability in the form of (socially inclusive) economic growth (Atkinson, 2015; Dixson-Declève et al., 2022; OECD, 2015b). There are furthermore strong hints that the slowdown of productivity gains in recent years is interlinked with rising or persistently high levels of inequality regarding income, wealth, and well-being (OECD, 2018b). Another example is of course the high costs associated with environmental degradation and pollution, although there is much debate about the right approaches for measuring such effects and discounting them as they lie in the future. The so-called *Stern Review on the Economics of Climate Change* (Stern, 2014) is a prominent example that gained much public awareness but also considerable criticism for its methods. The time horizon (and associated ways of calculating discounting rates) plays a crucial role in this regard. A measure, that has a positive economic impact in the short run, might in the long run have a negative economic effect when costs due to environmental externalities outweigh the benefits.

Another positive interconnection appears to exist between pro-environmental business practices and economic performance. In a study on the firm level, Di Maria et al. (2019) found that university-industry collaborations aiming at environmental sustainability also had a significant positive influence on the financial performance of the involved firms, thus improving their economic sustainability. A similar result is found by Duarte et al. (2008) in a study of collaborative university-industry partnership programs. As a result of the program, most firms reported improvements in economic, environmental, and social indicators. On the micro-level of firms, it seems no mission impossible to pursue several sustainability objectives simultaneously (Rauter, Globocnik, Perl-Vorbach, & Baumgartner, 2019). Increasing economic performance along with other sustainability aspects is feasible. On the macro-level, the idea of creating green jobs within a green economy that is less reliant on fossil resources and thus also more resilient toward resource-based shocks, is gaining attention globally (McCauley & Stephens, 2012). Scenarios in which improvements in social indicators (particularly regarding inequality and empowerment) and environmental indicators go hand-in-hand with globally rising GNP levels are plausible and feasible (Dixson-Declève et al., 2022). Understanding and addressing the interdependencies between the economic, social, and environmental aspects of sustainability are essential for developing effective and comprehensive strategies for sustainable development. Ignoring one dimension can lead to unintended consequences in the others, emphasizing the need for an integrated and balanced approach to sustainability.

2.2.5 *Public Debate on the Three Pillars*

The normative character of the three pillars and the potential for tensions between them imply an ongoing discussion within society regarding the definition of sustainability and the formulation of specific sustainability goals. This entails a discussion about the directionality, legitimacy, and responsibility in the context of a transformation toward sustainability (Schlaile et al., 2017). Directionality or goal orientation concerns the exact definition of the desired new state of sustainability, while legitimacy concerns the process of finding a way how to reach sustainability, and responsibility concerns the question of who is responsible or has the power to induce a transformation and who will have to carry the associated costs and benefits. As Anderson et al. (2016) illustrate, the question of sustainability concerns trade-offs between different values and raises questions about whose values count and how these trade-offs are negotiated. Authors such as Blättel-Mink and Kastenholz (2005) or Bisseleua et al. (2018) thus state that sustainability goals cannot be justified merely scientifically, but can only result from discussions within society, involving all relevant stakeholders. As with all normative issues of such complexity and extensive scope, this discussion will not necessarily find a conclusion that resolves all tensions and open questions (as mentioned before regarding the characteristics of wicked problems). Olde and Valentinov (2019) depict an example from the area of agriculture, showing that contradictory opinions from different stakeholder groups make it very unlikely that a consensus on sustainable farming practices will arise in the near future.

On a global scale, the United Nations' *Sustainable Development Goals* (SDGs) can be seen as internationally agreed normative goals, that constitute a compromise covering a broad range of different topics. There are however ample criticisms about the SDGs, ranging from claims about the underrepresentation of ecological concerns (Eisenmenger et al., 2020), to statements about the SDGs being too vague or too broad, making measuring the underlying targets and indicators very difficult if not impossible (see e. g. Hák et al., 2016).

The ongoing discussion, which has lasted for several decades now and has roots that are centuries old, indicates that sustainability is not a static condition but rather a dynamic, evolving concept that will change over time, with changing meanings, scopes, and implications (Strambach, 2017). This is also illustrated by the debates about the economic and social aspects of sustainability. In many countries (especially high-income countries) these discussions mostly take place under different labels. Debates about economic growth, unemployment, and standards of living are commonplace but are not referred to as discussions about sustainability issues. The same holds for the social dimension, which is discussed just as frequently, but generally in terms of social justice or the context of debates about poverty or welfare policy (confer Boström, 2012).

2.3 Scope of the Transformation toward Sustainability

The three pillars of sustainability illustrate the broad scope of the concept. It concerns almost all areas of human activity, ranging from local scale problems like urban traffic to global ones like climate change. Whether the topic is housing, agriculture, mobility, or more generally production and consumption of goods and services, they are all related to the global notion of sustainability. It is about the whole life-cycle of any product, from resource extraction to the production processes, which also include the generation of the energy used for these processes, to the use and re-use of each product and service, until disposal, re- or up-cycling (Grunwald, 2007). This broad scope is reflected in the scientific literature dealing with sustainability, which covers diverse sectors such as agriculture in developing countries (e. g. Akpo et al., 2015; Ayele et al., 2012; Bisseleua et al., 2018), the tourism industry (e. g. Jernsand, 2019), the transportation sector (e. g. Bakker et al., 2018), water management (e. g. Yarime, 2010), the health sector (e. g. Lehoux et al., 2018), or high-tech branches such as the chemical industry (Hajek & Stejskal, 2018), biotechnology and genetic engineering (e. g. Ervin et al., 2010), or nanotechnology (e. g. Glaser et al., 2016). The literature covers issues such as food waste valorization (e. g. Morone et al., 2019), the appeal of pre-owned possessions (e. g. Hood, 2016), new modes of consumption (e. g. Jaeger-Erben, Rückert-John, & Schäfer, 2015), private housing energy (e. g. Heiskanen & Lovio, 2010) and so forth. Papers focus on rural areas (e. g. Di Iacovo, Moruzzo, Rossignoli, & Scarpellini, 2014; Rinaldi & Cavicchi, 2016) as well as urban areas (e. g. Evans & Karvonen, 2014; Mehling & Kolleck, 2019), within diverse socioeconomic settings, from least developed or low-income countries (e. g. Hauser et al., 2011), respectively the most vulnerable groups of society (e. g. Kruss & Gastrow, 2017), to middle-income countries (e. g. Saad et al., 2008), and high-income countries (e. g. Glaser et al., 2016). While there are certainly differences regarding the sustainability challenges that high-income countries face compared to low-income countries (Strambach, 2017), there also seem to be similarities, such as similar principles regarding the (co-)creation of knowledge or value for sustainability purposes (Yun & Liu, 2019). This exemplary, non-exhaustive list of topics addressed in the frame of sustainability research demonstrates the broad scope, countless layers, and complexity of this theme.

2.3.1 Change of the Prevailing Socioeconomic Paradigm

Regarding its vast scope, a transformation toward sustainability implies far-reaching, fundamental changes in humanity's production and consumption patterns, comprising radical changes in individual behavior as well as systemic changes of the underlying institutions, structures, priorities, and principles of the prevailing global socio-economic systems (Grunwald, 2007; Jaeger-Erben et al., 2015; Luederitz et al., 2017; Pyka, 2017; Steward, 2012; Urmetzer, Schlaile, Bogner, Mueller, & Pyka, 2018). As Caniglia et al. (2021) put it, there are hundreds of reports expressing the need for interventions that induce systemic, transformative changes on a global scale to effectively deal with the current sustainability challenges. An example is provided by Jacobsson and Bergek (2011) with an analysis of the energy sector, illustrating the enormous scale of such a transformation. While the global hunger for energy is continuously rising, the shift toward a sustainable energy sector requires enormous adaptations in production capacities and power grids, implying massive investment in infrastructure based on a broad technology mix. In parallel, new rules, regulations, and business models are needed, which also account for the time lag in the diffusion and application of new technologies. As mentioned in Chap. 2.2.4, current statistics show that CO2 emissions from energy rebounded strongly after the COVID-19 decline, reaching a new record high of 39,3 billion tons in 2022, despite the massive growth of renewable sources of energy (Energy Institute, 2023).

Regarding the comprehensive scope of the required transformation, it is appropriate to talk about a change in the prevailing techno-economic paradigm (confer Altenburg & Pegels, 2012; Pyka, 2017; Schlaile et al., 2017). According to Dosi (1982), a technological paradigm refers to the currently established set of basic procedures and the corresponding knowledge, which is used to solve the problems that are deemed relevant within this paradigm. A paradigm furthermore defines what constitutes progress, shaped by the immanent limits and trade-offs of the paradigm. Within such a paradigm, there are technological trajectories, along which the technological advancement is progressing, within the boundaries defined by the paradigm. Dosi (1982) uses this concept to demonstrate explanatory limitations of market-based innovation-pull mechanisms, arguing that radical innovations (discontinuity) have different origins compared to incremental innovations (continuity), as radical innovations "stem from the interplay between scientific advances, economic factors, institutional variables, and unsolved difficulties on established technological paths" (Dosi, 1982, p. 147). The paradigm also helps to explain path-dependencies and lock-ins of techno-economic systems, such as the current carbon lock-in stemming from decades of reliance on fossil fuels (Seto et al., 2016). To overcome these lock-ins and open up the potential of new technological trajectories, a shift to a new techno-economic paradigm is necessary, based on technologies, institutions, and principles that are environmentally, socially, and economically sustainable.

The establishment of a new techno-economic (or socio-technical) paradigm is unlikely to be a linear process of incremental steps with a clear timeline and a foreseeable goal attainment in the near future. The transformation process will rather be long term, and open-ended, with changing speeds and the occurrence of disruptions and steps backward, characterized by uncertainty and changes in the precise definition of milestones, indicators, and the overall objective (Luederitz et al., 2017; Pyka, 2017; Rauschmayer et al., 2015; Rotmans et al., 2001).

2.3.2 Public Support and Vested Interests

Staying on the unsustainable path of tremendous resource depletion, environmental degradation, climate change, and prevailing inequality will induce massive (opportunity) costs and will most likely lead to catastrophic consequences. However, the transformation toward sustainability will also induce massive costs, but at the same time, it will offer the opportunity for economic growth, job creation, and prosperity. Despite the chances it offers, the transformation will most likely stay in contrast to existing business interests and will likely alter existing profit structures, which both would stay untouched if humanity stayed on the present, unsustainable path. It thus becomes obvious that the issue of sustainability is connected with conflicting interests of individuals and societal groups, as this transformation could in the short-run improve the situation of some while worsening the situation of others, even though in the long-run, there seems to be no alternative to a transformation toward sustainability.

However, this raises questions about the distribution of the costs and benefits associated with the transformation toward sustainability. That in turn raises questions about calculating the costs of such a transformation, implying the simulation of alternative scenarios (change versus no change), and being able to assess all negative externalities of specific measures and economic activities. A fair and just distribution of the burdens and gains of a transformation toward sustainability requires appropriate redistribution mechanisms. That includes, for example, accompanying measures such as lump-sum payments for low-income households that suffer financially from higher taxes on fossil fuels or burdens associated with new regulations.

It is therefore necessary to look at the political dimension of change and examine issues of power and public support in connection to transformation processes (Clark, van Kerkhoff, Lebel, & Gallopin, 2016; Rauschmayer et al., 2015; Wehrden et al., 2017). The fundamental change goes in most cases against the vested interests of someone (in most cases powerful incumbents) and raises fears about the loss of wealth, privileges, or influence. This is not without justification as radical transformation processes are likely to produce winners and losers. It is thus necessary to understand the implications of change processes, but also the sources and mechanisms of resistance against a transformation (confer Köhler et al., 2019). Reluctance against change can result from disbelief, lack of knowledge, or can be a consequence of opposing economic or power-related interests. This is, of course, related to the normative dimension of sustainability and the associated public debate about it, with all its contestations and disagreements. Numerous authors conclude that this has direct consequences for researchers working on these issues, stating that scholars should be aware of the political dimension of their work (Clark et al., 2016; Rauschmayer et al., 2015).

The political dimension furthermore implies that a radical transformation toward sustainability is unlikely to happen without broad public support (Sterman, 2008), especially in democratic societies. As this transformation implies trade-offs and is associated with (short-term) costs, questions about compensation mechanisms are highly relevant for the public acceptance of such a transformation (Altenburg & Pegels, 2012). It is, therefore, a matter of finding the right mechanisms, structures, and measures, while considering all stakeholders that could be affected. Bottom-up approaches and holistic strategies appear more likely to gain public support or at least avoid unrest, compared to essentially top-down, punctual measures. Generally, acceptance and public support for radical new practices will rise when those affected expect individual or social advantages (with regard to well-being) associated with the new practices (confer Ranacher et al., 2018; Urmetzer et al., 2018). A prominent example of civil unrest in connection with pro-climate reform is the Yellow Vests protests in France in 2018 and 2019. These (partly violent) political demonstrations were caused by the introduction of a new carbon tax. However, as Driscoll (2023) argues, the reason for the protests seems not to have been opposition against combating climate change. Although the people behind the Yellow Vests protests were a very heterogeneous group, it appears that they were very well concerned about climate change. The unrest was rather sparked by social justice considerations. The Yellow Vest protesters felt that the economic burden of the new tax was distributed unfairly among economically weak parts of French society. They furthermore criticized a lack of influence on the political process that led to the new tax (Driscoll, 2023). This example illustrates the interconnectedness of the economic, social, and environmental aspects of sustainability and the need for comprehensive considerations of these aspects in policy formulation (compare also Dixson-Declève et al., 2022).

The potential short-run burdens associated with the transformation and the resulting political and societal disputes illustrate that the means for achieving this transformation are more likely to be supported and thus successful if they generate short-run benefits that outweigh the burdens. Those benefits are not necessarily purely monetary but may imply increased well-being due to improvements in environmental and social conditions.

References

Abson, D. J., Wehrden, H. von, Baumgärtner, S., Fischer, J., Hanspach, J., Härdtle, W., et al. (2014). Ecosystem services as a boundary object for sustainability. Ecological Economics, 103, 29–37.

Akpo, E., Crane, T. A., Vissoh, P. V., & Tossou, R. C. (2015). Co-production of knowledge in multi-stakeholder processes: Analyzing joint experimentation as social learning. *Journal of Agricultural Education and Extension, 21*(4), 369–388. from https://www.scopus.com/inward/record.uri?eid=2-s2.0-84938966306&doi=10.1080%2f1389224X.2014.939201&partnerID=40&md5=be43d9e514c5e6d1be9f094f87437c32

Alexander, S. (2012). Planned economic contraction: The emerging case for degrowth. *Environmental Politics, 21*(3), 349–368.

Altenburg, T., & Pegels, A. (2012). Sustainability-oriented innovation systems—Managing the green transformation. *Innovation and Development, 2*(1), 5–22.

Amaral, L. P., Martins, N., & Gouveia, J. B. (2015). Quest for a sustainable university: A review. *International Journal of Sustainability in Higher Education, 16*(2), 155–172.

Anand, S., & Sen, A. (2000). Human development and economic sustainability. *World Development, 28*(12), 2029–2049.

Anderson, M. W., Teisl, M. F., & Noblet, C. L. (2016). Whose values count: Is a theory of social choice for sustainability science possible? *Sustainability Science, 11*(3), 373–383.

Arora, N. K., Fatima, T., Mishra, I., Verma, M., Mishra, J., & Mishra, V. (2018). Environmental sustainability: Challenges and viable solutions. *Environmental Sustainability, 1*(4), 309–340.

Arrow, K. J., Dasgupta, P., Goulder, L. H., Mumford, K. J., & Oleson, K. (2012). Sustainability and the measurement of wealth. *Environment and Development Economics, 17*(3), 317–353.

Atkinson, A. B. (2015). *Inequality: What can be done?* Harvard University Press.

Ayele, S., Duncan, A., Larbi, A., & Khanh, T. T. (2012). Enhancing innovation in livestock value chains through networks: Lessons from fodder innovation case studies in developing countries. *Science and Public Policy, 39*(3), 333–346. from https://www.scopus.com/inward/record.uri?eid=2-s2.0-84871418935&doi=10.1093%2fscipol%2fscs022&partnerID=40&md5=70c8d0d2b31bc3c7c0ea76b2f67398ec

Bakker, S., Guillen, M. D., Nanthachatchavankul, P., Zuidgeest, M., Pardo, C., & van Maarseveen, M. (2018). Hot or not? The role of cycling in ASEAN megacities: Case studies of Bangkok and Manila. *International Journal of Sustainable Transportation, 12*(6), 416–431.

Batie, S. S. (2008). Wicked problems and applied economics. *American Journal of Agricultural Economics, 90*(5), 1176–1191.

Bisseleua, D., Idrissou, L., Olurotimi, P., Ogunniyi, A., Mignouna, D., & Bamire, S. A. (2018). Multi-stakeholder process strengthens agricultural innovations and sustainable livelihoods of farmers in southern Nigeria. *Journal of Agricultural Education and Extension, 24*(1), 29–49. from https://www.scopus.com/inward/record.uri?eid=2-s2.0-85032832587&doi=10.1080%2f1389224X.2017.1392992&partnerID=40&md5=69d64c77313db12a24a15288c7d891a9

Blättel-Mink, B., & Kastenholz, H. (2005). Transdisciplinarity in sustainability research: Diffusion conditions of an institutional innovation. *International Journal of Sustainable Development and World Ecology, 12*(1), 1–12. from https://www.scopus.com/inward/record.uri?eid=2-s2.0-19544392116&doi=10.1080%2f13504500509469613&partnerID=40&md5=159c2c52e2bf79753a44222ff4b57faf

Boström, M. (2012). A missing pillar? Challenges in theorizing and practicing social sustainability: Introduction to the special issue. *Sustainability: Science, Practice and Policy, 8*(1), 3–14.

Bourguignon, F. (2003). The measurement of multidimensional poverty. *The Journal of Economic Inequality, 1*(1), 25–49.

Caniglia, G., Luederitz, C., Wirth, T. von, Fazey, I., Martín-López, B., Hondrila, K., et al. (2021). A pluralistic and integrated approach to action-oriented knowledge for sustainability. Nature Sustainability, 4(2), 93–100.

Carson, R. (1962). *Silent spring*. Houghton Mifflin.

Clark, W. C., van Kerkhoff, L., Lebel, L., & Gallopin, G. C. (2016). Crafting usable knowledge for sustainable development. *Proceedings of the National Academy of Sciences of the United States of America, 113*(17), 4570–4578.

Collier, P. (2008). *The bottom billion: Why the poorest countries are failing and what can be done about it (1. OUP paperback)*. Univ. Press.

Cuthill, M. (2010). Strengthening the 'social' in sustainable development: Developing a conceptual framework for social sustainability in a rapid urban growth region in Australia. *Sustainable Development, 18*(6), 362–373.

Dempsey, N., Bramley, G., Power, S., & Brown, C. (2011). The social dimension of sustainable development: Defining urban social sustainability. *Sustainable Development, 19*(5), 289–300.

Di Maria, E., Marchi, V. D., & Spraul, K. (2019). Who benefits from university-industry collaboration for environmental sustainability? *International Journal of Sustainability in Higher Education, 20*(6), 1022–1041.

Dixson-Declève, S., Gaffney, O., Ghosh, J., Randers, J., Rockström, J., & Stoknes, P. E. (2022). *Earth for all: A survival guide for humanity: A report to the Club of Rome (2022), fifty years after the limits of growth (1972)*. New Society Publishers.

Dosi, G. (1982). Technological paradigms and technological trajectories. *Research Policy, 11*(3), 147–162.

Duarte, A. P., Martins, P., & Alexandre, J. (2008). Pro-active behaviour induction by integration of sustainability in business strategic management: INOVE project case study. *Journal of Cleaner Production, 16*(10), 1127–1132.

Eisenmenger, N., Pichler, M., Krenmayr, N., Noll, D., Plank, B., Schalmann, E., et al. (2020). The sustainable development goals prioritize economic growth over sustainable resource use: A critical reflection on the SDGs from a socio-ecological perspective. *Sustainability Science, 15*(4), 1101–1110.

Energy Institute (2023). *Statistical Review of World Energy: 2023 - 72nd edition*, from https://www.energyinst.org/statistical-review.

Ervin, D. E., Glenna, L. L., Jussaume, J., & Raymond, A. (2010). Are biotechnology and sustainable agriculture compatible? *Renewable Agriculture and Food Systems, 25*(2, SI), 143–157.

Evans, J., & Karvonen, A. (2014). 'Give me a laboratory and I will lower your carbon footprint!' - Urban Laboratories and the governance of low-carbon futures. *International Journal of Urban and Regional Research, 38*(2), 413–430.

Georgescu-Roegen, N. (1971). *The entropy law and the economic process*. Harvard University Press.

Glaser, A., Ben Slimane, S., Auplat, C., & Coeurderoy, R. (2016). Enabling nanotechnology entrepreneurship in a French context towards a holistic theoretical framework. *Journal of Small Business and Enterprise Development, 23*(4), 1009–1031.

Goodland, R. (1995). The concept of environmental sustainability. *Annual Review of Ecology and Systematics, 26*(1), 1–24.

Grunwald, A. (2007). Working towards sustainable development in the face of uncertainty and incomplete knowledge. *Journal of Environmental Policy & Planning, 9*(3–4), 245–262.

Haas, R., Meixner, O., & Petz, M. (2016). Enabling community-powered co-innovation by connecting rural stakeholders with global knowledge brokers a case study from Nepal. *British Food Journal, 118*(6), 1350–1369.

Hajek, P., & Stejskal, J. (2018). R&D cooperation and knowledge spillover effects for sustainable business innovation in the chemical industry. *Sustainability, 10*(4).

Hák, T., Janoušková, S., & Moldan, B. (2016). Sustainable development goals: A need for relevant indicators. *Ecological Indicators, 60*, 565–573.

Hauser, M., Loiskandl, W., & Wurzinger, M. (2011). Innovation systems research sustainable natural resource use in least developed countries. *GAIA - Ecological Perspectives for Science and Society, 20*(1), 70–72.

Heiskanen, E., & Lovio, R. (2010). User-producer interaction in housing energy innovations. *Journal of Industrial Ecology, 14*(1), 91–102. from https://www.scopus.com/inward/record.uri?eid=2-s2.0-77954364479&doi=10.1111%2fj.1530-9290.2009.00196.x&partnerID=40&md5=5b64f38d46c4b0269aaf7db8739544a4

Hood, B. (2016). Make recycled goods covetable. *Nature, 531*(7595), 438–440.

Jacobsson, S., & Bergek, A. (2011). Innovation system analyses and sustainability transitions: Contributions and suggestions for research. *Environmental Innovation and Societal Transitions, 1*(1), 41–57.

Jaeger-Erben, M., Rückert-John, J., & Schäfer, M. (2015). Sustainable consumption through social innovation: A typology of innovations for sustainable consumption practices. *Journal of Cleaner Production, 108*, 784–798.

Jernsand, E. M. (2019). Student living labs as innovation arenas for sustainable tourism. *Tourism Recreation Research, 44*(3, SI), 337–347.

Köhler, J., Geels, F. W., Kern, F., Markard, J., Onsongo, E., Wieczorek, A., et al. (2019). An agenda for sustainability transitions research: State of the art and future directions. *Environmental Innovation and Societal Transitions, 31*, 1–32.

Konow, J. (2003). Which is the fairest one of all? A positive analysis of justice theories. *Journal of Economic Literature, 41*(4), 1188–1239. from https://www.aeaweb.org/articles?id=10.1257/002205103771800013

Kruss, G., & Gastrow, M. (2017). Universities and innovation in informal settings: Evidence from case studies in South Africa. *Science and Public Policy, 44*(1), 26–36.

Lehoux, P., Silva, H. P., Sabio, R. P., & Roncarolo, F. (2018). The unexplored contribution of responsible innovation in health to sustainable development goals. *Sustainability, 10*(11).

Leopold, A. (1949). *A sand county almanac and sketches here and there*. Oxford University Press.

Levin, K., Cashore, B., Bernstein, S., & Auld, G. (2012). Overcoming the tragedy of super wicked problems: Constraining our future selves to ameliorate global climate change. *Policy Sciences, 45*(2), 123–152.

Littig, B., & Griessler, E. (2005). Social sustainability: A catchword between political pragmatism and social theory. *International Journal of Sustainable Development, 8*(1/2), 65.

Lollar, G. S., Warr, O., Telling, J., Osburn, M. R., & Lollar, B. S. (2019). 'Follow the water': Hydrogeochemical constraints on microbial investigations 2.4 km below surface at the Kidd Creek deep fluid and deep life observatory. *Geomicrobiology Journal, 36*(10), 859–872.

Luederitz, C., Schäpke, N., Wiek, A., Lang, D. J., Bergmann, M., Bos, J. J., et al. (2017). Learning through evaluation—A tentative evaluative scheme for sustainability transition experiments. *Journal of Cleaner Production, 169*, 61–76.

Malthus, T. R. (1798). *An essay on the principle of population*. J. JOHNSON.

McCauley, S. M., & Stephens, J. C. (2012). Green energy clusters and socio-technical transitions: Analysis of a sustainable energy cluster for regional economic development in Central Massachusetts, USA. *Sustainability Science, 7*(2), 213–225.

Meadows, D. H., Meadows, D. L., Randers, J., & Behrens, W. W. (1972). *The limits to growth: A report for the club of rome's project on the predicament of mankind. A potomac associates book*. Universe Books.

Mehling, S., & Kolleck, N. (2019). Cross-sector collaboration in higher education institutions (HEIs): A critical analysis of an urban sustainability development program. *Sustainability, 11*(18).

Miller, T. R., Wiek, A., Sarewitz, D., Robinson, J., Olsson, L., Kriebel, D., & Loorbach, D. (2014). The future of sustainability science: A solutions-oriented research agenda. *Sustainability Science, 9*(2), 239–246.

Morelli, J. (2011). Environmental sustainability: A definition for environmental professionals. *Journal of Environmental Sustainability, 1*(1), 1–10.

Morone, P., Falcone, P. M., & Tartiu, V. E. (2019). Food waste valorisation: Assessing the effectiveness of collaborative research networks through the lenses of a COST action. *Journal of Cleaner Production, 238*.

OECD. (2015a). *Frascati manual 2015: Guidelines for collecting and reporting data on research and experimental development*. OECD Publishing.

OECD (2015b). In it together: Why less inequality benefits all: OECD.

OECD (2018). *Meeting policy challenges for a sustainable bioeconomy:* OECD.

Pyka, A. (2017). Dedicated innovation systems to support the transformation towards sustainability: Creating income opportunities and employment in the knowledge-based digital bioeconomy. *Journal of Open Innovation: Technology, Market, and Complexity, 3*(27), 1–18.

Ranacher, L., Höfferer, K., Lettner, M., Hesser, F., Stern, T., Rauter, R., & Schwarzbauer, P. (2018). What would potential future opinion leaders like to know? An explorative study on the perceptions of four wood-based innovations. *Die Bodenkultur: Journal of Land Management, Food and Environment, 69*(1), 47–59.

Rauschmayer, F., Bauler, T., & Schäpke, N. (2015). Towards a thick understanding of sustainability transitions — Linking transition management, capabilities and social practices. *Ecological Economics, 109*, 211–221.

Redpath, S. M., Young, J., Evely, A., Adams, W. M., Sutherland, W. J., Whitehouse, A., et al. (2013). Understanding and managing conservation conflicts. *Trends in Ecology & Evolution, 28*(2), 100–109.

Richardson, K., Steffen, W., Lucht, W., Bendtsen, J., Cornell, S. E., Donges, J. F., et al. (2023). Earth beyond six of nine planetary boundaries. *Science Advances, 9*(37), eadh2458.

Rinaldi, C., & Cavicchi, A. (2016). Universities' emerging roles to co-create sustainable innovation paths: Some evidences from the Marche region. *Aestimum, 69*, 211–224.

Rittel, H. W. J., & Webber, M. M. (1973). Dilemmas in a general theory of planning. *Policy Sciences, 4*(2), 155–169.

Rockström, J., Steffen, W., Noone, K., Persson, A., Chapin, F. S., Lambin, E. F., et al. (2009a). Planetary boundaries: Exploring the safe operating space for humanity. *Ecology and Society, 14*(2).

Rockström, J., Steffen, W., Noone, K., Persson, A., Chapin, F. S., Lambin, E. F., et al. (2009b). A safe operating space for humanity. *Nature, 461*(7263), 472–475.

Rotmans, J., Kemp, R., & van Asselt, M. (2001). More evolution than revolution: Transition management in public policy. *Foresight, 3*(1), 15–31.

Rydin, Y. (2007). Re-examining the role of knowledge within planning theory. *Planning Theory*, 6(1), 52–68.

Saad, M., Zawdie, G., & Malairaja, C. (2008). The triple helix strategy for universities in developing countries: The experiences in Malaysia and Algeria. *Science and Public Policy, 35*(6), 431–443. from https://www.scopus.com/inward/record.uri?eid=2-s2.0-49749131502&doi=10.3152%2f030234208X323316&partnerID=40&md5=cba483a7084a1f9b1b9a71c0d3728eea

Sachs, J. D. (2008). *Common wealth: Economics for a crowded planet*. Penguin Books.

Schlaile, M., Urmetzer, S., Blok, V., Andersen, A., Timmermans, J., Mueller, M., et al. (2017). Innovation Systems for Transformations towards sustainability?: Taking the normative dimension seriously. *Sustainability, 9*(12, 2253), 1–20.

Schneider, F., Kallis, G., & Martinez-Alier, J. (2010). Crisis or opportunity? Economic degrowth for social equity and ecological sustainability. Introduction to this special issue. *Journal of Cleaner Production, 18*(6), 511–518.

Schot, J., & Steinmueller, W. E. (2018). Three frames for innovation policy: R&D, systems of innovation and transformative change. *Research Policy, 47*(9), 1554–1567.

Schumacher, E. F. (1973). *Small is beautiful: Economics as if people mattered*. Blond & Briggs.

Seto, K. C., Davis, S. J., Mitchell, R. B., Stokes, E. C., Unruh, G., & Ürge-Vorsatz, D. (2016). Carbon lock-in: Types, causes, and policy implications. *Annual Review of Environment and Resources, 41*(1), 425–452.

Spangenberg, J. H. (2005). Economic sustainability of the economy: Concepts and indicators. *International Journal of Sustainable Development, 8*(1/2), 47.

Steffen, W., Richardson, K., Rockström, J., Cornell, S. E., Fetzer, I., Bennett, E. M., et al. (2015). Sustainability. Planetary boundaries: Guiding human development on a changing planet. *Science, 347*(6223), 1259855.

Stephens, J. C., Hernandez, M. E., Román, M., Graham, A. C., & Scholz, R. W. (2008). Higher education as a change agent for sustainability in different cultures and contexts. *International Journal of Sustainability in Higher Education, 9*(3), 317–338.

Sterman, J. D. (2008). Economics. Risk communication on climate: Mental models and mass balance. *Science, 322*(5901), 532–533.

Stern, N. (2014). The economics of climate *Change:* Cambridge University Press.

Steward, F. (2012). Transformative innovation policy to meet the challenge of climate change: Sociotechnical networks aligned with consumption and end-use as new transition arenas for a low-carbon society or green economy. *Technology Analysis & Strategic Management, 24*(4), 331–343.

Straka, T. M., Fritze, M., & Voigt, C. C. (2020). The human dimensions of a green–green-dilemma: lessons learned from the wind energy — Wildlife conflict in Germany. *Energy Reports, 6*, 1768–1777.

Strambach, S. (2017). Combining knowledge bases in transnational sustainability innovation: Microdynamics and institutional change. *Economic Geography, 93*(5), 500–526. from https://www.scopus.com/inward/record.uri?eid=2-s2.0-85030160222&doi=10.1080%2f00130095.2017.1366268&partnerID=40&md5=898772c879f5bad929c4fb7fc96e9b50

UNCED (1992). Agenda 21 - United Nations conference on Environment & Development: United Nations.

United Nations (1992). *Rio Declaration on Environment and Development.* Retrieved December 12, 2023, from https://www.un.org/en/development/desa/population/migration/generalassembly/docs/globalcompact/A_CONF.151_26_Vol.I_Declaration.pdf.

Urmetzer, S., Schlaile, M., Bogner, K., Mueller, M., & Pyka, A. (2018). Exploring the dedicated Knowledge Base of a transformation towards a sustainable bioeconomy. *Sustainability, 10*(6), 1694.

Olde, E. M. de, & Valentinov, V. (2019). The moral complexity of agriculture: A challenge for corporate social responsibility. Journal of Agricultural and Environmental Ethics, 32(3), 413–430.

Vallance, S., Perkins, H. C., & Dixon, J. E. (2011). What is social sustainability? *A clarification of concepts. Geoforum, 42*(3), 342–348.

Waddell, S. (2016). Societal change systems. *The Journal of Applied Behavioral Science, 52*(4), 422–449.

WCED. (1987). *Our common future.* Oxford University Press.

Wehrden, H. V., Luederitz, C., Leventon, J., & Russell, S. (2017). Methodological challenges in sustainability science: A call for method plurality, procedural rigor and longitudinal research. *Challenges in Sustainability, 5*(1).

Wiek, A., Ness, B., Schweizer-Ries, P., Brand, F. S., & Farioli, F. (2012). From complex systems analysis to transformational change: A comparative appraisal of sustainability science projects. *Sustainability Science, 7*(S1), 5–24.

Yarime, M. (2010). Understanding sustainability innovation as a social process of knowledge transformation. *Nanotechnology Perceptions, 6*(3), 143–153. from https://www.scopus.com/inward/record.uri?eid=2-s2.0-79958140442&doi=10.4024%2fN13YA10A.ntp.06.03&partnerID=40&md5=1f5c78f1ca103612df61e6b89d052cd9

Yun, J. J., & Liu, Z. (2019). Micro- and macro-dynamics of open innovation with a quadruple-helix model. *Sustainability, 11*(12).

Chapter 3
Innovations as a Means for the Transformation Toward Sustainability

3.1 Transformation Strategies

The issue of sustainability can be considered a wicked problem, as stated above (see Sect. 2.2). As further outlined, solution strategies to such problems require radical, multidimensional, and transformative approaches (Schlaile et al., 2017). Classical planning approaches seem unlikely to suffice for addressing such a complex, multi-layered problem with a strong normative dimension. Waddell (2016) argues for societal change systems, comprising thousands of organizations globally, to address the challenge of sustainability in a coordinated way, inducing fundamental changes to the current socio-economic system. Weber and Khademian (2008) also argue for the need for large networks to address wicked problems. Both papers emphasize the difficulties arising with such large networks, as coordinating and organizing such networks is incredibly demanding, especially regarding the exchange and transfer of knowledge between its members. As Grunwald (2007) argues, a transformation toward sustainability seems not feasible within classical political planning approaches. Abson et al. (2017) state that the classical policy instruments, which conventionally aim at adjusting parameters within a given framework, such as carbon pricing, environmental taxes, green procurement schemes, or regulations for limiting the emission of pollutants, are not enough regarding the required scope of change.

It is thus the question which mechanisms and instruments can facilitate the transformation toward sustainability. There are basically two possible solution strategies for addressing the limits of growth and the associated unsustainable levels of resource depletion and emission of pollutants and greenhouse gases (Pyka, 2017). One solution is sustainable degrowth, in the sense of a controlled downscaling of production and consumption for a defined period of time (the transition phase) for the purpose of enhancing human development and well-being while at the same time improving global ecological conditions (Alexander, 2012; Schneider et al., 2010). Current debates about this possible solution strategy address the political feasibility of such an approach. At the moment, public support and hence the prospect of

U. Wilke, *Towards Sustainable Innovations*, Economic Complexity and Evolution,
https://doi.org/10.1007/978-3-032-31024-8_3

success of planned degrowth appear very low due to hindering factors stemming from structural (cultural, social, economic) barriers and potential short-term losses of well-being that stand in contrast to the expectations and desires of large parts of society (Büchs & Koch, 2019).

The other solution is the decoupling of growth and resource employment (Pyka, 2017). This implies fundamental alterations to the current production and consumption patterns. The following chapters of this thesis argue that innovations can provide the basis for such new modes of production and consumption. They can furthermore render short-term gains possible regarding economic, social, and environmental benefits, and thus are likely to gain widespread support. The transformation toward sustainability can thus be significantly fostered by transformative, systemic innovations.[1]

3.2 Innovations as Novelties that Induce Change

The Oslo Manual (OECD/Eurostat, 2018) gives the following definition of the term innovation:

> An innovation is a new or improved product or process (or combination thereof) that differs significantly from the unit's previous products or processes and that has been made available to potential users (product) or brought into use by the unit (process). (OECD/Eurostat, 2018, p. 20)

The broad formulation is intended to cover innovations in all areas, with the term "unit" referring to either business, government, households, or non-profit organizations. The definition of the Oslo Manual illustrates several important aspects of innovations. On the one hand, an innovation is characterized by its novelty. It is furthermore implemented or used, which distinguishes it from an idea, invention, or concept. In this regard, innovation in an industrial context could be simply defined as a commercialized invention (Freeman & Soete, 2000). This concise definition emphasizes another relevant point that is implicitly included in the Oslo Manual's definition and more fully formulated at another position in the document (OECD/Eurostat, 2018, pp. 47–48): The introduction of an innovation is driven by expectations of additional value or other benefits, which are supposed to result from the implementation of that novelty. Conventionally, this benefit is of an economic or monetary nature.

Following this initial presentation of a widely used definition of innovation, it seems appropriate to take a step back in the history of economic thought to look at the broader implications of innovations and technological change. Such an economic

[1] This argument should not be misunderstood as downplaying the importance of other components necessary for the transformation towards sustainability, such as processes of cultural evolution. Government policies and international political agreements also play fundamental roles, not least by providing regulatory push and pull mechanisms that induce innovations (confer Jaffe et al., 2002).

analysis of the concept of innovation can hardly be conducted without reference to Alois Schumpeter, who could be named "'Godfather' of innovation studies" (Tidd et al., 2005, p. 7) and whose work is "at the heart of economic of innovation" (Antonelli, 2009, p. 619).

In his seminal works *Theorie der wirtschaftlichen Entwicklung* (Schumpeter, 1997, originally published in 1911/1912), and *Capitalism, socialism, and democracy* (Schumpeter, 1994, originally published in 1942), Schumpeter introduced much of his famous concept of "creative destruction", depicting the economic process as being driven by innovations, which are novel ways of producing goods or services, and which can be of such disruptive character that they lead to the vanishing of whole industries via the creation of new ones.[2] Schumpeter distinguishes between different phases of the innovation process, emphasizing the role of the entrepreneur who reaps the monopolistic benefits of innovation until imitating entrepreneurs bring those benefits down in a new market equilibrium until the next innovation disrupts the prevailing economic activities. Hence, innovations are a decisive factor influencing long-term economic progress, implying a dynamic, non-linear sequence of market disequilibria induced by novel technologies, processes, approaches, new methods of production, new distribution channels, new sources for the supply of resources or production inputs, or new organizational forms.[3] Innovations emerge as recombination or new combinations of existing production factors and can be of an incremental or radical nature, leading to adoption or disruption.

The aspect of novelty implies that innovation is basically a concept of change, whereby this change can refer to products, processes, position (meaning the context in which a product or service is introduced), or paradigms, which refer to the underlying basic principles of an organization (Tidd et al., 2005). This change can affect entire industries or national economies. The degree of novelty or change compared to the current state defines the position of an innovation on the continuum from small step, incremental innovation, to synthetic innovation (creative recombination of existing methods and technologies), to radical, disruptive, or groundbreaking innovations (Boer & During, 2001).

The idea of creative destruction highlights another aspect associated with innovations: New products, processes or approaches can not only generate benefits but can also induce costs, especially for incumbent firms. These costs of innovations are associated with expertise and skills becoming obsolete, making certain jobs redundant, causing whole business models to not function anymore, and making infrastructure and equipment outdated (Foray, 2004). In this context, Hall and Vredenburg (2003) talk about the "double-edged sword" of innovations from the perspective of an individual firm, as innovations can be the source of sustained competitive advantage or the cause of major competitive disruptions and distress.

---

[2] See e. g. Antonelli, 2009 or Blättel-Mink, 2021 for a more detailed portrayal of Schumpeter's concept of innovation.

[3] This line of argument already gave rise to portraying the economic progress as an evolutionary process (Pyka, 2021).

3.3 Innovations and Sustainability

Innovations can be a major driver of sustainable development (Brodhag, 2013). Novelties that incorporate social and environmental aspects, in addition to economic considerations, have the potential to substantially foster the transformation toward sustainability (Dwyer, 2013; Pyka, 2017; Strambach, 2017). Innovations can thus be considered a tool to make economic development more environmentally friendly and socially inclusive (Veiga Ávila et al., 2019). Put differently, innovations are effective means to maintain competitiveness and high living standards while simultaneously addressing environmental concerns (Mazzanti, 2018). The idea, that innovations can act as drivers for the transformation toward sustainability has also found its way into application in the context of handbooks, policy papers, and reports of international organizations such as the World Bank (World Bank, 2021; World Bank Group, 2014), and the OECD (OECD, 2011; OECD, 2017). It is furthermore prominently featured in the context of the European Union's Green Deal (European Commission, 2019) and the European Union's current industrial strategy (European Commission, 2020).

However innovations are not per se conducive to sustainability (Schlaile et al., 2017), and there are numerous examples of innovations that entail negative impacts on sustainability (Schot & Steinmueller, 2018). We can thus distinguish between a rather conventional notion of innovation referring to novelties with a primarily commercial or economic value, and other innovations that also induce positive impacts regarding the social and environmental aspects of sustainability (Strambach, 2017). During the last two to three decades, numerous concepts for such sustainability-enhancing innovations have emerged. Table 3.1 provides an overview of a few prominent examples of how scholars define such concepts.

There are other terms used for innovations incorporating positive effects on sustainability, such as green innovation, socio-ecological innovation, or socially responsible innovation, to give a non-exhaustive list. Some of those notions explicitly focus on the ecological dimension of sustainability, which is also reflected in the chosen terms for those concepts, such as eco-innovations or environmental innovations. Other concepts explicitly refer to sustainability in their wording but still incorporate only environmental aspects and are often used to primarily describe innovations that lessen the burden of a firm's activities on the natural environment (Varadarajan, 2017).

There is no universally agreed definition of any of these terms and there is certainly conceptual overlap. Franceschini et al. (2016) however caution against using those terms synonymously. Concentrating on the four terms "eco-innovation", "environmental innovation", "green innovation", and "sustainable innovation", they demonstrate that those notions not only depict similarities but also differences, as these notions are associated with different topics and scientific communities.

Despite the differences regarding the exact definition, those concepts have a common denominator: Economic success or profitability is no longer the sole decisive factor for whether a novelty is considered to be an innovation. Other aspects play a role as well, such as environmental considerations, social considerations, or

Table 3.1 Different innovation concepts entailing social and ecological aspects

Concept and definition	Author(s)
"Ecological innovation includes the development and implementation of new products, new technologies, new production processes, new resources, new markets and new systems that integrate economy and ecology, i.e. introduce ecological aspects in economic strategies."	Blättel-Mink (1998)
"Eco-innovation is the process of developing new products, processes or services which provide customer and business value but significantly decrease environmental impact."	Fussler and James (1996)
"Eco-innovations are all measures of relevant actors (firms, politicians, unions, associations, churches, private households) which develop new ideas, behavior, products and processes, apply or introduce them and which contribute to a reduction of environmental burdens or to ecologically specified sustainability targets."	Rennings (2000)
"Sustainable innovation as a process where sustainability considerations (environmental, social, financial) are integrated into company systems from idea generation through to research and development (R&D) and commercialisation. This applies to products, services, and technologies, as well as new business and organisation models."	Clark and Charter (2007)
"In a market system, sustainable development requires sustainability innovation and entrepreneurs who can achieve environmental or social goals with superior products or processes that are successful in the marketplace of mainstream customers."	Schaltegger and Wagner (2011)
"… eco-innovation (e.g. eco-design, cleaner production) and sustainability-oriented innovations (SOIs), that is, the integration of ecological and social aspects into products, processes, and organizational structures."	Klewitz and Hansen (2014)
"Sustainability oriented innovation (SOI) involves making intentional changes to an organization's philosophy and values, as well as to its products, processes or practices, to serve the specific purpose of creating and realizing social and environmental value in addition to economic returns"	Adams et al. (2016)
"Sustainable innovation is a firm's implementation of a new product, process, or practice, or modification of an existing product, process, or practice that significantly reduces the impact of the firm's activities on the natural environment. Sustainable product innovation is a firm's introduction of a new product or modification of an existing product whose environmental impact during the lifecycle of the product, spanning resource extraction, production, distribution, use, and post-use disposal, is significantly lower than existing products for which it is a substitute."	Varadarajan (2017)

a combination of both. Some authors argue that the different objectives of such innovations are likely to go hand-in-hand, meaning that environmental innovations, induced by environmental policy, can improve industrial competitiveness by creating absolute advantages for a firm, compared to other foreign firms not affected by the environmental policy (Barbieri et al., 2016; Porter & van der Linde, 1995). However, these "win-win" theories are not uncontested, on a theoretical and an empirical level

(Jaffe et al., 2002). Sustainable innovations also seem more demanding, as firms need to consider more primary and secondary stakeholders and have to deal with ambiguous, or even contradictory demands, while at the same time, radical (sustainable) innovations are more risky for firms, as disruptive novelties can turn knowledge and expertise of their value chain partners obsolete (Hall & Vredenburg, 2003).

In general, the connection of economic, social, and environmental considerations reflects the normative directionality, which is the central idea of the concept of sustainable innovation and the various other terms in use (Strambach, 2017). This also appears to be one of the sources for the lack of conceptual clarity. Referring to the normative nature of sustainability, the economic, social, and environmental criteria will have different meanings within different spatial and cultural contexts, leading to different meanings associated with sustainable innovations (Boons et al., 2013). An example is provided by Baek et al. (2019), who describe the development of a soil sensor, done in collaboration between partners from Myanmar and South Korea, for the purpose of improving sustainability in agriculture.[4] The partners involved in the collaboration assessed the intended innovations differently. While the South Korean partners approached the development of a technological innovation, the partners from Myanmar thought of it as a social innovation, indicating different normative assessments and practices (Baek et al., 2019). This highlights the fact that specific technological innovations developed in high-income countries tend to require a certain amount of adaptation to fit into the local context of low-income countries to induce positive impacts on sustainability (Khumairoh et al., 2019). This approach however is unlikely to work for any technological novelty, meaning that in low-income countries, those innovations (products, processes, or others) that fit the local context need to be "picked" (Martin, 2019). That also implies the existence of a demand for low-income, country-specific sustainable innovations for purposes such as eradicating extreme poverty and focusing on low-tech sectors and local markets (Boons et al., 2013; Martin, 2019).

Scholars furthermore differ in their assessment regarding the degree of novelty and the scope of impact of sustainable innovations. Numerous studies examine gradual technological improvements, new products, and processes, often on a firm level, framing them as sustainable innovations. Other authors, such as Adams et al. (2016), discuss the concept of sustainability-oriented innovations on different levels, from internally oriented shifts on the firm level to more radical and systemic changes building upon multi-actor collaborations and new business paradigms. Yet other authors emphasize that the transformation toward sustainability implies a shift from one socio-technological system to another and thus requires paradigm-changing novelties with system-wide impacts (Boons et al., 2013; Caniglia et al., 2021; Geels, 2005; Schlaile et al., 2017). Such system innovations (Elzen & Wieczorek, 2005) involve multiple actors, induce change in regulatory, technological, behavioral, and societal factors, and work on various levels (micro, macro, and meso). This is connected to the multiple dimensions of sustainability and its broad range of impact concerning production, consumption, energy, housing, and most other

---

[4] See Sect. 7.5.2.1 for a detailed description of this project.

areas of human activity. Comprehensive economic concepts incorporating sustainability considerations, such as the knowledge-based sustainable bioeconomy (see for example Pyka & Prettner, 2018) or a sustainable circular economy (Geissdoerfer et al., 2017) frequently refer to systemic and transformative innovations.

Summing up, the conceptual ambiguity regarding the various terms for sustainable innovations is no surprise, considering the normative character of the underlying term sustainability itself and the resulting multitude of interpretations. However, there exist various commonalities of the different notions for sustainable innovations, namely the incorporation of ecological and social aspects, and those factors distinguish them from conventional innovations.

3.3.1 Technological Novelties and Social Innovations

Numerous authors question whether purely technological solutions to sustainability challenges are feasible at all (see for example Adams et al., 2016; Dwyer, 2013; Grunwald, 2007; Mazzanti, 2018; Sterman, 2008; Steward, 2012). On the one hand, there are countless examples of technological novelties that were designed to counteract environmental degradation and resource overuse but proved inefficient or even counterproductive in reality (Hauser et al., 2011). More generally, history shows that new technologies tend at best to postpone the depletion of natural resources but they do not stop it, either because the technologies are unsustainable themselves or they are being used in an unsustainable manner (Goncz et al., 2007).[5] One reason is that technological novelties can lead to rebound effects, in which efficiency gains are offset by lower costs and subsequent income and substitution effects (Berkhout et al., 2000). This can even result in higher overall levels of resource consumption if the efficiency gains lead to additional economic growth (Zink & Geyer, 2017).

Another reason is the ongoing growth of the global population (which is even more severe in combination with global GDP per capita). The world population is likely to grow for another 60 to 80 years, reaching 10.4 billion in the year 2100 (medium scenario, see United Nations—Department of Economic and Social Affairs (DESA), 2023). Figure 3.1 shows the range of the current prediction. This rise in global population will put further pressure on the world's ecological and social systems, meaning that technologies alone would need to more than offset this growth (in addition to the growth of GDP), to stop resource depletion and environmental degradation.

Hence, many new technologies can potentially have positive effects on sustainability, but the realization of these effects depends on the prevailing political and economic framework conditions and the resulting application and use of these new technologies (Grunwald, 2007; Steward, 2012). In other words, a technology per se hardly constitutes a sustainable innovation, as it is rather the use and the (long-run) application of that technology that determines its impact regarding ecological and

[5] See the statistics on global material footprint and energy consumption and related emissions of greenhouse gas in Sect. 2.2.4.

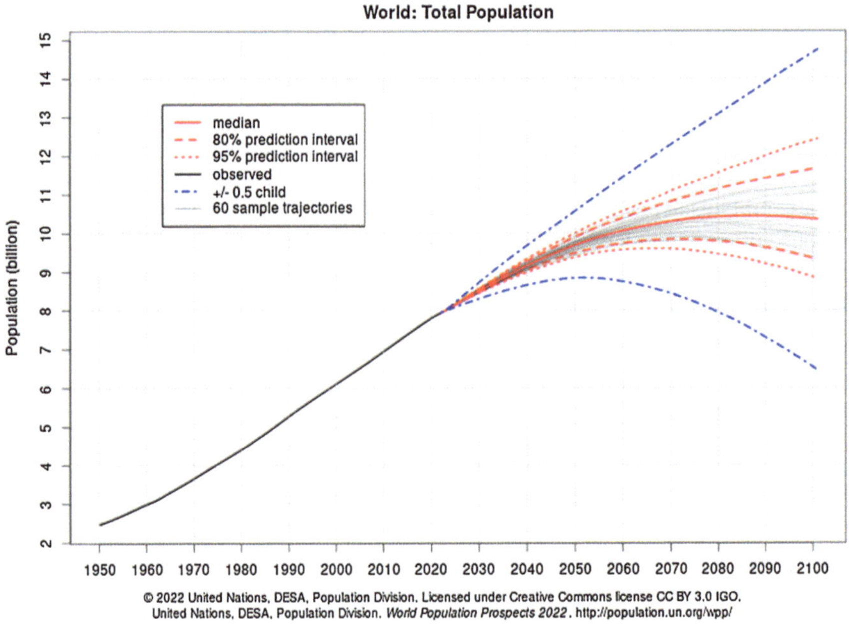

Fig. 3.1 Global population growth. *Source* https://population.un.org/wpp/Graphs/Probabilistic/POP/TOT/900—extracted 20 October 2023

social aspects. Technology itself is merely a set of opportunities for society to be used in the pursuit of a specific goal, which can be the transformation toward sustainability, or profit and wealth maximization regardless of its social and ecological implications.

Addressing sustainability challenges thus seems to require a mixture of new technologies, new institutions, and new societal and economic practices (Grunwald, 2007; Steward, 2012). And the technological part, regardless of whether a technological solution is actually possible or not, is not the decisive factor. It is the prevailing economic and political arrangement that is likely to make the difference (Lehoux et al., 2018; Sterman, 2008), not least because of time lags in market-driven diffusion and application of new technologies, making accompanying technology-specific policies necessary (Jacobsson & Bergek, 2011).

Considering the limited impact of technological novelties, it is not surprising that social innovations are expected to play a pivotal role in the transmission toward sustainability (confer Koenig, 2015; Rennings, 2000; Schlaile et al., 2017). Although there is no commonly accepted definition of the term social innovation, with many existing definitions being vague, very broad, or fuzzy (Koenig, 2015; Pol & Ville, 2009), and even though the literature on the topic presents several different phenomena with quite differing characteristic as social innovations (Jaeger-Erben et al., 2015), the idea behind the concept of social innovation has proven very useful.

Pol and Ville (2009) distinguish between business innovations and social innovations and state that there is a large overlap. Social innovation is a novelty that has the potential to improve either the quality or the quantity of life, whereby the quality is associated with individual well being and valuable options at the macro-level of society. For Pol and Ville (2009) social innovations are not per se good for a society, as they might be detrimental to the normatively defined goals of that society. Young (2011) on the other hand sees social innovations in the area of social norms and institutions, which are mechanisms that facilitate coordination between individuals. A social innovation is thus a new and improved mechanism, in the sense that it increases the welfare of the individuals who apply it, compared to the existing mechanisms. Social innovations are not necessarily of commercial value (Jones & Zubielqui, 2017), and as a consequence, there tends to be under-investment in such innovations if left to private markets, resulting in an under-provision of such novelties compared to the desired state derived from the existing societal goals (Dasgupta & David, 1994; Pol & Ville, 2009).

To better grasp the concept of social innovations and their potential contribution to a transformation toward sustainability, it appears helpful to look at examples from the literature. Pol and Ville (2009) depict new and more effective methods of teaching and learning as a social innovation. Rennings (2000) cites changes in consumption patterns and alternative lifestyles, such as a modal split toward ecological alternatives as a social innovation. Young (2011) sees social innovations in the areas of legal institutions such as private property rights, contractual arrangements, and the systems to protect them, as well as in novel forms of corporate governance. Jaeger-Erben et al. (2015) see social innovations in the field of alternative consumption styles which explicitly incorporate normative considerations such as community-empowering consumption, resource-light, and waste-avoiding consumption, or need- and utility-oriented consumption.

Social innovations can thus take many forms. They are often associated with the provision of public goods, such as education, public health care, or environmental management, illustrating their non-commercial character. Social innovations in these areas can be linked to lower (transaction) costs or higher effectiveness. But they can also apply to areas in which private commercial interests and the provision of public goods can overlap or even substitute each other, such as public transportation systems and individual mobility. To facilitate the transformation toward sustainability, social innovations can relate to new and better steering mechanisms for such a transformation. They can concern the “rules of the game” such as improved approaches to public governance, more inclusive societal decision processes, or new ways to organize economic transactions.

Social innovations tend to be more complex compared to product, process, or organizational innovations. They can be based on new technologies, such as blockchain-based smart contracts for decentralized trading of privately produced renewable energy. Or they can incorporate old technologies such as bicycles (see for example Bakker et al., 2018), or be linked to rediscovered ancient concepts such as shared or community-based ownership (confer Schot & Steinmueller, 2018), and hence even might lack the element of novelty in a conventional sense (Jaeger-Erben et al., 2015). This overlap and the inclusion of various elements make a sharp distinction between different kinds of innovation at times impossible (Rennings, 2000). The assessment of whether a novelty is a technological innovation or a social one as it comes along with new social practices, can depend on the cultural and socio-economic context, as the above-mentioned example of the collaborative development of a soil sensor demonstrates (Baek et al., 2019).

3.3.2 Assessing the Sustainability Impact of an Innovation

A fundamental challenge regarding sustainable innovations is the assessment of the actual sustainability impacts of an innovation. Generally, sustainability assessments are not trivial tasks, due to the complex, multidimensional, and normative nature of sustainability (Matthews et al., 2019). Nonetheless, numerous different indicators, tools, techniques, and metrics exist for measuring and evaluating sustainability and its change over time. Singh et al. (2012) give an excellent overview in this regard, from rather simple indices relying on a few measured variables to highly sophisticated ones that incorporate a broad range of variables covering the social, economic, and environmental aspects of sustainability.

Despite the existence of such indices, the challenges of measuring the sustainability impact of an innovation are manifold. First, it should be recognized that the assessment of sustainability has a strong normative element as well. The inclusion of specific indicators and their weighting is a value-based decision, depending on the definition of sustainability that is being used (Singh et al., 2012). Every assessment is a simplified representation of the enormous complexity of our highly dynamic reality, plus there are different measurement approaches for most variables. Regarding innovations, a comprehensive sustainability assessment must consider the distribution of benefits and burdens for the whole life-cycle of the innovation (Grunwald, 2007). For products, this includes resource extraction, energy being used for production and distribution, and finally disposal, reuse, or recycling. One approach is thus to compare new technologies with the existing alternatives to evaluate their potential contribution to sustainability (Horbach et al., 2013). But this again leads to the difficulty stated above, that the actual impact of a new technology depends on its usage determined mainly by the prevailing economic, social, and political framework conditions. The intergenerational component of sustainability further complicates this issue, as the long-term impacts of nascent technologies on the environment can hardly be measured (Glaser et al., 2016). Assessing the sustainability impacts of social innovations seems even more demanding, as they tend to be more complex, often involving new technologies, institutional change, and novel social practices. Corresponding approaches aiming at developing such innovations and the necessary knowledge, thus require sophisticated evaluation approaches with a broad measurement of baseline variables and a comparison to adequate control groups (confer Evans & Karvonen, 2014; Luederitz et al., 2017).

Approaches to specifically measure an innovation's impact on the social and environmental aspects of sustainability include for example the "Sustainability Innovation Cube" developed by Hansen et al. (2009). Their framework consists of three dimensions, leading to 27 possible domains in which an innovation could induce sustainability effects. 71 assessment methods are assigned to these domains, illustrating the complexity of such an endeavor. Another framework is described by Matthews et al. (2019) who follow a procedural approach for assessing the potential sustainability effects of emerging technologies. Their framework strongly relies on stakeholder involvement in the assessment process and incorporates a broad range of different methods for measuring sustainability effects, while always keeping an eye on the context to which the technology is sought to be applied.

Generally, involving relevant stakeholders seems highly relevant for sustainability assessment approaches (confer Falcone et al., 2019). The scope and timing of such an involvement can differ considerably. While some approaches aim at involving stakeholders early in the design phase of an assessment scheme, others include stakeholders rather late and primarily for collecting data.

Assessing the overall sustainability impact of an innovation with metrics that are composed of different indicators can lead to ambiguous results, if the innovation has beneficial effects on some sustainability indicators, while simultaneously having negative effects on others. The ideal type of sustainable innovation would thus be an innovation that induces improvements in all sustainability areas. This raises questions about the classification of innovations that lead to an improvement in some indicators while keeping others stable or even worsening them. One question is, under which circumstances such innovations still could be considered sustainable. An answer could refer to the overall effect on sustainability and depend on whether the improvements outweigh the negative effects, which in turn requires value-based weightings of the different indicators. This comes along with the normative judgment about the desirability of improvements in specific indicators and the acceptable costs of such improvements. Regarding the long-term time horizon of a transformation toward sustainability, assessing an innovation's impact is also an issue of temporal dynamics that could occur, especially if effects change from positive to negative or vice versa. This in turn raises questions about time-based discounting of long-term effects, and how to arrive at the necessary discount rates.

Empirical investigations about sustainable innovations barely provide details regarding the methods used for assessing the sustainability effects of innovations (see for example Ayele et al., 2012; Di Maria et al., 2019; Hajek & Stejskal, 2018; Rauter et al., 2019). In some cases, it is not clear whether the actual impact of supposedly sustainable innovations has been assessed at all. Studies based on surveys regularly rely on the respondents' appraisement of whether innovations have had positive effects. Numerous other studies, especially those focusing on environmental aspects of sustainability, use patent data as a proxy for sustainable innovations.[6]

[6] Section 7.3 provides further details about such approaches, also regarding their shortcomings.

References

Abson, D. J., Fischer, J., Leventon, J., Newig, J., Schomerus, T., Vilsmaier, U., et al. (2017). Leverage points for sustainability transformation. *Ambio, 46*(1), 30–39.

Adams, R., Jeanrenaud, S., Bessant, J., Denyer, D., & Overy, P. (2016). Sustainability-oriented innovation: A systematic review. *International Journal of Management Reviews, 18*(2), 180–205.

Alexander, S. (2012). Planned economic contraction: The emerging case for degrowth. *Environmental Politics, 21*(3), 349–368.

Antonelli, C. (2009). The economics of innovation: From the classical legacies to the economics of complexity. *Economics of Innovation and New Technology, 18*(7), 611–646.

Ayele, S., Duncan, A., Larbi, A., & Khanh, T. T. (2012). Enhancing innovation in livestock value chains through networks: Lessons from fodder innovation case studies in developing countries. *Science and Public Policy, 39*(3), 333–346. https://www.scopus.com/inward/record.uri?eid=2-s2.0-84871418935&doi=10.1093%2fscipol%2fscs022&partnerID=40&md5=70c8d0d2b31bc3c7c0ea76b2f67398ec

Baek, J. S., Kim, S., & Harimoto, T. (2019). The effect of cultural differences on a distant collaboration for social innovation: A case study of designing for precision farming in Myanmar and South Korea. *Design and Culture, 11*(1, SI), 37–58.

Bakker, S., Guillen, M. D., Nanthachatchavankul, P., Zuidgeest, M., Pardo, C., & van Maarseveen, M. (2018). Hot or not? The role of cycling in ASEAN megacities: Case studies of Bangkok and Manila. *International Journal of Sustainable Transportation, 12*(6), 416–431.

Barbieri, N., Ghisetti, C., Gilli, M., Marin, G., & Nicolli, F. (2016). A survey of the literature on environmental innovation based on Main path analysis. *Journal of Economic Surveys, 30*(3), 596–623.

Berkhout, P. H., Muskens, J. C., Velthuijsen, W., & J. (2000). Defining the rebound effect. *Energy Policy, 28*(6–7), 425–432.

Blättel-Mink, B. (1998). Innovation towards sustainable economy—The integration of economy and ecology in companies. *Sustainable Development, 6*(2), 49–58.

Blättel-Mink, B. (2021). Das Innovationsverständnis von Joseph A. Schumpeter. In B. Blättel-Mink, I. Schulz-Schaeffer, & A. Windeler (Eds.), *Handbuch Innovationsforschung* (pp. 63–82). Springer Fachmedien Wiesbaden.

Boer, H., & During, W. E. (2001). Innovation, what innovation? A comparison between product, process and organisational innovation. *International Journal of Technology Management, 22*(1/2/3), 83.

Boons, F., Montalvo, C., Quist, J., & Wagner, M. (2013). Sustainable innovation, business models and economic performance: An overview. *Journal of Cleaner Production, 45*, 1–8.

Brodhag, C. (2013). Research universities, technology transfer, and job creation: What infrastructure, for what training? *Studies in Higher Education, 38*(3, SI), 388–404.

Büchs, M., & Koch, M. (2019). Challenges for the degrowth transition: The debate about wellbeing. *Futures, 105*, 155–165.

Caniglia, G., Luederitz, C., Wirth, T. von, Fazey, I., Martín-López, B., Hondrila, K., et al. (2021). A pluralistic and integrated approach to action-oriented knowledge for sustainability. *Nature Sustainability, 4*(2), 93–100.

Clark, T., & Charter, M. (2007). *Sustainable innovation: Key conclusions from sustainable innovation conferences 2003–2006 organised by the Centre for Sustainable Design.* Sustainable Innovation.

Dasgupta, P., & David, P. A. (1994). Toward a new economics of science. *Research Policy, 23*(5), 487–521.

Di Maria, E., Marchi, V. de, & Spraul, K. (2019). Who benefits from university-industry collaboration for environmental sustainability? International Journal of Sustainability in Higher Education, 20(6), 1022–1041.

Dwyer, J. (2013). Transformation for sustainable agriculture: What role for the second pillar of CAP? *Bio-Based and Applied Economics, 2*(1), 29–47. https://www.scopus.com/inward/record.uri?eid=2-s2.0-84937425588&partnerID=40&md5=34516af279bbf1427da971e3d16aed30

Elzen, B., & Wieczorek, A. (2005). Transitions towards sustainability through system innovation. *Technological Forecasting and Social Change, 72*(6), 651–661.

European Commission. (2019). Communication from the commission to the European Parliament, the European council, the council, the European economic and social committee and the Committee of the Regions 'the European green Deal' COM (2019) 640 final, Brussels. https://eur-lex.europa.eu/legal-content/EN/TXT/?uri=CELEX:52019DC0640

European Commission. (2020). Communication from the commission to the European Parliament, the European council, the council, the European economic and social committee and the Committee of the Regions—a new industrial strategy for Europe. https://eur-lex.europa.eu/legal-content/EN/TXT/?uri=CELEX:52020DC0102&qid=1683118489896

Evans, J., & Karvonen, A. (2014). 'Give me a laboratory and I will lower your carbon footprint!'—Urban Laboratories and the governance of low-carbon futures. *International Journal of Urban and Regional Research, 38*(2), 413–430.

Falcone, P. M., González García, S., Imbert, E., Lijó, L., Moreira, M. T., Tani, A., et al. (2019). Transitioning towards the bio-economy: Assessing the social dimension through a stakeholder lens. *Corporate Social Responsibility and Environmental Management, 26*(5), 1135–1153.

Foray, D. (2004). *Economics of knowledge*. MIT Press.

Franceschini, S., Faria, L. G., & Jurowetzki, R. (2016). Unveiling scientific communities about sustainability and innovation. A bibliometric journey around sustainable terms. *Journal of Cleaner Production, 127*, 72–83.

Freeman, C., & Soete, L. (2000). *The economics of industrial innovation* (3. ed., reprinted ed.). MIT Press.

Fussler, C., & James, P. (1996). *Driving eco-innovation: A breakthrough discipline for innovation and sustainability*. Pitman publ.

Geels, F. W. (2005). Processes and patterns in transitions and system innovations: Refining the co-evolutionary multi-level perspective. *Technological Forecasting and Social Change, 72*(6), 681–696.

Geissdoerfer, M., Savaget, P., Bocken, N. M., & Hultink, E. J. (2017). The circular economy—A new sustainability paradigm? *Journal of Cleaner Production, 143*, 757–768.

Glaser, A., Ben Slimane, S., Auplat, C., & Coeurderoy, R. (2016). Enabling nanotechnology entrepreneurship in a French context towards a holistic theoretical framework. *Journal of Small Business and Enterprise Development, 23*(4), 1009–1031.

Goncz, E., Skirke, U., Kleizen, H., & Barber, M. (2007). Increasing the rate of sustainable change: A call for a redefinition of the concept and the model for its implementation. *Journal of Cleaner Production, 15*(6), 525–537.

Grunwald, A. (2007). Working towards sustainable development in the face of uncertainty and incomplete knowledge. *Journal of Environmental Policy & Planning, 9*(3–4), 245–262.

Hajek, P., & Stejskal, J. (2018). R&D cooperation and knowledge spillover effects for sustainable business innovation in the chemical industry. *Sustainability, 10*(4).

Hall, J., & Vredenburg, H. (2003). The challenges of innovating for sustainable development. *MIT Sloan Management Review*. https://sloanreview.mit.edu/article/the-challenges-of-innovating-for-sustainable-development/

Hansen, E. G., Grosse-Dunker, F., & Reichwald, R. (2009). Sustainability innovation cube—A framework to evaluate sustainability-oriented innovations. *International Journal of Innovation Management, 13*(4), 683–713.

Hauser, M., Loiskandl, W., & Wurzinger, M. (2011). Innovation systems research sustainable natural resource use in least developed countries. *GAIA—Ecological Perspectives for Science and Society, 20*(1), 70–72.

Horbach, J., Oltra, V., & Belin, J. (2013). Determinants and specificities of eco-innovations compared to other innovations-an econometric analysis for the French and German industry based on the community innovation survey. *Industry and Innovation, 20*(6), 523–543. https://www.scopus.com/inward/record.uri?eid=2-s2.0-84887093794&doi=10.1080%2f13662716.2013.833375&partnerID=40&md5=f48e51984dde023f1b8f624e409a203e

Jacobsson, S., & Bergek, A. (2011). Innovation system analyses and sustainability transitions: Contributions and suggestions for research. *Environmental Innovation and Societal Transitions, 1*(1), 41–57.

Jaeger-Erben, M., Rückert-John, J., & Schäfer, M. (2015). Sustainable consumption through social innovation: A typology of innovations for sustainable consumption practices. *Journal of Cleaner Production, 108*, 784–798.

Jaffe, A. B., Newell, R. G., & Stavins, R. N. (2002). Environmental policy and technological change. *Environmental and Resource Economics, 22*(1/2), 41–70.

Jones, J., & de Zubielqui, G. C. (2017). Doing well by doing good: A study of university-industry interactions, innovationess and firm performance in sustainability-oriented Australian SMEs. *Technological Forecasting and Social Change, 123*, 262–270.

Khumairoh, U., Lantinga, E. A., Suprayogo, D., Schulte, R., & Groot, J. (2019). Modifying the farmer field school method to support on-farm adaptation of complex rice systems. *Journal of Agricultural Education and Extension, 25*(3), 227–243. https://www.scopus.com/inward/record.uri?eid=2-s2.0-85064638550&doi=10.1080%2f1389224X.2019.1604391&partnerID=40&md5=497f640fe79957ac38c816e18f70f149

Klewitz, J., & Hansen, E. G. (2014). Sustainability-oriented innovation of SMEs: A systematic review. *Journal of Cleaner Production, 65*, 57–75.

Koenig, A. (2015). Towards systemic change: On the co-creation and evaluation of a study programme in transformative sustainability science with stakeholders in Luxembourg. *Current Opinion in Environmental Sustainability, 16*, 89–98.

Lehoux, P., Silva, H. P., Sabio, R. P., & Roncarolo, F. (2018). The unexplored contribution of responsible innovation in health to sustainable development goals. *Sustainability, 10*(11).

Luederitz, C., Schäpke, N., Wiek, A., Lang, D. J., Bergmann, M., Bos, J. J., et al. (2017). Learning through evaluation—A tentative evaluative scheme for sustainability transition experiments. *Journal of Cleaner Production, 169*, 61–76.

Martin, D. P. (2019). Knowledge transfer models and poverty alleviation in developing countries: Critical approaches and foresight. *Third World Quarterly, 40*(7), 1209–1226.

Matthews, N. E., Stamford, L., & Shapira, P. (2019). Aligning sustainability assessment with responsible research and innovation: Towards a framework for constructive sustainability assessment. *Sustainable Production and Consumption, 20*, 58–73.

Mazzanti, M. (2018). Eco-innovation and sustainability: Dynamic trends, geography and policies. *Journal of Environmental Planning and Management, 61*(11), 1851–1860. https://www.scopus.com/inward/record.uri?eid=2-s2.0-85055419592&doi=10.1080%2f09640568.2018.1486290&partnerID=40&md5=14f8556d894a42be04285f021df037b8

OECD. (2011). *Towards green growth*. OECD Publishing.

OECD. (2017). *Investing in climate, investing in growth*. OECD Publishing.

OECD/Eurostat. (2018). *Oslo manual 2018: Guidelines for collecting, reporting and using data on innovation* (4th ed.). OECD Publishing.

Pol, E., & Ville, S. (2009). Social innovation: Buzz word or enduring term? *The Journal of Socio-Economics, 38*(6), 878–885.

Porter, M. E., & van der Linde, C. (1995). Toward a new conception of the environment-competitiveness relationship. *Journal of Economic Perspectives, 9*(4), 97–118. https://www.aeaweb.org/articles?id=10.1257/jep.9.4.97

Pyka, A. (2017). Dedicated innovation systems to support the transformation towards sustainability: Creating income opportunities and employment in the knowledge-based digital bioeconomy. *Journal of Open Innovation: Technology, Market, and Complexity, 3*(27), 1–18.

Pyka, A. (2021). Evolutorische Innovationsökonomik. In B. Blättel-Mink, I. Schulz-Schaeffer, & A. Windeler (Eds.), *Handbuch Innovationsforschung* (pp. 83–101). Springer Fachmedien Wiesbaden.

Pyka, A., & Prettner, K. (2018). Economic growth, development, and innovation: The transformation towards a knowledge-based bioeconomy. In I. Lewandowski (Ed.), *Bioeconomy* (pp. 331–342). Springer International Publishing.

Rauter, R., Globocnik, D., Perl-Vorbach, E., & Baumgartner, R. J. (2019). Open innovation and its effects on economic and sustainability innovation performance. *Journal of Innovation & Knowledge, 4*(4), 226–233.

Rennings, K. (2000). Redefining innovation—Eco-innovation research and the contribution from ecological economics. *Ecological Economics, 32*(2), 319–332.

Schaltegger, S., & Wagner, M. (2011). Sustainable entrepreneurship and sustainability innovation: Categories and interactions. *Business Strategy and the Environment, 20*(4), 222–237.

Schlaile, M., Urmetzer, S., Blok, V., Andersen, A., Timmermans, J., Mueller, M., et al. (2017). Innovation systems for transformations towards sustainability?: Taking the normative dimension seriously. *Sustainability, 9*(12, 2253), 1–20.

Schneider, F., Kallis, G., & Martinez-Alier, J. (2010). Crisis or opportunity? Economic degrowth for social equity and ecological sustainability. Introduction to this special issue. *Journal of Cleaner Production, 18*(6), 511–518.

Schot, J., & Steinmueller, W. E. (2018). Three frames for innovation policy: R&D, systems of innovation and transformative change. *Research Policy, 47*(9), 1554–1567.

Schumpeter, J. A. (1994). *Capitalism, socialism, and democracy*. Routledge.

Schumpeter, J. A. (1997). *Theorie der wirtschaftlichen Entwicklung: Eine Untersuchung über Unternehmergewinn, Kapital, Kredit, Zins und den Konjunkturzyklus (Neunte Auflage, unveränderter Nachdruck der 1934 erschienen vierten Auflage). ProQuest Ebook Central.* Duncker & Humblot.

Singh, R. K., Murty, H. R., Gupta, S. K., & Dikshit, A. K. (2012). An overview of sustainability assessment methodologies. *Ecological Indicators, 15*(1), 281–299.

Sterman, J. D. (2008). Economics. Risk communication on climate: Mental models and mass balance. *Science, 322*(5901), 532–533.

Steward, F. (2012). Transformative innovation policy to meet the challenge of climate change: Sociotechnical networks aligned with consumption and end-use as new transition arenas for a low-carbon society or green economy. *Technology Analysis & Strategic Management, 24*(4), 331–343.

Strambach, S. (2017). Combining knowledge bases in transnational sustainability innovation: Microdynamics and institutional change. *Economic Geography, 93*(5), 500–526. https://www.scopus.com/inward/record.uri?eid=2-s2.0-85030160222&doi=10.1080%2f00130095.2017.1366268&partnerID=40&md5=898772c879f5bad929c4fb7fc96e9b50

Tidd, J., Bessant, J. R., & Pavitt, K. L. R. (2005). *Managing innovation: Integrating technological, market and organizational change* (3rd. ed.). Wiley.

United Nations—Department of Economic and Social Affairs (DESA). (2023). *World population prospects 2022: Summary of results*. United Nations Publications.

Varadarajan, R. (2017). Innovating for sustainability: A framework for sustainable innovations and a model of sustainable innovations orientation. *Journal of the Academy of Marketing Science, 45*(1), 14–36.

Veiga Ávila, L., Beuron, T. A., Brandli, L. L., Damke, L. I., Pereira, R. S., & Klein, L. L. (2019). Barriers to innovation and sustainability in universities: An international comparison. *International Journal of Sustainability in Higher Education, 20*(5), 805–821. https://www.scopus.com/inward/record.uri?eid=2-s2.0-85068372697&doi=10.1108%2fIJSHE-02-2019-0067&partnerID=40&md5=af1ca70222e89de9f0cf51d447f341b9

Waddell, S. (2016). Societal change systems. *The Journal of Applied Behavioral Science, 52*(4), 422–449.

Weber, E. P., & Khademian, A. M. (2008). Wicked problems, knowledge challenges, and collaborative capacity builders in network settings. *Public Administration Review, 68*(2), 334–349.

World Bank. (2021). *Green, resilient, and inclusive development*. World Bank.

World Bank Group. (2014). *Building competitive green industries: The climate and clean technology opportunity for developing countries*. Washington, DC.

Young, H. P. (2011). The dynamics of social innovation. *Proceedings of the National Academy of Sciences of the United States of America, 108*(Suppl 4), 21285–21291.

Zink, T., & Geyer, R. (2017). Circular economy rebound. *Journal of Industrial Ecology, 21*(3), 593–602.

Chapter 4
Innovation Systems

While Sect. 3.2 has provided an introductory discussion of the defining elements of innovations, Chap. 4 goes into more detail regarding the dynamic nature of innovations and the processes that lead to their emergence. The innovation system approach serves as the analytical frame for this purpose, as it has proven to be a powerful tool for examining the occurrence of innovations and the patterns of technological and economic change.

4.1 Innovations as an Outcome of Interactive Processes

Innovation is a complex and dynamic phenomenon that defies a linear and sequential approach, as it encompasses numerous interactions and feedback loops in the creation and utilization of knowledge (Lundvall, 1992; Nelson, 1993; OECD, 1997). It is based upon a continuous interactive learning process that relies on diverse inputs and necessitates ongoing problem-solving. Individuals and organizations interact and engage in knowledge exchange, collaboration, and experimentation. Innovations exhibit systemic and evolutionary characteristics, transcending isolated advancements to influence and reshape entire systems and industries (Dosi, 1988). The innovative process is highly path-dependent and cumulative, building upon past knowledge, experiences, and achievements. Each innovation serves as a stepping stone, laying the foundation for subsequent breakthroughs and contributing to economic progress (Arbo & Benneworth, 2007; Dosi, 1988). This perspective of "innovation as an interactive process" might be the reason why the traditional divide between those emphasizing the significance of supply-side factors and those advocating for the influence of demand factors in shaping the speed and trajectory of innovation, has been overcome (Jensen et al., 2007).

The innovation system approach takes these considerations into account. It is a holistic concept for analyzing the occurrence of innovations. It encompasses the set

U. Wilke, *Towards Sustainable Innovations*, Economic Complexity and Evolution,
https://doi.org/10.1007/978-3-032-31024-8_4

of institutions, actors, and further structural elements, as well as their relationships, that act and interact in the production, diffusion, and application of knowledge and economically useful novelties. Seminal works that introduced the concept came from Lundvall (1992) and Nelson (1993) for the national level (NIS—national innovation system), while Cooke (1992) introduced the concept at the regional level (RIS—regional innovation system). Table 4.1 provides an overview of prominent definitions.

The innovation system approach draws its intellectual foundations from the pioneering work of Friedrich List and Alois Schumpeter, as well as from the fields of evolutionary economics and systems thinking (Acs et al., 2017; Hanusch & Pyka, 2007; Lundvall, 2016; Weber & Truffer, 2017). Friedrich List was among the early scholars to emphasize the role of technology in driving economic development, while Schumpeter's prominent role in the analysis of innovation has already been highlighted in Sect. 3.2. Evolutionary economics as a discipline examines the dynamics of change over time, employing explanations that incorporate random elements for creating variation and mechanisms for selection and retention (Dosi & Nelson, 1994). Thus, the focus lies on understanding learning processes and the influence of path dependencies, which are central to this approach. Path dependency has two key implications in this context (Pierson, 2000). Firstly, it encompasses the overarching idea that "history matters," often used to challenge explanations that overlook historical factors. This assertion can be distilled into the simple notion that the future trajectory of an economic system is influenced by its historical path. Secondly, it involves

Table 4.1 Definitions of innovation systems with partly different geographical scopes

Definition	Author(s)
"… A system of innovation is constituted by the elements and relationships which interact in the production, diffusion and use of new, and economically useful, knowledge … and are either located within or rooted inside the borders of a nation state."	Lundvall (1992)
"… a set of institutions whose interactions determine the innovative performance … of national firms."	Nelson (1993)
"A national system of innovation is the system of interacting private and public firms (either large or small), universities and government agencies, aiming at the production of science and technology within national borders. Interaction among those units may be technical, commercial, legal, social and financial, inasmuch as the goal of the interaction is the development, protection, financing or regulation of new science and technology."	Niosi et al. (1993)
"Our own concept of a national system of innovation builds on these earlier contributions, and can be defined as follows: The national institutions, their incentive structures and their competencies, that determine the rate and direction of technological learning (or the volume and composition of change-generating activities) in a country."	Patel and Pavitt (1994)
"It can be thought of as a system which creates and distributes knowledge, utilizes this knowledge by introducing it into the economy in the form of innovations, diffuses it and transforms it into something valuable, for example, international competitiveness and economic growth."	Gregersen and Johnson (1997)

a more precise assertion regarding how past events or decisions disproportionately impact future events or decisions, employing mechanisms like increasing returns, positive feedback effects, lock-ins, or other similar mechanisms (Pierson, 2000). Since its introduction in the late 1990s, the innovation system approach has been applied widely to examine questions about the innovative performance or competitiveness of specific regions or countries and has furthermore considerably influenced politics (Fagerberg, 2017).

The innovation system approach helps understand the processes that lead to innovations and thus generates insights for adopting policies that address inefficiencies within the system. These inefficiencies can arise from various factors such as infrastructure limitations, transition challenges, institutional shortcomings, network failures, and capabilities deficits (Jacobsson & Bergek, 2011). By recognizing and addressing these failures, policies can be developed to improve the innovation system and promote more effective and sustainable innovation processes. The innovation system approach can help identify the most severe weaknesses and hence those components and processes where policy interventions are likely to have the biggest effect (Jacobsson & Bergek, 2011).

Different authors have proposed frameworks for mapping core functions of innovation systems, see for example Hekkert et al. (2007), Hekkert and Negro (2009), Jacobsson and Bergek (2011), or Weber and Truffer (2017). Those approaches emphasize similar aspects, illustrating the importance of the following topics for innovation systems theory: entrepreneurial activities, development, and diffusion of knowledge, guidance of the search, market formation, resource mobilization, and legitimization. Table 4.2 provides an overview of these central features.

Knowledge plays a decisive role in innovation systems, as can be seen in the definition by Gregersen and Johnson (1997), as shown in Table 4.1, who put knowledge at the center. Knowledge must be understood as the most important resource within an innovation system as it lies at the core of any innovation process, making learning the most important activity (Lundvall, 2016). Respectively, the innovation systems approach places a strong emphasis on knowledge and the corresponding processes. The generation of knowledge, encompassing both explicit and implicit knowledge, as well as its dissemination and assimilation, represent pivotal elements in innovation systems theory (Wehn & Montalvo, 2018). Such flows of technology and information between individuals, businesses, and institutions can occur in various forms such as joint research activities, technical collaborations, co-patenting, co-publications, via informal linkages between organizations and individuals, as well as via the adoption and application of new machinery and equipment or via personnel mobility, to give a non-exhaustive list of examples (OECD, 1997). Those different modes of exchange can be distinguished into formal processes of research and development and informal approaches focusing on interactive learning, whereby those firms and organizations that practice both modes seem to be the most successful ones (Jensen et al., 2007).

In relation to the history of neoclassical economic thought, innovation systems theory differs regarding the understanding of the dynamic, path-dependent, and disruptive nature of change and innovations, entailing the existence of disequilibria

Table 4.2 Innovation system core functions according to Hekkert et al. (2007)

Function	Description
Entrepreneurial activities	Entrepreneurs play a crucial role in innovation systems. Their role lies in translating the potential of new knowledge development, networks, and markets into tangible actions, thereby creating, and seizing business opportunities
Development and diffusion of knowledge	Learning mechanisms form the core of every innovation process. Consequently, research and development alongside knowledge development are essential prerequisites within the innovation system. The function of networks revolves around the exchange of information. Especially in a diverse context where research and development intersect with government, competitors, and the market, policy decisions, including standards and long-term targets, should align with the latest technological insights, and concurrently, research agendas are likely to be influenced by evolving norms and values. Networks serve as channels for diffusing such information and the corresponding knowledge
Guidance of the search	This system function encompasses activities within the innovation system that can enhance the recognition and clarity of specific needs among technology users. Expectations play a role as well, as there are instances where expectations align on a particular issue, creating momentum for change
Market formation	New technologies frequently face challenges when competing with established technologies. Hence, it becomes crucial to establish protected environments for the introduction of these new technologies. Approaches include the creation of temporary niche markets or favorable tax structures
Resource mobilization	Essential for all activities within the innovation system are resources, encompassing both financial and human aspects. Providing adequate supply and ensuring accessibility to resources are thus critical functions
Legitimization	For a new technology to prosper, it must integrate into an existing regime or, in some cases, disrupt it entirely. Opposition from vested interests is common in the face of this "creative destruction". In such situations, advocacy coalitions can serve as a catalyst, working to establish legitimacy for the new technology and counteracting resistance to change

and fluctuations (Jensen et al., 2007). Another significant difference to the neoclassical approach stems from the understanding of the nature and role of knowledge. The innovation system approach treats knowledge as a resource that doesn't float freely but is sticky (Hippel, 1994). It furthermore requires absorptive capacity on the side of a receiving agent to be acquired (Cohen & Levinthal, 1990), and exhibits limited accessibility (confer Jensen et al., 2007; Schot & Steinmueller, 2018).[1]

Since its introduction, the innovation system approach has been adapted and extended to focus on specific sectors, industries, or technologies. This resulted in

[1] These points will be further elaborated in Sect. 5.1.2.

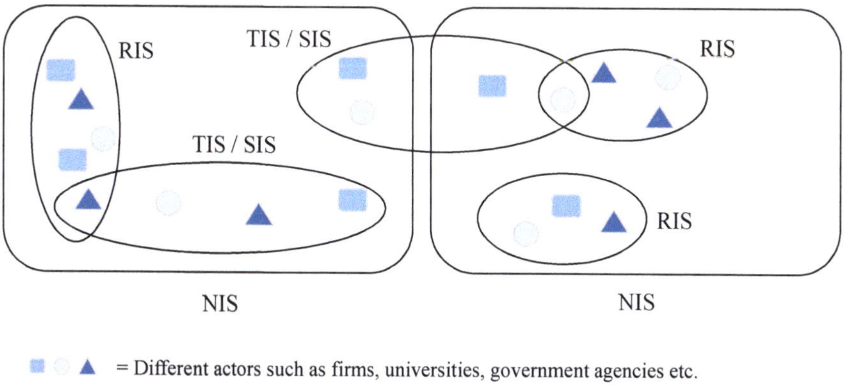

Fig. 4.1 Relation of NIS, RIS, and TIS/SIS

concepts such as sectoral innovation systems (Malerba, 2002) or technological innovation systems (Binz et al., 2014). The various innovation system approaches differ in the definition of the borders of the examined systems, and hence allow investigation of different research questions. They can be considered to be interdependent to a certain extent (Jacobsson & Bergek, 2011), whereby the industry-specific and technology-specific systems can also show geographical patterns and are not per se without geographical borders (Binz et al., 2014). However, the different types of systems can also relate to each other (Hekkert et al., 2007). Figure 4.1 shows the geographical relation between national innovation systems (NIS), regional innovation systems (RIS), and technological innovation systems (TIS), respectively sectoral innovation systems (SIS).

4.2 Innovation Systems Bearing Sustainable Innovations

A transformation toward sustainability entails the collaborative creation of social, behavioral, and technological change, interconnectedly impacting skills, industry structures, regulations, products, infrastructures, user preferences, and cultural settings. The sustainable innovations that can facilitate such a change differ from conventional innovations that focus purely on economic aspects. Schot and Steinmueller (2018) hence suggest, that the prevalent innovation system approaches, which focus on analyzing such conventional innovation, might not be appropriate for analyzing sustainable innovations. The approach thus needs to be adjusted to incorporate considerations of ecological and social impacts of the desired sustainable innovations, while recognizing the significance of social innovations and the potential values of old technologies. The transformative character of sustainable innovations and the disruptive nature of associated changes imply different working mechanisms and creation processes. This also implies the inclusion of different actors and further fields of knowledge to cover non-market-related impacts of the desired innovations.

An early example of an extended innovation system approach is presented by Segura-Bonilla (2003), who, based on a study of the forest sector, introduces natural elements and economy–ecology relationships into the system, allowing for a more accurate mapping of all relevant factors and aiming at deriving innovations that foster sustainable forestry and sustainable development in the long run. In such a sustainable system of innovation, learning and the creation of economically useful knowledge occur in the context of human interactions as well as in the context of interactions with environmental endowments of nature. Apart from industry, government, and academia, such innovation systems also involve consumers and indigenous groups, presuming that access to the tacit knowledge of such groups bears valuable insights regarding ecological aspects (Segura-Bonilla, 2003).

Altenburg and Pegels (2012) propose a sustainability-oriented innovation system with a strong role for the government, which is supposed to use incentives and regulations to promote the development and deployment of sustainable technologies. The approach aims to overcome market failures and drive a fundamental socio-technological paradigm shift within a limited timeframe. Achieving consensus on the direction of change and compensating stakeholders affected by reforms become critical aspects of effective governance, alongside the harmonization of national and international policy frameworks. However, implementing government interventions carries inherent risks, such as making costly wrong technology choices and potential rent-seeking behaviors with long-term subsidies. To address these challenges and adapt to changing circumstances, a dynamic mix of policy instruments, including incentives, orders, and innovative policies, is needed. Overall, the success of sustainability-oriented innovation systems hinges on robust and adaptive governance mechanisms. By balancing incentives and regulations, fostering collaboration, and staying responsive to emerging information, governments can effectively drive transformative changes toward sustainability while minimizing potential pitfalls (Altenburg & Pegels, 2012).

Jacobsson and Bergek (2011) argue in a similar direction, emphasizing the need for technology-specific policies for addressing sustainability challenges. Market-based economic incentives and R&D support are essential but insufficient to tackle the diverse challenges posed by different technologies. To effectively promote sustainable alternatives to fossil fuels, policymakers should adopt a comprehensive approach that considers the unique features and contexts of each technology within the different technological innovation systems. These policies should target all critical components of the innovation process to support the development and diffusion of eco-friendly solutions (Jacobsson & Bergek, 2011).

Ghazinoory et al. (2020) present the concept of a problem-oriented innovation system for tackling macro-level societal issues. They emphasize the need for a dual approach, integrating technical innovations and social innovations to address the different technological, social, and economic aspects of major challenges such as sustainability. This combination appears crucial for comprehensive problem-solving. Such a problem-oriented innovation system implies additional functionalities, including system monitoring and guidance, fostering public awareness, and promoting standardization (Ghazinoory et al., 2020). At its core, the problem-oriented innovation system aims to achieve problem resolution through the synergistic collaboration of various levels of innovation systems, thus harnessing the potential of both technological advancements and social changes for identifying promising avenues for tackling issues such as sustainability.

A further approach is the dedicated innovation system (Pyka, 2017; Schlaile et al., 2017; Urmetzer et al., 2018), which goes beyond traditional innovation system approaches by aiming for systemic change toward sustainability rather than focusing solely on technological change and economic growth. Dedicated innovation systems are understood as complex adaptive systems, involving various actors and institutions from industrial, scientific, political, fiscal, and civil society domains. These actors are interconnected, creating a creative environment that fosters mutual learning and knowledge creation, all to pursue socially desirable and sustainable innovations. Dedicated innovation systems differ from conventional approaches by striving for balance among regulatory push, demand-driven market pull, science-based technology push, and societal and ethical considerations (see Fig. 4.2). To achieve sustainable progress, it appears important to integrate social innovations alongside technological advancements, ensuring a wider positive impact on citizens while increasing their willingness to participate in the transformative process. This approach furthermore underlines that the interconnectedness between economic growth, human development, social inclusion, and sustainability heavily relies on a nation's innovation capabilities and its capacity to absorb technological advancements effectively (Pyka, 2017; Schlaile et al., 2017).

Introducing a clear goal orientation toward sustainability incorporates a normative dimension which is a significant alteration to the innovation system model (Schlaile et al., 2017). This implies looking at the level of underlying paradigms, which comprise fundamental assumptions and beliefs guiding human behavior, elucidating co-evolutionary dependencies between paradigms and social practices. In this context, technological innovation, competition, entrepreneurship, and knowledge creation and diffusion play pivotal roles in driving societal transformation. Understanding these interconnected dynamics offers valuable insights into leveraging innovation's potential for addressing challenges and promoting sustainable development (Pyka, 2017).

The normative aspect of such an innovation system approach gives rise to questions concerning its directionality, legitimacy, and responsibility (Schlaile et al., 2017). Addressing these questions is essential before determining the "how" of the transformation process. Directionality refers to defining a specific goal of the transformation process and then choosing the right pathway toward it. This is an intricate issue as sustainability is a wicked problem. It is further aggravated by the evolutionary character of innovations, which question the prospects of success of a planning approach. Identifying the direction requires understanding which agents or groups possess the capacity and influence to guide societies toward socially desirable

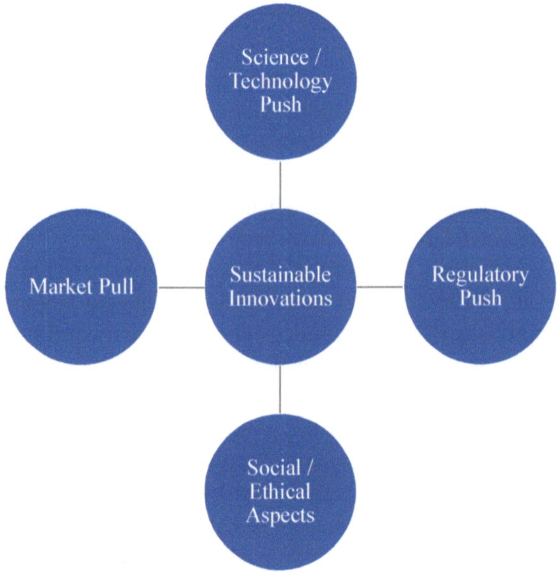

Fig. 4.2 Push and pull factors regarding sustainable innovations

outcomes. Secondly, the legitimacy of transformation toward sustainability comes into question. While top-down approaches are no longer self-evident, bottom-up approaches may struggle to find the optimal innovative solution without achieving a critical mass (Schlaile et al., 2017). Cultural evolutionary processes further shape values, goals, and norms, creating barriers and enablers for both the "what" and "why" questions of sustainability. Finally, the question of responsibility emerges, involving considerations of who wields the power to bring about change and who bears the consequences of these transformative efforts. Addressing these complex questions is crucial for ensuring a purposeful and inclusive transformation toward a sustainable future.

The systemic borders of such sustainability-oriented innovation systems are given by the problem they address, namely the issue of sustainability. The corresponding innovation networks can have various geographical scales, in correspondence to the specific sustainability challenges they address. They can be regional, national, or cross-border, for example when it comes to transnational problems such as the pollution of large lakes, oceans, border rivers, or cross-border ecosystems. Sustainability-oriented innovation networks can also consist of actors who are dispersed around the globe due to the international nature of large-scale sustainability issues such as climate change, or because the relevant knowledge for addressing specific (local) sustainability challenges can be found among highly specialized actors who are globally dispersed (confer Baek et al., 2019; Haas et al., 2016).

4.3 Actors in Sustainability-oriented Innovation Systems

The turn toward sustainability as an overarching goal is leading to a fundamental change in the orientation of an innovation system. It shifts attention away from companies (and to a lesser extent universities) as the key players toward a more comprehensive approach that involves the capacities of the public sector and civil society to a greater extent (Healy & Morgan, 2012). Reasons for this are on the one hand the normative character of sustainability, implying that the formulation of particular goals is a result of the societal discourse.[2] On the other hand, the required knowledge for sustainable innovations is dispersed among a wide range of different actors outside the business world (Hojnik & Ruzzier, 2016; Horbach et al., 2013; Strambach, 2017).[3] The inclusion of diverse actors helps to get access to this knowledge and enables a better combination of complementary capabilities (Ayele et al., 2012). This also puts a focus on the users of innovations, either as consumers of goods and services that are distributed via markets, or as recipients of public goods, or as citizens applying new social practices. Von Hippels (2006) considerations of consumer-driven innovations are thus of high relevance for analyzing sustainable innovation systems. As Grundel and Dahlström (2016) put it, such consumer-driven innovations must be considered more democratic and hence are more likely to adequately represent the underlying normative concerns, as the users of innovations are directly involved in the innovation process. This is linked to the idea of a stronger role of consumers in transition processes in general, which is reflected in notions such as active consumerism or responsible consumption (confer Wilke et al., 2021). Consumers' choices influence the outcomes of market-based selection processes. Consumers can furthermore act as co-creators of value and can become the decisive factor in consumer-driven business models and networks.

Next to (organized) consumers and civil society organizations, other actors such as specific interest groups, international organizations, or intermediaries are deemed relevant for sustainable innovations. The literature mentions various actor groups in this regard. Table 4.3 provides a non-exhaustive list of examples of such groups.

Sustainability-oriented innovation systems thus include a wide variety of different actors on local, regional, national, and international levels. The collaboration of such diverse actors is demanding, and the literature is rich in examples of difficulties that can occur (confer Klenk & Hickey, 2012; McCauley & Stephens, 2012; Polk, 2015; Pyka & Nelson, 2018). Obstacles might stem from different motivations, goals, and ideas about the results of the collaboration, different understandings of sustainability and its numerous aspects, different vocabulary and subject-specific background, differing methods and approaches, different incentive structures, organizational cultures, time horizons, and so forth. Figure 4.3 provides a graphical representation of the enlarged scope of potential actors in sustainability-oriented innovation systems. The fact alone, that there is an additional group of stakeholders involved in such innovation systems increases the need for coordination mechanisms.

---

[2] Compare Sect. 2.2.5.

[3] This point is further detailed in Sect. 5.2.

Table 4.3 Non-business/non-academic actor groups in sustainability-oriented innovation systems

Actors	Author(s)
Ethical businesses, social entrepreneurs	Barron et al. (2017), Haas et al. (2016)
Indigenous groups	Klenk and Hickey (2012), Kruss and Gastrow (2017)
Non-governmental organizations	Klenk and Hickey (2012), Bisseleua et al. (2018),
Farmers associations	Bisseleua et al. (2018), Middendorf et al. (2020)
Workers unions	Klenk and Hickey (2012)
International organizations	Glaser et al., 2016)
Civil right movements	Hall & Vredenburg, 2003)
Cooperatives	Kruss & Gastrow, 2017)

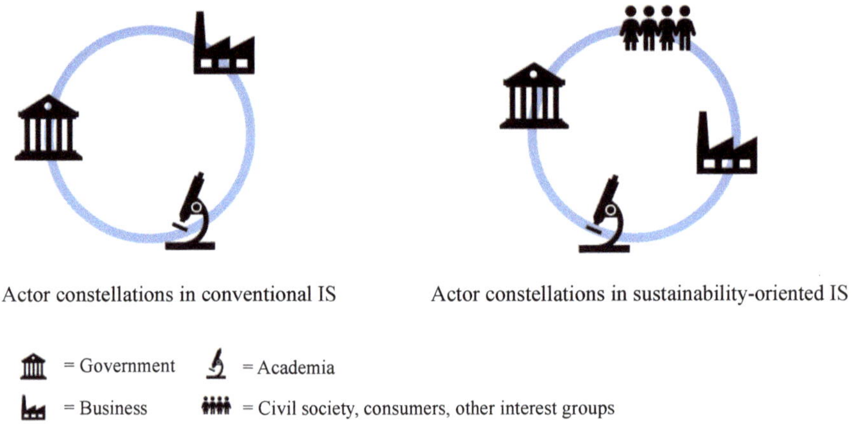

Fig. 4.3 Differing stakeholder groups typically involved in different kinds of innovation systems

Comparing the different actor groups, it appears that higher education institutions play a vital role in sustainability-oriented innovation networks. First, they serve as hubs for generating new knowledge (Dobers et al., 2008). Universities hold a unique position in society, fostering independent and free-thinking research and idea exchange. They are widely recognized as centers for creating, preserving, disseminating, and exchanging knowledge across various disciplines (Stephens et al., 2008). With their significant role in educating a large portion of the population and generating knowledge, universities stand as key organizations within contemporary, knowledge-driven societies (Perkmann et al., 2013). Their extensive expertise spans natural and social sciences, engineering, business, arts, and humanities, making them well-equipped to tackle multifaceted sustainability challenges (Hart et al., 2015). Indeed, modern society has yet to produce an institution that rivals universities in their capacity for generating new knowledge (Nowotny et al., 2001).

In addition to their knowledge-generating capabilities, higher education institutions possess the potential to forge long-term partnerships required to address sustainability problems effectively (Hart et al., 2015; Medici et al., 2018). Universities are trusted and stable institutions, often with centuries-long traditions, which are not driven by electoral or market pressures, allowing them to focus on their mission and pursue long-term goals (Adomssent, 2013). Their neutrality is considered an asset in regional collaborations, as they are less influenced by political or commercial tensions and are seen as more impartial (Rinaldi et al., 2018). Creating neutral spaces for networking meetings and events with businesses, state agencies, and civil society actors, and sharing resources for knowledge exchange further enhances their collaborative role. Hence, the involvement of universities in initiatives like green energy clusters has been pivotal since their inception (McCauley & Stephens, 2012).

Today, most higher education institutions have evolved beyond their traditional roles of teaching and research (Henke et al., 2016). Instead, they pursue a variety of activities, including formal adult education, knowledge transfer initiatives, and support programs for start-ups, collectively referred to as the "third mission" (Henke et al., 2016; Peer & Stoeglehner, 2013). The transformation toward sustainability has led universities to take on further roles beyond the traditional academic approach (Wittmayer & Schäpke, 2014). As knowledge brokers, process facilitators, and change managers, universities play crucial roles in the creation, transfer, and application of knowledge dedicated to sustainability. Embracing missions such as education, research, technology transfer, and co-creation, these roles complement one another and further universities' potential as powerful generators of social and technological innovation. Their long-term focus and non-profit orientation are particularly valuable attributes that contribute to their ability to foster sustainable thinking and action.

References

Acs, Z. J., Audretsch, D. B., Lehmann, E. E., & Licht, G. (2017). National systems of innovation. *The Journal of Technology Transfer, 42*(5), 997–1008.

Adomssent, M. (2013). Exploring universities' transformative potential for sustainability-bound learning in changing landscapes of knowledge communication. *Journal of Cleaner Production, 49*, 11–24.

Altenburg, T., & Pegels, A. (2012). Sustainability-oriented innovation systems—Managing the green transformation. *Innovation and Development, 2*(1), 5–22.

Arbo, P., & Benneworth, P. (2007). Understanding the regional contribution of higher education institutions: A literature review. *OECD Education Working Papers, 9*, 0–78.

Ayele, S., Duncan, A., Larbi, A., & Khanh, T. T. (2012). Enhancing innovation in livestock value chains through networks: Lessons from fodder innovation case studies in developing countries. *Science and Public Policy, 39*(3), 333–346. https://www.scopus.com/inward/record.uri?eid=2-s2.0-84871418935&doi=10.1093%2fscipol%2fscs022&partnerID=40&md5=70c8d0d2b31bc3c7c0ea76b2f67398ec

Baek, J. S., Kim, S., & Harimoto, T. (2019). The effect of cultural differences on a distant collaboration for social innovation: A case study of designing for precision farming in Myanmar and South Korea. *Design and Culture, 11*(1, SI), 37–58.

Barron, N. J., Kuller, M., Yasmin, T., Castonguay, A. C., Copa, V., Duncan-Horner, E., et al. (2017). Towards water sensitive cities in Asia: An interdisciplinary journey. *Water Science and Technology, 76*(5), 1150–1157.

Binz, C., Truffer, B., & Coenen, L. (2014). Why space matters in technological innovation systems—Mapping global knowledge dynamics of membrane bioreactor technology. *Research Policy, 43*(1), 138–155.

Bisseleua, D., Idrissou, L., Olurotimi, P., Ogunniyi, A., Mignouna, D., & Bamire, S. A. (2018). Multi-stakeholder process strengthens agricultural innovations and sustainable livelihoods of farmers in southern Nigeria. *Journal of Agricultural Education and Extension, 24*(1), 29–49. https://www.scopus.com/inward/record.uri?eid=2-s2.0-85032832587&doi=10.1080%2f1389224X.2017.1392992&partnerID=40&md5=69d64c77313db12a24a15288c7d891a9

Cohen, W. M., & Levinthal, D. A. (1990). Absorptive capacity: A new perspective on learning and innovation. *Administrative Science Quarterly, 35*(1), 128.

Cooke, P. (1992). Regional innovation systems: Competitive regulation in the new Europe. *Geoforum, 23*(3), 365–382.

Dobers, P., Linderstrom, M., & Mobjork, M. (2008). Institutional entrepreneurship in an academic organisation: Sustainability at Malardalen university. *International Journal of Innovation and Sustainable Development, 3*(3–4), 201–216. https://www.scopus.com/inward/record.uri?eid=2-s2.0-58149337360&doi=10.1504%2fIJISD.2008.022226&partnerID=40&md5=65d44f37c1ccda3897f664dd94f61c10

Dosi, G. (1988). Sources, procedures, and microeconomic effects of innovation. *Journal of Economic Literature, 26*(3), 1120–1171.

Dosi, G., & Nelson, R. R. (1994). An introduction to evolutionary theories in economics. *Journal of Evolutionary Economics, 4*(3), 153–172.

Fagerberg, J. (2017). Innovation policy: Rationales, lessons an challenges. *Journal of Economic Surveys, 31*(2), 497–512.

Ghazinoory, S., Nasri, S., Ameri, F., Montazer, G. A., & Shayan, A. (2020). Why do we need 'problem-oriented innovation system (PIS)' for solving macro-level societal problems? *Technological Forecasting and Social Change, 150*, 119749.

Glaser, A., Ben Slimane, S., Auplat, C., & Coeurderoy, R. (2016). Enabling nanotechnology entrepreneurship in a French context towards a holistic theoretical framework. *Journal of Small Business and Enterprise Development, 23*(4), 1009–1031.

Gregersen, B., & Johnson, B. (1997). Learning economies, innovation systems and European integration. *Regional Studies, 31*(5), 479–490.

Grundel, I., & Dahlström, M. (2016). A quadruple and quintuple helix approach to regional innovation Systems in the Transformation to a forestry-based bioeconomy. *Journal of the Knowledge Economy, 7*(4), 963–983.

Haas, R., Meixner, O., & Petz, M. (2016). Enabling community-powered co-innovation by connecting rural stakeholders with global knowledge brokers a case study from Nepal. *British Food Journal, 118*(6), 1350–1369.

Hall, J., & Vredenburg, H. (2003). The challenges of innovating for sustainable development. *MIT Sloan Management Review*. https://sloanreview.mit.edu/article/the-challenges-of-innovating-for-sustainable-development/

Hanusch, H., & Pyka, A. (2007). Principles of neo-Schumpeterian economics. *Cambridge Journal of Economics, 31*(2), 275–289.

Hart, D. D., Bell, K. P., Lindenfeld, L. A., Jain, S., Johnson, T. R., Ranco, D., & McGill, B. (2015). Strengthening the role of universities in addressing sustainability challenges: The Mitchell center for sustainability solutions as an institutional experiment. *Ecology and Society, 20*(2).

Healy, A., & Morgan, K. (2012). Spaces of innovation: Learning, proximity and the ecological turn. *Regional Studies, 46*(8), 1041–1053.

Hekkert, M. P., & Negro, S. O. (2009). Functions of innovation systems as a framework to understand sustainable technological change: Empirical evidence for earlier claims. *Technological Forecasting and Social Change, 76*(4), 584–594.

Hekkert, M. P., Suurs, R., Negro, S. O., Kuhlmann, S., & Smits, R. (2007). Functions of innovation systems: A new approach for analysing technological change. *Technological Forecasting and Social Change, 74*(4), 413–432.

Henke, J., Pasternack, P., & Schmid, S. (2016). *Third Mission bilanzieren: Die dritte Aufgabe der Hochschulen und ihre öffentliche Kommunikation. HoF-Handreichungen: Vol. 8.* Wittenberg: Institut für Hochschulforschung (HoF) Halle-Wittenberg.

Hojnik, J., & Ruzzier, M. (2016). What drives eco-innovation? A review of an emerging literature. *Environmental Innovation and Societal Transitions, 19*, 31–41.

Horbach, J., Oltra, V., & Belin, J. (2013). Determinants and specificities of eco-innovations compared to other innovations-an econometric analysis for the French and German industry based on the community innovation survey. *Industry and Innovation, 20*(6), 523–543. from https://www.scopus.com/inward/record.uri?eid=2-s2.0-84887093794&doi=10.1080%2f13662716.2013.833375&partnerID=40&md5=f48e51984dde023f1b8f624e409a203e

Jacobsson, S., & Bergek, A. (2011). Innovation system analyses and sustainability transitions: Contributions and suggestions for research. *Environmental Innovation and Societal Transitions, 1*(1), 41–57.

Jensen, M. B., Johnson, B., Lorenz, E., & Lundvall, B. Å. (2007). Forms of knowledge and modes of innovation. *Research Policy, 36*(5), 680–693.

Klenk, N. L., & Hickey, G. M. (2012). Improving the social robustness of research networks for sustainable natural resource management: Results of a delphi study in Canada. *Science and Public Policy, 39*(3), 357–372. https://www.scopus.com/inward/record.uri?eid=2-s2.0-84871442822&doi=10.1093%2fscipol%2fscs024&partnerID=40&md5=bb6ba96108e54d21c582dd44da47aaaf

Kruss, G., & Gastrow, M. (2017). Universities and innovation in informal settings: Evidence from case studies in South Africa. *Science and Public Policy, 44*(1), 26–36.

Lundvall, B.-Å. (Ed.). (1992). *National systems of innovation: Towards a theory of innovation and interactive learning* (Paperback ed., 1. publ ed.). Pinter.

Lundvall, B.-Å. (2016). *The learning economy and the economics of Hope.* Anthem Press.

Malerba, F. (2002). Sectoral systems of innovation and production. *Research Policy, 31*(2), 247–264.

McCauley, S. M., & Stephens, J. C. (2012). Green energy clusters and socio-technical transitions: Analysis of a sustainable energy cluster for regional economic development in Central Massachusetts, USA. *Sustainability Science, 7*(2), 213–225.

Middendorf, B. J., Prasad, P., & Pierzynski, G. M. (2020). Setting research priorities for tackling climate change. *Journal of Experimental Botany, 71*(2), 480–489, https://www.scopus.com/inward/record.uri?eid=2-s2.0-85077668026&doi=10.1093%2fjxb%2ferz360&partnerID=40&md5=07c47b92f3a09f5b028e88c1c9f16573

Nelson, R. R. (Ed.). (1993). *National innovation systems: A comparative analysis.* Oxford Univ. Press.

Niosi, J., Saviotti, P., Bellon, B., & Crow, M. (1993). National systems of innovation: In search of a workable concept. *Technology in Society, 15*(2), 207–227.

Nowotny, H., Scott, P., & Gibbons, M. (2001). *Re-thinking science: Knowledge and the public in an age of uncertainty.* Sage Publ.

OECD (1997). *National innovation systems.* Paris, France.

Patel, P., & Pavitt, K. (1994). National Innovation Systems: Why they are important, and how they might be measured and compared. *Economics of Innovation and New Technology, 3*(1), 77–95.

Peer, V., & Stoeglehner, G. (2013). Universities as change agents for sustainability—Framing the role of knowledge transfer and generation in regional development processes. *Journal of Cleaner Production, 44*, 85–95.

Perkmann, M., Tartari, V., McKelvey, M., Autio, E., Broström, A., D'Este, P., et al. (2013). Academic engagement and commercialisation: A review of the literature on university–industry relations. *Research Policy, 42*(2), 423–442.

Pierson, P. (2000). Increasing returns, path dependence, and the study of politics. *American Political Science Review, 94*(2), 251–267.

Polk, M. (2015). Transdisciplinary co-production: Designing and testing a transdisciplinary research framework for societal problem solving. *Futures, 65*, 110–122.
Pyka, A. (2017). Dedicated innovation systems to support the transformation towards sustainability: Creating income opportunities and employment in the knowledge-based digital bioeconomy. *Journal of Open Innovation: Technology, Market, and Complexity, 3*(27), 1–18.
Pyka, A., & Nelson, R. R. (2018). Schumpeterian competition and industrial dynamics. In R. R. Nelson, G. Dosi, C. E. Helfat, A. Pyka, S. G. Winter, P. P. Saviotti, et al. (Eds.), *Modern evolutionary economics. An overview* (pp. 104–128). Cambridge University Press.
Medici, S. de, Riganti, P., & Viola, S. (2018). Circular economy and the role of universities in urban regeneration: The case of Ortigia, Syracuse, *Sustainability,* 10(11).
Rinaldi, C., Cavicchi, A., Spigarelli, F., Lacche, L., & Rubens, A. (2018). Universities and smart specialisation strategy from third mission to sustainable development co-creation. *International Journal of Sustainability in Higher Education, 19*(1), 67–84.
Schlaile, M., Urmetzer, S., Blok, V., Andersen, A., Timmermans, J., Mueller, M., et al. (2017). Innovation Systems for Transformations towards sustainability?: Taking the normative dimension seriously. *Sustainability, 9*(12, 2253), 1–20.
Schot, J., & Steinmueller, W. E. (2018). Three frames for innovation policy: R&D, systems of innovation and transformative change. *Research Policy, 47*(9), 1554–1567.
Segura-Bonilla, O. (2003). Competitiveness, systems of innovation and the learning economy: The forest sector in Costa Rica. *Forest Policy and Economics, 5*(4), 373–384.
Stephens, J. C., Hernandez, M. E., Román, M., Graham, A. C., & Scholz, R. W. (2008). Higher education as a change agent for sustainability in different cultures and contexts. *International Journal of Sustainability in Higher Education, 9*(3), 317–338.
Strambach, S. (2017). Combining knowledge bases in transnational sustainability innovation: Microdynamics and institutional change. *Economic Geography, 93*(5), 500–526. https://www.scopus.com/inward/record.uri?eid=2-s2.0-85030160222&doi=10.1080%2f00130095.2017.1366268&partnerID=40&md5=898772c879f5bad929c4fb7fc96e9b50
Urmetzer, S., Schlaile, M., Bogner, K., Mueller, M., & Pyka, A. (2018). Exploring the dedicated knowledge base of a transformation towards a sustainable bioeconomy. *Sustainability, 10*(6), 1694.
von Hippel, E. (1994). "Sticky Information" and the Locus of problem solving: Implications for innovation. *Management Science, 40*(4), 429–439.
von Hippel, E. (2006). *Democratizing innovation.* The MIT Press.
Weber, K. M., & Truffer, B. (2017). Moving innovation systems research to the next level: Towards an integrative agenda. *Oxford Review of Economic Policy, 33*(1), 101–121.
Wehn, U., & Montalvo, C. (2018). Knowledge transfer dynamics and innovation: Behaviour, interactions and aggregated outcomes. *Journal of Cleaner Production, 171*, S56–S68.
Wilke, U., Schlaile, M. P., Urmetzer, S., Mueller, M., Bogner, K., & Pyka, A. (2021). Time to say 'good buy' to the passive consumer? A conceptual review of the consumer in the bioeconomy. *Journal of Agricultural and Environmental Ethics, 34*(4).
Wittmayer, J. M., & Schäpke, N. (2014). Action, research and participation: Roles of researchers in sustainability transitions. *Sustainability Science, 9*(4), 483–496.

Chapter 5
Knowledge as the Basis for Innovations and Development

As already mentioned in Sect. 4.1, knowledge is seen as pivotal for the occurrence of innovations, which in turn, can be understood as drivers of economic progress, as already argued by Schumpeter (1994, 1997). The importance of knowledge has long been recognized. The neoclassic school of economic thought highlights the role of knowledge in explaining economic development, with the Solow Growth Model (Solow, 1956) being one of the most prominent examples, putting improved technological and organizational knowledge in the form of Solow's residual at the center of explaining economic growth (Johnson et al., 2009).[1] Evolutionary economics emphasizes the importance of learning and the accumulation of knowledge for explaining trajectories of change, since knowledge is a central element in the processes of variation, selection, and retention of economic traits (Dosi & Nelson, 1994) In innovation system theory, the creation, diffusion and transfer of knowledge in multi-actor settings are key processes which lay the foundation for the occurrence of innovations (Acs et al., 2017; Arbo & Benneworth, 2007; Lundvall, 2016).

Although knowledge has always been important for economic activity, the contemporary era is often described as a knowledge society, as the prevalence of knowledge-intensive activities has reached unprecedented heights (Foray, 2004). Knowledge has thus become a central resource in every modern economy. In this context, knowledge not only fuels economic development but also forms the foundation for effective public planning, as it enables (positive) change and progress based on well-informed decisions (Rydin, 2007).

Innovation as a knowledge-based process implies that the practical applications of existing or newly developed knowledge can lead to the creation of new products, services, processes, approaches, or practices (OECD, 1997; OECD/Eurostat, 2018). The development of such novelties is thus inherently rooted in knowledge-based activities (Tidd et al., 2005). Put differently, the capacity for innovation in firms,

[1] Aghion and Howitt (2009) provide a comprehensive overview on growth models with endogenous technological change, clustered in four classes: neoclassical growth models, AK models, product variety models and Schumpeterian models.

U. Wilke, *Towards Sustainable Innovations*, Economic Complexity and Evolution,
https://doi.org/10.1007/978-3-032-31024-8_5

organizations, regions, or nations depends on their ability to introduce novel elements of knowledge or combine existing knowledge in original ways to create new and purposeful solutions, products, or processes that address evolving challenges and meet the changing needs of their respective markets or communities. This dynamic interplay between ingenuity and adaptability fosters continuous improvement and enables competitiveness and economic growth in an ever-evolving global landscape (OECD, 1997).

5.1 What Is Knowledge

Countless great minds have extensively elaborated on this question without arriving at a consensus (Grant, 1996). The notion of knowledge proves to be a complex and elusive concept. Expressed in general terms, knowledge refers to the understanding, information, facts, skills, and insights that individuals or groups acquire through experience, education, observation, and reflection. It encompasses awareness and familiarity with concepts, theories, data, events, or practices in various fields of study or areas of life. Knowledge is not just the accumulation of information but also involves the ability to process, analyze, interpret, and apply that information to solve problems, make decisions, and contribute to meaningful discussions or actions.

From an epistemological perspective, there is no clear-cut, widely accepted definition of knowledge (Pritchard, 2014). The traditional philosophical understanding of knowledge as justified true belief was rendered obsolete with Gettier's seminal work in 1963, presenting the so-called Gettier cases that undermined the traditional view (Gettier, 1963).

Instead of a singular definition, a more pragmatic approach to understanding knowledge is to view it as a cluster term with multiple dimensions (Gottschalk-Mazouz, 2007). It encompasses the idea of causal relationships (Rydin, 2007), granting individuals the power for intellectual or physical action (Foray, 2004), and providing the capacity to discern nuances within a collective domain of action, driven by an awareness of context and theory, or both (Tsoukas & Vladimirou, 2001).

Weber and Khademian (2008) offer three conceptualizations of knowledge to navigate its complexities. Firstly, knowledge can be seen as a tangible entity that can be captured, stored, transferred, and managed. Secondly, adopting a "semantic lens," knowledge is viewed in terms of its reception and the vital role interpretation plays in disseminating it. Lastly, the "pragmatic view of knowledge" portrays it as localized, embedded, and intricately connected to practice. Here, recognition is given to the interplay between knowledge and practice, understanding that what people and organizations know is deeply rooted in what they put into practice. This perspective underscores the significance of "local" knowledge, highlighting that knowledge is uniquely produced within specific contexts or settings (Weber & Khademian, 2008).

Put differently, knowledge can refer to the stock of facts, theories, information, and the corresponding interpretations and rules for application, available to a person, a group, or an organization. From a different perspective, knowledge can be understood as one of humanity's basic concepts (in an ontological sense) used to describe and order abstract items and relations, similar to other concepts such as truth, feelings, belief, consciousness, and the alike. This notion refers to the intellectual realm as part of our abstract understanding of the surrounding reality and human existence. From yet another perspective, knowledge is a concept used to describe the cognitive relation of a person, a group of persons, or all of humanity about a subject, whereby the subject can be a physical object, an abstract concept, or another person or group of persons. The cognitive relation implies an understanding of the subject and its characteristics, the availability of facts and information about the subject, and the ability to order these facts, derive implications, and place them in relation to other subjects and their characteristics.

For analytical clarity and subsequent investigations, it is useful to distinguish between data, information, and knowledge, as this differentiation holds significant implications regarding their generation, transfer, and application (Boisot & Canals, 2004). For instance, the process of reproducing knowledge primarily occurs through learning, demanding substantial time and effort, while in contrast, reproducing information in the digital era is as simple as copying and pasting (Foray, 2004). Following Tsoukas and Vladimirou (2001), data represents an ordered sequence of given items or events, information arranges items contextually, revealing relationships between them, and knowledge involves judging the significance of events and items based on specific contexts or theories. However, drawing a clear distinction between these three notions is not straightforward. A set of characters (e.g., letters from the Latin alphabet) can be interpreted differently, depending on context factors and the prior knowledge of a person seeking to interpret them. For a person who is not familiar with the Latin alphabet, the letters appear as incomprehensible scribble, while for another, it could be meaningless data, a sequence of words without meaning, and for a third person, it could hold valuable knowledge as this person possesses context information, that the second person does not have (compare Boisot & Canals, 2004). The differences between data, information, and knowledge can be delineated along several continua. One is the cost of reproduction, which is low for data and information but high for knowledge, as it involves learning. Another is the risk of loss. Knowledge is more susceptible to being lost, while information is relatively less so, and data is the least vulnerable (Boisot & Canals, 2004).

5.1.1 *Knowledge Typologies*

Several scholars have proposed categories and criteria for distinguishing different kinds of knowledge. Table 5.1 gives an overview of prominent examples of such typologies. They vary in the number of underlying dimensions and the resulting number of knowledge types. Other typologies arrange knowledge along continua, resulting in a non-discrete classification. One example is the approach of Carayannis and Campbell (2010), who use two axes for describing different kinds of knowledge:

one ranging from codified to tacit and the other from user-independent to user-dependent. Yet another approach is exemplified by Rydin (2007). She distinguishes between knowledge categories and knowledge types. Examining social planning processes, different knowledge claims exist, pertaining to the current and future socio-economic circumstances, the processes of planning and actual societal and economic change, and the normative considerations underlying the formulation of goals for a planning process. This results in six knowledge types, each assigned to one of three categories, namely empirical/descriptive knowledge, process-oriented knowledge, and predictive/normative knowledge (Rydin, 2007).

The knowledge classification of Pritchard (2014) is somewhat more fundamental compared to the others. He distinguishes between ability knowledge and propositional knowledge. The first refers to the capability of performing a specific task of physical activity such as running, climbing, drawing, typing, cutting, or sewing. The second, propositional knowledge, refers to the understanding of facts, rules, relations, and abstract concepts. Many complex tasks require proficiency in a combination of both knowledge types, such as playing an instrument, engaging in rule-based sports, acting, singing, giving a speech, or performing heart surgery. In contrast to Pritchard's (2014) classification, the other typologies in Table 5.1 predominantly focus on propositional knowledge. This is no surprise, as for most economic activities, and in particular, regarding the occurrence of innovations, propositional knowledge, the comprehension of information, regulations, connections, and theoretical ideas, is the relevant type of knowledge.

The four categories of Lundvall (2016) are *know-what*, which is knowledge about facts, *know-why*, which refers to knowledge of principles and scientific laws, *know-who*, which refers to social relations and being familiar with relevant persons possessing specific knowledge, and *know-how*, which refers to skills. Each of these knowledge types shows different characteristics when treated as a good. There are furthermore different modes of learning associated with each knowledge type,

Table 5.1 Examples of knowledge typologies

Author(s)	Number of items	Notations
Pritchard (2014)	2	Propositional knowledge, ability knowledge
Lundvall (2016)	4	Know-what, know-why, know-who, know-how
Foray (2004)	3	Certified knowledge, uncertified knowledge, integrative knowledge
Jong and Ferguson-Hessler (1996)	16	Matrix consisting of two dimensions: type of knowledge (situational, conceptual, procedural, and strategic) and qualities of knowledge (level (surface versus deep), structure, automation, modality, and generality
Gorman (2002)	8	Information (what), skills (how), judgment (when), wisdom (why)—each in an explicit (declarative) and an implicit (tacit) form

implying different mechanisms for knowledge transfer and acquisition. Finally, each of these different knowledge types discerns different characteristics regarding the possibilities and challenges associated with the codification of a specific item of knowledge.

The classification by Jong and Ferguson-Hessler (1996) follows an epistemological approach, suggesting that components within the knowledge base can be defined by the role they play in accomplishing a specific task. Their typology consists of a matrix with two dimensions: type of knowledge and quality of knowledge. The first dimension comprises four elements, namely situational, conceptual, procedural, and strategic knowledge. The second dimension, quality of knowledge, covers the level, structure, and modality of knowledge, and distinguishes between "automated (compiled) versus nonautomated knowledge" (Jong & Ferguson-Hessler, 1996, p. 108) and between general and domain-specific knowledge. Different kinds of knowledge can thus be described as a function of the two dimensions, allowing for a differentiated description of knowledge items, with a focus on the problem-solving skills of individuals.

Gorman (2002) differentiates between different classes of knowledge to study technology transfer. Taking a specific emphasis on the transfer of knowledge without explicit documentation, Gorman (2002) underscores the limitations of relying solely on documentation for effective knowledge transfer. His classification into explicit (declarative) and implicit (tacit) forms aligns with the widely accepted notion that individuals often possess knowledge beyond what they can explicitly put into words. This distinction sheds light on the intricacies of knowledge transfer, particularly in situations where reliance on explicit documentation alone may prove inadequate for a comprehensive and successful transfer process. Gorman's (2002) study captures the nuanced interplay between documented and tacit knowledge, revealing the depth of understanding required for effective knowledge transfer.

The distinction between explicit and implicit forms of knowledge was introduced by Polanyi (1966). Implicit, or tacit knowledge refers to the knowledge and understanding that individuals possess but find difficult to express or articulate explicitly. Such knowledge is generally deemed more difficult to transfer because it is highly subjective, context-dependent, and difficult to codify (Foray, 2004). In contrast to tacit knowledge, explicit knowledge is formal, codified, and can be readily communicated through language, documents, or manuals. The interplay between tacit and explicit knowledge is crucial for effective knowledge management and organizational learning (Nonaka, 1994). Recognizing and harnessing tacit knowledge is essential for fostering innovation and expertise within individuals and organizations (Jensen et al., 2007; Leonard & Sensiper, 1998). Whereby the challenge of handling tacit knowledge is threefold: first, the context of its production is relevant; the second question is how to find and appropriate tacit knowledge within an organization; and the third problem refers to mechanisms for sharing implicit knowledge with other actors (Gertler, 2003).

5.1.2 Knowledge as Good

The costs of knowledge creation and the potential benefits in the form of profitable innovations raise questions about the commercialization of scientific findings and the characteristics of knowledge as a good. The first issue concerns the problem of appropriability (Grant, 1996) and is connected to considering knowledge as intellectual property that has to be protected (Nowotny et al., 2001). According to Nelson (1989), there are generally three main ways of appropriating returns on knowledge and innovations. One is the patent systems, granting companies (but also universities or other for-profit or hybrid actors) exclusive rights to exploit a novelty for a limited period. The second possibility is secrecy. Some firms choose to keep their innovations a secret instead of seeking patents. By keeping their technology confidential, they can maintain a competitive advantage and prevent rivals from accessing their knowledge. The third possible way is the advantages of having a head start, in the tradition of Schumpeter's pioneering entrepreneurs (Schumpeter, 1997). Such strategies can also imply knowledge disclosure to establish industry-wide standards and norms for new technologies. The idea behind such strategies is to harness advantages associated with belonging to the standard-setting firms (confer Foray, 2004).

The appropriability of knowledge and innovations has to be seen as an incentive for private actors to invest in research and development, and more generally the production of knowledge by private actors (Levin et al., 1987). It prevents competitors from free-riding and allows firms to protect their commercial interests or even establish market dominance and secure returns before competitors catch up (Nelson, 1989). For the economy as a whole, this is not necessarily beneficial, since allowing existing technology to spread freely benefits not only consumers but also those who seek to enhance it. Technological progress often relies on an interactive and cumulative process, and strict protection of individual accomplishments could hinder overall advancement (Levin et al., 1987).[2]

The question, of what type of good a specific piece of knowledge is, is subject to vivid discussions. Stiglitz (1999) argues that much of knowledge is a global public good, based on the fact that knowledge is non-rivalrous and, with some exceptions, non-excludable, making it an "impure" public good. Moreover, it can spread freely across borders, which gives it a global character. Nelson (1989) argues that knowledge (technology) is partly a private and partly a public good, which gives rise to the concept of latent public good. He argues that generic knowledge might indeed have characteristics of a public good as the whole society benefits from it, and it is inexpensive or even costless to teach and learn compared with the costs of the initial knowledge production. In contrast to that, industry-specific knowledge might be very expensive for other firms to acquire and adapt for application (Nelson, 1989). Other authors argue that it depends on the type of knowledge in question, calling most

[2] The negative implications of appropriability can of course be understood in the line of welfare losses due to incomplete (monopolistic or oligopolistic) markets, whereas at the same time, counteracting effects of welfare enhancement due to economic growth driven by technological progress or entrepreneurial leadership have to be considered as well.

knowledge neither strictly public nor strictly private (Lundvall, 2016), or calling it partially non-excludable (Foray, 2004), or stating that it exhibits differing degrees of excludability (Romer, 2006).

The different assessments regarding the properties of knowledge as a good are closely linked to the underlying theoretical approaches and they can lead to quite different implications.[3] The neoclassical view of knowledge having a public good character leads to the well-known conclusion of market failure and under-provision of science, research, and development, caused by a lack of returns on potential investments (Schot & Steinmueller, 2018; Stiglitz, 1999). The innovation system approach treats knowledge differently, acknowledging the costs of learning and the benefits that firms can draw from generating new knowledge. Low and inadequate levels of knowledge, insufficient knowledge transfer, and underinvestment in knowledge generation are thus seen as system failures (Urmetzer et al., 2018).

Neoclassical economic theory approaches knowledge in a rather mechanistic manner, often involving a research and development sector that generates new knowledge based on a conventional production function, such as a generalized Cobb–Douglas function (confer Aghion & Howitt, 2009; Romer, 2006). These approaches do not appear to be suitable for explaining cross-national income differences related to knowledge. Economic growth rates show a rather mixed picture of convergence and divergence over time. While certain groups of economies tend to become more similar over time, others tend to become more dissimilar. Neoclassical theory cannot satisfactorily explain this observation (Aghion & Howitt, 2009). In this context, Boisot and Canals (2004) state that approaches such as the game theory do not seem helpful as they impose increasingly unrealistic cognitive conditions on economic agents. While the neoclassical homo economicus model has proven inadequate for explaining processes of knowledge creation, transfer, and learning, evolutionary economics has offered a more realistic perspective on human behavior in this regard.

5.2 Knowledge for the Transformation Toward Sustainability

As outlined in Sect. 3.3, innovations conducive for a transformation toward sustainability differ from conventional innovations, which primarily serve economic purposes and aim at increasing efficiency. One major difference between the two types of innovations is distinct knowledge bases. Sustainable innovations, which encompass social and environmental objectives, require further expertise compared to purely market-driven innovations (Hojnik & Ruzzier, 2016; Horbach et al., 2013; Strambach, 2017). Achieving environmental and social objectives demands a comprehensive understanding of various additional aspects, such as environmental impact measurement, relevant regulations, industry standards, and certificates, as well as insight into the needs and demands of customers, interest groups, and public

---

[3] Compare Sect. 4.1.

policymakers. Additionally, expertise in social impact assessment and awareness of the externalities of products and processes throughout their entire life cycle are essential. As a result, the corresponding knowledge relevant for sustainable innovations appears to be more dispersed and more complex (Ghassim, 2018; Urmetzer et al., 2018; van Geenhuizen & Ye, 2014). Companies pursuing such innovations often engage in more extensive collaborations with external partners (Aldieri et al., 2020; Marchi & Grandinetti, 2013), as they demand a greater reliance on external sources of knowledge and information in comparison to other forms of innovation (Horbach et al., 2013). As pointed out in Sect. 4.3, these partners do not solely originate from the business world or academia. In numerous instances, they encompass governmental organizations, NGOs, consumer groups, civil society organizations, or indigenous groups. This inclusion is due to their specialized expertise in social and environmental aspects of sustainability, especially regarding local or context-specific intricacies. The broader array of potential stakeholders, each with potentially conflicting demands, makes the development of sustainable innovations much more demanding compared to purely market-driven innovations (Hall & Vredenburg, 2003). Achieving sustainability transformation necessitates the emergence of radical new knowledge. Nevertheless, this knowledge must also establish connections with existing innovation systems (Clark et al., 2016).

It is helpful to look at the findings of sustainability science, which shed light on the essential knowledge types needed for a transition toward sustainability. Three classes of knowledge are widely acknowledged as crucial for this endeavor, as depicted in Fig. 5.1: systems knowledge, normative knowledge, and transformative knowledge (Abson et al., 2014, 2017; Grunwald, 2007; Hart et al., 2015; ProClim, 1997; Rauschmayer et al., 2015; Urmetzer et al., 2018; Wehrden et al., 2017; Wiek et al., 2012). In brief, systems knowledge encompasses a comprehensive understanding of the Earth as a complex system, consisting of interconnected subsystems, including techno-economic and socio-environmental systems. It delves into all aspects of human production and consumption patterns (institutional, technological, organizational) and their impact on the natural environment. This type of knowledge involves analyzing and describing existing sustainability challenges. Normative knowledge focuses on defining the desired state of the Earth system and its subsystems. It outlines the normative goal of sustainability, specifying the ideal target for the transformation process. Transformative knowledge pertains to the strategic and operational aspects of the transition. It explores viable and promising pathways for achieving the desired state of the Earth system. This knowledge deals with societal change toward sustainability, identifying feasible strategies, considering uncertainties, the chances of success, and the costs of change, and preparing for potential adaptations and corrections in the future. Put differently, systems knowledge refers to what the world looks like and could look like, comprising the set of all production and consumption possibilities. Normative knowledge refers to how the world should look, specifying the preferred subset of production and consumption possibilities. Finally, transformative knowledge refers to how to get from what the world looks like today to what it should look like in the future, meaning how to reach the desired subset of production and consumption possibilities.

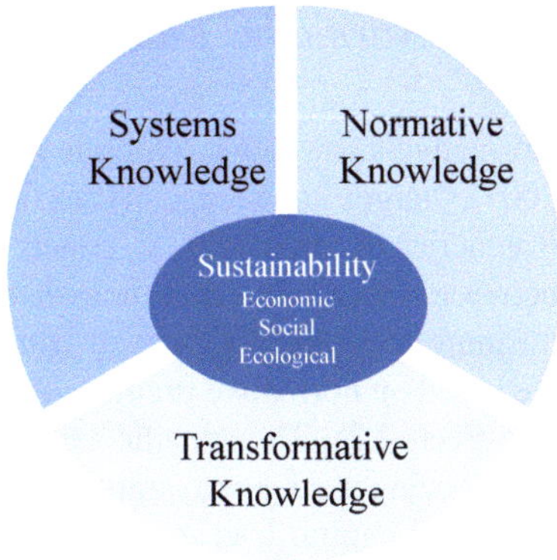

Fig. 5.1 Knowledge types relevant for the transformation toward sustainability

5.2.1 Systems Knowledge

Systems knowledge, or "explanatory knowledge" (Grunwald, 2007), entails a deep understanding of natural and societal systems and their interactions, as all resources utilized by humans are integrated within intricate social-ecological systems, which in turn comprise several subsystems (Ostrom, 2009). Systems knowledge serves as a necessary foundation for successful action in sustainable development initiatives. It pertains to understanding the dynamics and reasons behind a transition toward sustainability (Rauschmayer et al., 2015). It involves a comprehensive grasp of the functioning of social and ecological systems, including their interactions and flows of ecosystem services (Clark et al., 2016). It is thus about the coupled dynamics of human societies and the natural environment, emphasizing the interdependence of social and environmental factors (Hart et al., 2015). Systems knowledge covers past, present, and future states (Wiek et al., 2012) and entails analytical and descriptive knowledge of sustainability problems.

The societal system comprises technology as a constituting aspect of human culture and societies. Systems knowledge thus entails technological knowledge and the impacts of technology on other systems such as the ecological system, to the extent known. It furthermore entails knowledge of the underlying principles of these systems, referring to the functioning of geological, atmospheric, and biological systems and processes and the corresponding fundamental laws of physics, but also to the basic principles that shape human interaction and form culture, politics, economies, and societies. As such, the relevant systems knowledge is widely spread among different disciplines and often characterized by specific disciplinary points of view and methodologies (Urmetzer et al., 2018; Wehrden et al., 2017). As a result, one major challenge stems from integrating such diverse knowledge.

5.2.2 *Normative Knowledge*

Normative knowledge, which is also denoted "orientation knowledge" (Grunwald, 2007), "target knowledge" (Rauschmayer et al., 2015), or "actionable knowledge" (Luederitz et al., 2017), is concerned with establishing criteria that differentiate between sustainable and non-sustainable factors. These criteria are normative, meaning they are not derived from empirical observation or experimentation but are based on normative premises, as is the underlying concept of sustainability itself (see Sect. 2.2). The specific criteria depend on the respective concept of sustainability being used. For example, differences in assumptions about the substitutability of natural capital lead to distinct criteria. Additionally, the normative foundation, whether based on the finite carrying capacity of natural and societal systems or justice-theoretical principles, influences the criteria used for sustainability appraisals (Grunwald, 2007).

Normative knowledge is thus forward-looking and focuses on the future state of the system that sustainability efforts aim to achieve. It involves understanding why this particular state is the desired goal. This type of knowledge sets the vision and direction for sustainability transitions (Rauschmayer et al., 2015). It is anticipatory and involves knowledge about sustainability goals and objectives, providing guidance for decision-making and shaping future actions. Normative knowledge enables stakeholders to take concrete steps toward achieving sustainability targets and address complex challenges (Luederitz et al., 2017).

Ethical clarifications are essential regarding sustainability knowledge (ProClim, 1997). The concept of sustainability itself, along with the understanding of humanity's role in nature, necessitates a clear ethical foundation. This helps to address questions related to values, responsibilities, and considerations of what is deemed acceptable or unacceptable in the pursuit of sustainability. It thus deals with the rationalization of value judgments related to evaluating alternative potential states of the world (Wehrden et al., 2017).

As outlined in Sect. 2.2, norms and values differ across space and time. They are dynamic, evolve, and change, meaning that normative knowledge also entails the understanding of differing or conflicting norms and the processes of cultural evolution that influence norms and their alteration over time.

5.2.3 *Transformative Knowledge*

Transformative or transformational knowledge refers to the knowledge that focuses on the practical realization of desired states within a system (Rauschmayer et al., 2015). It comprises knowledge of viable transition pathways and solutions to sustainability problems. This knowledge delves into understanding how human–environment systems can transition toward sustainability and identifies the operational strategies to achieve these goals (Wiek et al., 2012). It is essential for making informed decisions and taking active steps toward sustainability. That involves understanding how to address weak spots in sustainability and tackle implementation problems. It also includes strategies to convince and motivate stakeholders and induce societal change. Notably, transformative knowledge acknowledges the uncertainty and incompleteness of our understanding and suggests courses of action even under uncertainty (Grunwald, 2007).

Transformative knowledge is needed to develop tangible strategies for managing ecosystems toward societal goals derived from normative knowledge and encompasses various strategic elements, including participation, empowerment, education, and communication (Abson et al., 2014). In this regard, understanding the contextual frameworks and conditions that facilitate sustainable development is crucial for designing effective strategies (ProClim, 1997).

Another aspect is the understanding of how to influence and steer processes of cultural dynamics and cultural evolution (confer Kashima, 2016; Wilson, 2016). This is connected to the underlying normative knowledge and concerns making processes of blind variation and selective retention regarding cultural practices, norms, and values, more intentional (Wilson, 2016). It entails understanding how cultural information is created, interpreted, passed on, and memorized to be retained by individuals and within groups (Kashima, 2016).

Transformative knowledge furthermore entails understanding how to measure impact and trace change, and the use of appropriate indicators and measurements (confer Singh et al., 2012). Such sustainability assessments serve to evaluate transformative strategies and their success or failure. They are a valuable tool for learning and adapting the approaches to facilitate the transformation toward sustainability (Amaral et al., 2015; Luederitz et al., 2017).

In conclusion, transformative knowledge is about strategies, pathways, and practical actions that can foster a transformation toward sustainability. It is about knowing which instruments and mechanisms work on which level while considering the interdependencies between micro, meso, and macro levels. It is about concrete actions for triggering, implementing, and steering change processes and identifying the right leverage points for inducing systemic change (Abson et al., 2017; Schlaile et al., 2017). Transformative knowledge is crucial for guiding decision-making, implementing effective measures, and inducing positive societal changes. Acknowledging uncertainty and embracing transformative knowledge can enable progress toward a more sustainable future.

References

Abson, D. J., von Wehrden, H., Baumgärtner, S., Fischer, J., Hanspach, J., Härdtle, W., et al. (2014). Ecosystem services as a boundary object for sustainability. *Ecological Economics, 103*, 29–37.

Abson, D. J., Fischer, J., Leventon, J., Newig, J., Schomerus, T., Vilsmaier, U., et al. (2017). Leverage points for sustainability transformation. *Ambio, 46*(1), 30–39.

Acs, Z. J., Audretsch, D. B., Lehmann, E. E., & Licht, G. (2017). National systems of innovation. *The Journal of Technology Transfer, 42*(5), 997–1008.

Aghion, P., & Howitt, P. (2009). *The economics of growth.* MIT Press.
Aldieri, L., Kotsemir, M., & Vinci, C. P. (2020). The role of environmental innovation through the technological proximity in the implementation of the sustainable development. *Business Strategy and the Environment, 29*(2), 493–502.
Amaral, L. P., Martins, N., & Gouveia, J. B. (2015). Quest for a sustainable university: A review. *International Journal of Sustainability in Higher Education, 16*(2), 155–172.
Arbo, P., & Benneworth, P. (2007). Understanding the regional contribution of higher education institutions: A literature review. *OECD Education Working Papers, 9*, 1–78.
Boisot, M., & Canals, A. (2004). Data, information and knowledge: Have we got it right? *Journal of Evolutionary Economics, 14*(1), 43–67.
Carayannis, E., & Campbell, D. (2010). Triple helix, Quadruple helix and Quintuple helix and how do Knowledge, Innovation and the Environment relate to Each other? a proposed framework for a trans-disciplinary analysis of sustainable development and social ecology. *International Journal of Social Ecology and Sustainable Development, 1*(1), 41–69. https://www.scopus.com/inward/record.uri?eid=2-s2.0-84864553399&doi=10.4018%2fjsesd.2010010105&partnerID=40&md5=5eb73922347c6a295357cd738c1d388d.
Clark, W. C., van Kerkhoff, L., Lebel, L., & Gallopin, G. C. (2016). Crafting usable knowledge for sustainable development. *Proceedings of the National Academy of Sciences of the United States of America, 113*(17), 4570–4578.
Dosi, G., & Nelson, R. R. (1994). An introduction to evolutionary theories in economics. *Journal of Evolutionary Economics, 4*(3), 153–172.
Foray, D. (2004). *Economics of knowledge.* MIT Press.
Gertler, M. S. (2003). Tacit knowledge and the economic geography of context, or The undefinable tacitness of being (there). *Journal of Economic Geography, 3*(1), 75–99.
Gettier, E. L. (1963). Is justified true belief knowledge? *Analysis, 23*(6), 121–123.
Ghassim, B. (2018). Sustainability-oriented innovation in the minerals industry: An empirical study on the effect of non-geographical proximity dimensions. *Sustainability, 10*(2), 282.
Gorman, M. E. (2002). Types of knowledge and their roles in technology transfer. *Journal of Technology Transfer, 27*, 219–231.
Gottschalk-Mazouz, N. (2007). Was ist Wissen? In S. Ammon, C. Heineke, & K. Selbmann (Eds.), *Wissen in Bewegung. Dominanz, Synergien und Emanzipation in den Praxen der 'Wissensgesellschaft'* (pp. 21–40). Velbrück Wissenschaft.
Grant, R. M. (1996). Toward a knowledge-based theory of the firm. *Strategic Management Journal, 17*, 109–122.
Grunwald, A. (2007). Working towards sustainable development in the face of uncertainty and incomplete knowledge. *Journal of Environmental Policy & Planning, 9*(3–4), 245–262.
Hall, J., & Vredenburg, H. (2003). The challenges of innovating for sustainable development. *MIT Sloan Management Review.* https://sloanreview.mit.edu/article/the-challenges-of-innovating-for-sustainable-development/.
Hart, D. D., Bell, K. P., Lindenfeld, L. A., Jain, S., Johnson, T. R., Ranco, D., & McGill, B. (2015). Strengthening the role of universities in addressing sustainability challenges: the Mitchell Center for Sustainability Solutions as an institutional experiment. *Ecology and Society, 20*(2).
Hojnik, J., & Ruzzier, M. (2016). What drives eco-innovation? A review of an emerging literature. *Environmental Innovation and Societal Transitions, 19*, 31–41.
Horbach, J., Oltra, V., & Belin, J. (2013). Determinants and specificities of eco-innovations compared to other innovations-an econometric analysis for the French and German industry based on the community innovation survey. *Industry and Innovation, 20*(6), 523–543. https://www.scopus.com/inward/record.uri?eid=2-s2.0-84887093794&doi=10.1080%2f13662716.2013.833375&partnerID=40&md5=f48e51984dde023f1b8f624e409a203e
Jensen, M. B., Johnson, B., Lorenz, E., & Lundvall, B. Å. (2007). Forms of knowledge and modes of innovation. *Research Policy, 36*(5), 680–693.
Johnson, B., Müller, J., Gregersen, B., & Orozco, J. (2009). Pitfalls and opportunities in knowledge sharing: experiences from a research capacity building project in Central America.

International Journal of Technological Learning, Innovation and Development, 2(4), 250–273. https://www.scopus.com/inward/record.uri?eid=2-s2.0-84897056348&doi=10.1504%2fIJTLID.2009.026817&partnerID=40&md5=25eb04d759600d092a235e1d3622ccd1
de Jong, T., & Ferguson-Hessler, M. G. (1996). Types and qualities of knowledge. *Educational Psychologist, 31*(2), 105–113.
Kashima, Y. (2016). Cultural dynamics. *Current Opinion in Psychology, 8*, 93–97.
Leonard, D., & Sensiper, S. (1998). The role of tacit knowledge in group innovation. *California Management Review, 40*(3), 112–132.
Levin, R. C., Klevorick, A. K., Nelson, R. R., Winter, S. G., Gilbert, R., & Griliches, Z. (1987). Appropriating the returns from industrial research and development. *Brookings Papers on Economic Activity, 1987*(3), 783.
Luederitz, C., Schäpke, N., Wiek, A., Lang, D. J., Bergmann, M., Bos, J. J., et al. (2017). Learning through evaluation—A tentative evaluative scheme for sustainability transition experiments. *Journal of Cleaner Production, 169*, 61–76.
Lundvall, B.-Å. (2016). *The learning economy and the economics of hope.* Anthem Press.
de Marchi, V., & Grandinetti, R. (2013). Knowledge strategies for environmental innovations: The case of Italian manufacturing firms. *Journal of Knowledge Management, 17*(4), 569–582.
Nelson, R. R. (1989). What is private and what is public about technology? *Science, Technology, & Human Values, 14*(3), 229–241.
Nonaka, I. (1994). A dynamic theory of organizational knowledge creation. *Organization Science, 5*(1), 14–37.
Nowotny, H., Scott, P., & Gibbons, M. (2001). *Re-thinking science: knowledge and the public in an age of uncertainty.* Sage Publ.
OECD. (1997). *National innovation systems.* France.
OECD/Eurostat. (2018). *Oslo manual 2018: Guidelines for collecting, reporting and using data on innovation* (4th ed.). OECD Publishing.
Ostrom, E. (2009). A general framework for analyzing sustainability of social-ecological systems. *Science, 325*(5939), 419–422.
Polanyi, M. (1966). *The tacit dimension.* Doubleday.
Pritchard, D. (2014). *What is this thing called knowledge?* Routledge.
ProClim. (1997). *ProClim—Research on sustainability: ProClim—Schweizerische Akademie der Naturwissenschaften SANW.*
Rauschmayer, F., Bauler, T., & Schäpke, N. (2015). Towards a thick understanding of sustainability transitions — Linking transition management, capabilities and social practices. *Ecological Economics, 109*, 211–221.
Romer, D. (2006). *Advanced macroeconomics* (3rd ed.). McGraw-Hill/Irwin.
Rydin, Y. (2007). Re-examining the role of knowledge within planning theory. *Planning Theory, 6*(1), 52–68.
Schlaile, M., Urmetzer, S., Blok, V., Andersen, A., Timmermans, J., Mueller, M., et al. (2017). Innovation systems for transformations towards sustainability?: Taking the normative dimension seriously. *Sustainability, 9*(12, 2253), 1–20.
Schot, J., & Steinmueller, W. E. (2018). Three frames for innovation policy: R&D, systems of innovation and transformative change. *Research Policy, 47*(9), 1554–1567.
Schumpeter, J. A. (1997). *Theorie der wirtschaftlichen Entwicklung: Eine Untersuchung über Unternehmergewinn, Kapital, Kredit, Zins und den Konjunkturzyklus* (Neunte Auflage, unveränderter Nachdruck der 1934 erschienen vierten Auflage). *ProQuest Ebook Central.* Duncker & Humblot.
Schumpeter, J. A. (1994). *Capitalism, socialism, and democracy.* Routledge.
Singh, R. K., Murty, H. R., Gupta, S. K., & Dikshit, A. K. (2012). An overview of sustainability assessment methodologies. *Ecological Indicators, 15*(1), 281–299.
Solow, R. M. (1956). A contribution to the theory of economic growth. *The Quarterly Journal of Economics, 70*(1), 65.

Stiglitz, J. E. (1999). Knowledge as a global public good. In I. Kaul (Ed.), *Global public goods. International cooperation in the 21st century* (pp. 308–325). Oxford University Press.

Strambach, S. (2017). Combining knowledge bases in transnational sustainability innovation: Microdynamics and institutional change. *Economic Geography, 93*(5), 500–526. https://www.scopus.com/inward/record.uri?eid=2-s2.0-85030160222&doi=10.1080%2f00130095.2017.1366268&partnerID=40&md5=898772c879f5bad929c4fb7fc96e9b50

Tidd, J., Bessant, J. R., & Pavitt, K. L. R. (2005). *Managing innovation: Integrating technological, market and organizational change* (3rd ed.). Wiley.

Tsoukas, H., & Vladimirou, E. (2001). What is organizational knowledge? *Journal of Management Studies, 38*(7), 973–993.

Urmetzer, S., Schlaile, M., Bogner, K., Mueller, M., & Pyka, A. (2018). Exploring the dedicated knowledge base of a transformation towards a sustainable bioeconomy. *Sustainability, 10*(6), 1694.

van Geenhuizen, M., & Ye, Q. (2014). Responsible innovators: Open networks on the way to sustainability transitions. *Technological Forecasting and Social Change, 87*, 28–40.

Weber, E. P., & Khademian, A. M. (2008). Wicked problems, knowledge challenges, and collaborative capacity builders in network settings. *Public Administration Review, 68*(2), 334–349.

Wehrden, H. von, Luederitz, C., Leventon, J., & Russell, S. (2017). Methodological challenges in sustainability science: A call for method plurality, procedural rigor and longitudinal research. *Challenges in Sustainability, 5*(1).

Wiek, A., Ness, B., Schweizer-Ries, P., Brand, F. S., & Farioli, F. (2012). From complex systems analysis to transformational change: A comparative appraisal of sustainability science projects. *Sustainability Science, 7*(S1), 5–24.

Wilson, D. S. (2016). Intentional cultural change. *Current Opinion in Psychology, 8*, 190–193.

Chapter 6
Knowledge Processes

As outlined in the previous chapter, knowledge should not be considered a public good that is easily accessible and floats freely, waiting to be put into application at no cost. Rather, knowledge is a highly dynamic substance, permanently subject to change, becoming obsolete, or getting lost while new knowledge is continuously created (Foray, 2004). Knowledge is characterized by path dependencies (Dosi, 1982), it is cumulative in nature (Foray, 2004), sticky (Hippel, 1994), dispersed, and context-specific (Galunic & Rodan, 1998). Some knowledge is tacit and therefore hardly codifiable (Polanyi, 1966). Agents seeking to acquire a new piece of knowledge need absorptive capacity to do so (Cohen & Levinthal, 1990).

To further the investigation of knowledge as the foundation for innovations, it is helpful to look at knowledge processes. For analytical purposes, it makes sense to differentiate between the three processes of creation, transfer, and application, whereby knowledge application is closely linked to the introduction of innovations, in the sense that an innovation is the result of a creative use or exploitation of (novel) knowledge (confer Ayele et al., 2012; Spielman et al., 2009). For the application, the context specificity and local characteristics of knowledge are relevant. In this regard, the introduction of an innovation as an effective solution strategy to a sustainability problem implies that the underlying knowledge is adapted to the local context, meaning that knowledge is transformed into action (confer Batie, 2008; Clark et al., 2016; Urmetzer et al., 2018). This is in most cases connected to a certain degree of uncertainty as to whether an innovation will provide the intended effects regarding sustainability, especially in the long run.[1]

While it is helpful to separate the three knowledge processes for analytical reasons, it is essential to recognize that in reality these processes are often interconnected and there is no strict chronological or causal sequence between them, as depicted in Fig. 6.1. Instead, they are dynamically linked, and each process can influence and contribute to the others in complex ways (Kates et al., 2001; Urmetzer et al., 2018).

[1] See Sect. 3.3 about sustainable innovations.

U. Wilke, *Towards Sustainable Innovations*, Economic Complexity and Evolution,
https://doi.org/10.1007/978-3-032-31024-8_6

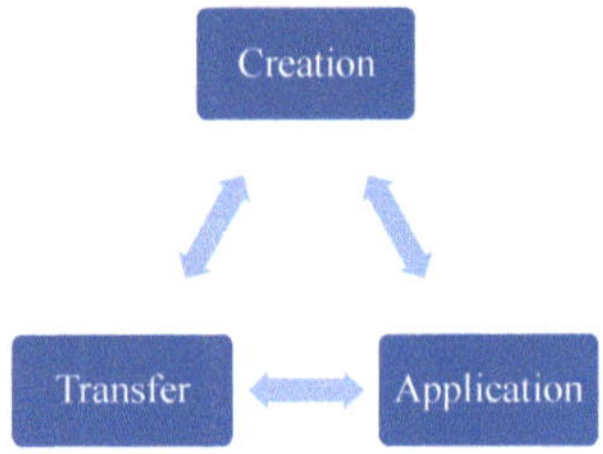

Fig. 6.1 The interdependent knowledge processes

For instance, the application of existing knowledge can lead to the transfer of that knowledge to different contexts, individuals, or groups. Likewise, when knowledge is applied and innovations are introduced into a specific context, this can in turn generate new insights and ideas, leading to the creation of new knowledge. Furthermore, the transfer of knowledge between individuals or organizations can stimulate the formation of new knowledge or result in new innovative applications of that knowledge.

This interlinkage of the different processes is particularly evident in the area of sustainability, which can be considered a "wicked problem"[2] due to its complex and multifaceted nature, involving social, environmental, and economic aspects. Addressing such challenges requires a continuous and adaptive process of knowledge creation, diffusion, and application (Grunwald, 2007). With increased comprehension of the complexities involved and the accumulation of feedback from real-world applications, the corresponding knowledge evolves and new insights emerge. The iterative nature of this process allows for the effective handling of the dynamic and evolving aspects inherent in sustainability challenges.

To comprehensively understand knowledge processes, it is imperative to examine their institutional dimensions (van Kerkhoff, 2014). That encompasses various aspects, ranging from mechanisms to govern those knowledge processes to considerations about acknowledging access to knowledge as a fundamental human right. The dynamics of knowledge creation, sharing, access, and utilization play a pivotal role in the transformation toward sustainability.

Higher education institutions hold a central position in both the creation and dissemination of knowledge. However, their involvement in applying knowledge is relatively less pronounced compared to other entities such as companies, political bodies, and public administrations, which are responsible for translating knowledge into practical applications through the provision of innovations in the forms of products, services, laws, regulations, and public goods (Stephens et al., 2008).

---

[2] See Sect. 2.2.

6.1 Knowledge Creation

The creation of new knowledge is a path-dependent and cumulative process (Dosi, 1982; Foray, 2004). New knowledge and innovative ideas emerge from the (re-)combination of previously disparate knowledge elements, as a consequence of reshaping, reconfiguring, and reordering existing knowledge (Schumpeter, 1997). It thus requires a pre-existing foundation for comprehension which is shaped and influenced by its historical trajectories. This significance of prior knowledge becomes particularly pronounced as knowledge becomes more intricate and specialized, especially within specific industries or scientific domains (Kirat & Lung, 1999; Tsoukas & Vladimirou, 2001). The more intricate the domain, the greater the reliance on background knowledge and the interlinking of ideas.

Some authors suggest distinguishing between two ideal types of knowledge creation: one is via deliberate research and development endeavors aimed at generating new knowledge; and the second is through the dynamic process of experiential learning, encompassing both "learning by doing" and "learning by using" (Foray, 2004; Rosenberg, 1982). Those two modes of knowledge generation are also referred to as the science, technology, and innovation mode (STI) and the doing, using, and interacting (DUI) mode (see for example Jensen et al., 2007). The first mode revolves around the cultivation and application of formally codified scientific and technical knowledge. In contrast, the other mode thrives on experience-driven learning, rooted in practical engagement, utilization, and interaction. It is linked to the fact that in numerous domains, a substantial portion of practice remains only partially comprehended, and a significant proportion of engineering design activities revolves around devising solutions for intricate professional challenges. Both ideal types of knowledge production seem to be highly relevant for the occurrence of innovations. Furthermore, it must be noted that there is not one common method or approach being applied in all scientific disciplines which unequivocally characterizes all research approaches (Chalmers, 2013). Hence the differentiation between scientific activities and non-scientific activities can be cumbersome. Major industrial development projects as well as endeavors in the applied sciences can involve both types of knowledge creation in a complementarily or iterative manner.

The STI mode can be further divided into ideal types of scientific-based knowledge-creation mechanisms, as depicted in Fig. 6.2. The underlying differentiation is based on the applicability of the knowledge to be generated. Basic research aims at creating fundamental new scientific insights that are not directed toward a specific application possibility. Applied research pertains to activities that seek to expand scientific insights in the pursuit of generating new knowledge with a focus on specific practical applications and consequently (economic) utilization. The third category, experimental development refers to activities that aim to apply previously gained scientific knowledge in a specific context or to solve a clearly defined problem, such as the construction of prototypes and models (confer Foray, 2004; OECD, 2015a). However, such a distinction contains subjective elements: It is mainly the participating researchers themselves who determine which goals they pursue with

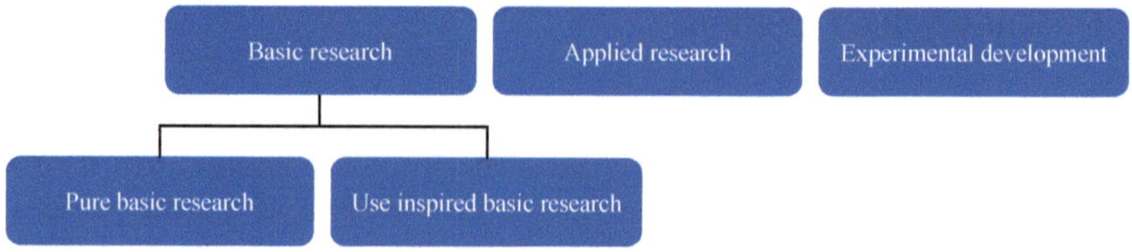

Fig. 6.2 Ideal-types of science-based knowledge creation

their work. Moreover, there are interrelationships between basic research, applied research, and experimental development, occurring in the form of both feedforward and feedback relationships (confer Corsten et al., 2016).

A widespread differentiation of different types of knowledge creation associated with sustainability transformations is aptly presented by Roux et al. (2006). This approach distinguishes between two different types of science-based knowledge creation: mode 1 or classic mode, which mainly refers to fundamental research, and mode 2 research which is transdisciplinary, spread across society, heterogeneous, focusing on application, and intended for solving real-world problems. The concept of mode 2 knowledge creation was introduced by Nowotny et al. (2001) and Gibbons (1994) and has since spread widely in the scientific literature. Roux et al. (2006) furthermore describe three distinct realms of knowledge creation that can be regarded as DUI modes, namely policy and strategy development, operational management, and local communities. Each of these fields of knowledge creation encompasses distinct knowledge elements, including goals, operating principles, plans, strategies, and desired outcomes.

6.2 Knowledge Transfer

6.2.1 Rationale and Relevant Knowledge Characteristics

Knowledge is the paramount resource driving sustainable innovations. The mere creation of novel insights does however not automatically result in the emergence of innovations. Especially in the academic context, much knowledge about sustainability is created but not put into practice (Clark et al., 2016; Trencher et al., 2017). This elucidates the necessity of disseminating and transferring knowledge to other actors within the innovation system. In general, the past decades have witnessed a growing acknowledgment of the pivotal role played by the dynamics of knowledge diffusion and transfer (Morone & Taylor, 2004). Weber and Khademian (2008) state that a major challenge of effectively addressing any public challenge in a networked environment hinges on the successful transfer, reception, and integration of knowledge between participants. Within the business world, inter-organizational knowledge transfer is seen as a major driver for enhancing a firm's knowledge pool for sustaining innovative capacities and competitiveness (Easterby-Smith et al., 2008). Due to the highly dynamic nature of knowledge (Gottschalk-Mazouz, 2007), it is susceptible to becoming obsolete and firms (as well as other actors) need to consistently maintain its relevance, which necessitates ongoing investments, involving a reflective assessment of the existing knowledge reservoir and the continuous acquisition of new knowledge.

Especially the transfer of complex, state-of-the-art knowledge is difficult, and a successful transmission is no trivial task. A critical characteristic of knowledge regarding its transfer is the issue of stickiness. This concept derives from the expenditure that is necessary to relocate a piece of information or knowledge from one context to another (Hippel, 1994). Another crucial aspect of transfer dynamics is the growing dispersion of knowledge, caused by its ongoing fragmentation as it delves into more specialized divisions and disperses into disciplinary and local contexts, which can refer to a specific site, institute, laboratory, or factory, where the knowledge was created (Foray, 2004). Furthermore, the tacitness of a piece of knowledge can pose a serious challenge to its transfer. Implicit, context-specific knowledge that is deeply rooted in an individual's experiences, insights, and expertise, can hardly be codified or even articulated, making it challenging to transfer or communicate that knowledge to others (Foray, 2004).

Knowledge transfer and learning are costly processes, with no guarantee of success (Easterby-Smith et al., 2008). An agent receiving a piece of knowledge needs appropriate absorptive capacity (Cohen & Levinthal, 1990), meaning that this agent already needs to possess a certain stock of knowledge to be able to understand and apply the new piece of knowledge. The dynamism of knowledge is underscored by the individual costs associated with its acquisition, retention, and regular updates. This can potentially give rise to challenges concerning the credibility of knowledge, and the acquisition of new pieces of knowledge if they do not fit into the existing stock of knowledge of an individual.

6.2.2 Modelling Knowledge Transfer

In the past, the concept of knowledge transfer was regularly regarded as a relatively straightforward and one-way process. As noted by (Jacobson et al., 2003), the traditional perspective on knowledge transfer involved a unidirectional and logical flow of information, primarily from researchers to policy-makers, firms, or other practitioners (see Fig. 6.3). This model, often referred to as the "science push" or knowledge-driven model, centered on researchers providing information. Alternatively, it encompassed policy-makers or firms commissioning information from researchers to address well-defined issues, known as the "demand pull" or problem-solving model.

However, several significant changes have emerged over time (Fazey et al., 2013) Firstly, the conventional notion of knowledge sharing as a one-way process from researchers to practitioners has evolved into a multidirectional process valuing

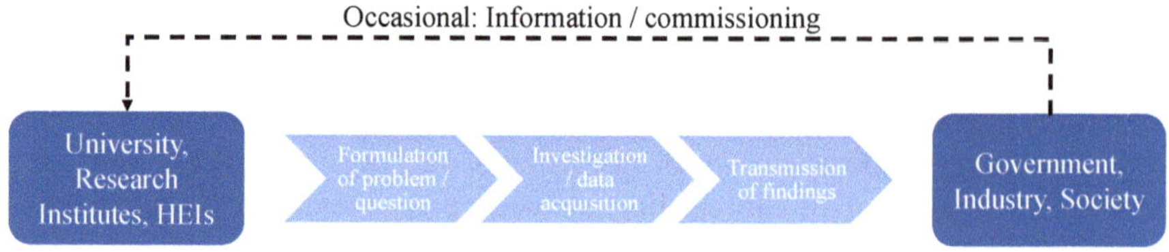

Fig. 6.3 Unidirectional model of transfer

diverse forms of knowledge from various groups. Secondly, the boundaries between different groups and between the realms of science and society have become less distinct. And thirdly, there is a growing emphasis on interdisciplinarity, as different fields of knowledge increasingly intersect and contribute to a more holistic understanding of complex issues.

Current approaches model knowledge transfer as an iterative, reciprocal, multifaceted process (see Fig. 6.4). It involves at least two parties whereby one party makes available an item of knowledge not yet possessed by the other party. It is in most cases an intentional process, although other constellations are common, but are labeled differently, such as unintended knowledge drain. Such occurrences range from normal business practices such as reverse engineering to illegal activities such as industrial espionage or idea theft (confer Battistella et al., 2016).

Due to the processual nature of knowledge transfer, four distinct stages can be identified: initiation, implementation, ramp-up, and integration (Szulanski, 2000). The initiation phase confers to recognizing opportunities for transfer and assessing their costs and the set-up of transfer. Important aspects in this phase are the perceived reliability and trustworthiness of the involved actors. The implementation phase concerns the actual process of transmitting knowledge from one party to the other, while the ramp-up phase concerns the initial use of the acquired knowledge and the integration phase refers to the subsequent phase when the acquired knowledge is perceived as valuable and thus routinized (Szulanski, 2000).

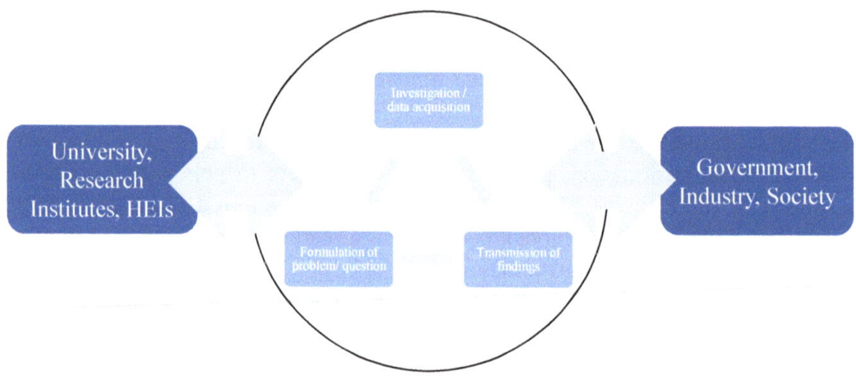

Fig. 6.4 Iterative and reciprocal model of transfer

For analyzing the different elements relevant for understanding transfer processes, many authors refer to the signaling metaphor of the Shannon–Weaver model of communication (Shannon, 1948), which specifies the following basic elements of a transfer: source, channel, message, recipient, and context (confer Szulanski, 2000). Figure 6.5 provides a graphical presentation of the basic elements. The source and recipient can be understood as the actors involved in a transfer activity, whereby other actors such as intermediaries could be involved as well (Battistella et al., 2016). Important for the transfer process are the resources and capabilities of both the actors giving knowledge and the actors receiving knowledge, as well as their motivation to teach and respectively their motivation to learn (Easterby-Smith et al., 2008). The channel of transfer refers to the means that are being used for transferring knowledge. This includes a wide variety of different mechanisms and procedures, covering codified output such as patents and publications, collaborative and contract research, joint ventures, testing and consulting, innovation services, training and education, staff exchange, or informal contacts (confer Bekkers & Bodas Freitas, 2008; Fritsch & Schwirten, 1999). The channels being used depend on the actors and their preferences, the content being transferred, and the relationship between the actors. In the signaling metaphor, the message can be understood as the content of transfer, which is a specific element of knowledge with its nature being determined by aspects such as tacitness, ambiguity, and complexity (Easterby-Smith et al., 2008). The context is given by inter-organizational dynamics between the involved actors, such as power structures, trust, and formal ties, but is also shaped by the environment in which the knowledge was produced and the reference context. Even in the case of transferring codified knowledge, it is necessary to adapt and tailor it to the specific requirements at hand (confer Battistella et al., 2016; Bekkers & Bodas Freitas, 2008; Fritsch & Schwirten, 1999).

Despite the importance of knowledge transfer for deriving innovations, a limiting factor must be mentioned. Transfer is not an efficient mechanism for knowledge integration (Grant, 1996). While knowledge integration depends on a certain level of knowledge transfer establishing a basis of common knowledge, which includes a shared language, shared meaning, and common specialized knowledge, excessive knowledge transfer is inefficient. It would require enormous amounts of resources and would quickly reach natural limits. Put simply, not everybody can (or must) know

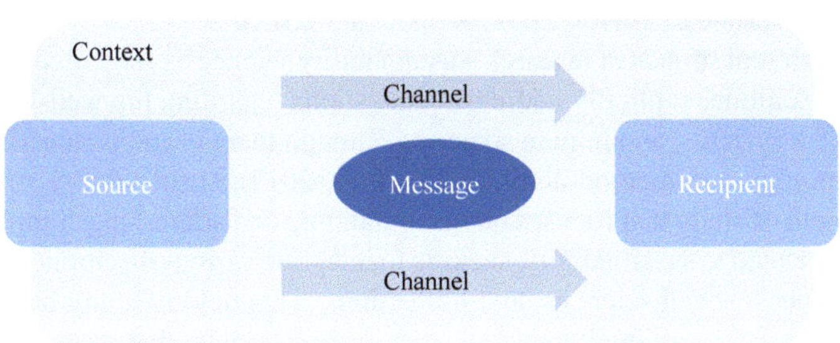

Fig. 6.5 Depiction of the signaling metaphor

everything. In the context of complex social problems such as the transformation toward sustainability, this can however imply certain trade-offs between straightforward yet limited approaches to transfer and understanding and more intricate ones where suitable actions and implications are less evident (van Kerkhoff & Lebel, 2006). In combination with the high relevance of tacit knowledge, especially in high-end technology and current state-of-the-art knowledge, transfer via heads, such as staff exchange, plays an important role in knowledge transfer (confer Gorman, 2002).

6.3 Specific Features in the Context of Sustainability

During the last decades, numerous authors have analyzed processes that aim at the generation and transfer of knowledge for a transformation toward sustainability, suggesting new approaches and changing roles of science and research, associated with different notions and concepts such as post-normal science, action research, co-design, co-creation, co-production, mode 2 science, mode 3 science, transformative science, and social learning (confer Luks & Siebenhüner, 2007; Scholz, 2017). One of the underlying ideas of these concepts concerns the fact that every form of knowledge is situated within a specific context, emerging within a certain cultural backdrop and under specific social structures (Nowotny et al., 2001). The conventional approaches for knowledge creation and transfer seem to not fit into the realm of sustainability knowledge (van Kerkhoff & Lebel, 2006). Within innovation systems aiming at sustainable solutions, different mechanisms are required, as the setting of such systems is more complex and involves various actors of different natures (van Horne & Dutot, 2017).

Science and society co-evolve, as the advancement of science, along with its institutions, norms, techniques, tools, and methodologies, is intricately linked to social and political institutions, power dynamics, cultural norms, customs, and traditions (Jasanoff, 2004). Social learning in this regard is a process in which large parts of society acquire new knowledge in the context of real-world problems and interpersonal exchange, delivering an increased understanding of the complex and systemic nature of sustainability and the transformation pathways toward it (confer Miller et al., 2014; Morone & Taylor, 2004; Wiek et al., 2012).

Out of different strands of research, sustainability science has emerged as a distinct scientific discipline, explicitly addressing questions regarding the well-being of the planet, its ecosystems, and human societies. Though there is ambivalence regarding its epistemology and methodology (Wiek et al., 2012), sustainability science is a coherent field of study that focuses on understanding and addressing complex global challenges related to sustainability, seeking to integrate various disciplines, including natural sciences, social sciences, and humanities. This field of study has identified numerous aspects regarding knowledge creation and transfer that are deemed highly relevant in the context of approaching the wicked problem of sustainability. Those

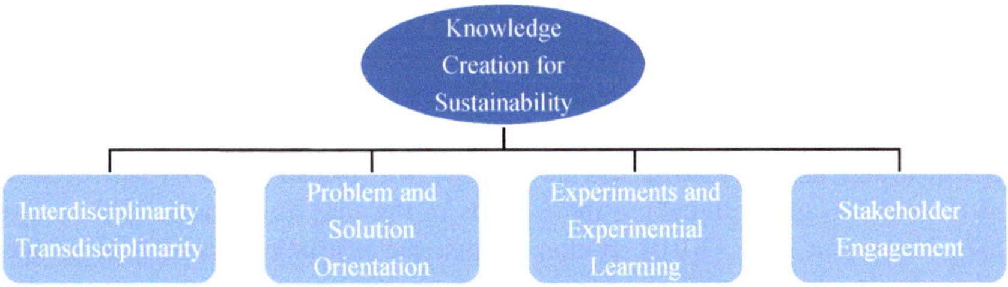

Fig. 6.6 Relevant aspects of knowledge creation for sustainable innovations

aspects evolve around the issues of inter- and transdisciplinary approaches, an orientation toward problems and solutions, the use of experiments and learning by doing, and the engagement of all relevant stakeholders (see Fig. 6.6).

Before detailing each of these aspects in the following, it must be noted that for a successful transformation toward sustainability, it appears essential to strike a balance between sustainability co-creation for practical solutions and fostering curiosity-driven, discipline-oriented basic research, whose applicability and value for attaining societal goals is often not obvious until many years later (Rau et al., 2018; Trencher et al., 2017). Solely concentrating on transdisciplinary approaches for addressing specific problems and solutions could inadvertently sideline the potential of fundamental research, which can lead to radical innovations and entirely new solutions in the long run (Batie, 2008; Foray, 2004). It thus seems more appropriate to combine solution-oriented idea generation, basic research, and knowledge and technology development into a cohesive, iterative process involving similar stakeholders and shared challenges (van Horne & Dutot, 2017). Such a holistic perspective underscores the interconnected nature of these phases and the necessity of ongoing interactions and adjustments. This way, actors from various domains can collaboratively address emerging challenges and seize opportunities throughout the innovation process.

6.3.1 Problem- and Solution-Oriented Research Programs

The focus on concrete problems for elaborating workable solutions represents a shift toward generating usable knowledge that effectively addresses real-world sustainability challenges (Abson et al., 2017; Kates et al., 2001). This approach is based on the understanding that vast amounts of knowledge are produced that lack relevance to actual problems, local contexts, and institutional settings and thus are not usable (Clark et al., 2016). Hence, the goal must be to bridge the gap between social-ecological systems knowledge and actionable societal interventions and innovations by producing knowledge that fits the system context and can effectually induce change (Hart et al., 2015). Considering specific sustainability problems as a starting point for knowledge creation aligns with the notion that innovation is grounded in knowledge-based problem-solving processes (Kirat & Lung, 1999). Innovations that encompass social and environmental goals consequently require knowledge that refers to the specific challenges in these areas.

As mentioned in the previous chapter, an exclusive focus on specific problems is met with criticism. One drawback is the disregard for curiosity-driven basic research, which can yield groundbreaking innovations in the long run (Batie, 2008; Foray, 2004). Perry and May (2010) caution against the instrumentalization of science and emphasize the importance of preserving a space for research that is not solely geared toward immediate application. Rau et al. (2018) highlight the potential risk of marginalizing disciplines especially from the areas of arts and humanities in favor of economistic impact assessments, particularly favoring engineering- and technology-focused disciplines, as the contribution of arts and humanities might be diverse and difficult to capture but highly valuable for societal development. Scholz (2017) sees the risk that science is increasingly influenced by a simplified problem-and-solution framework that does not adequately incorporate the intricacies and epistemic inherent to scientific progress.

In light of these critiques and considerations, proponents of the problem- and solution-oriented research approach underscore the need for a balance between contributing to specific case solutions and advancing a general body of theoretical knowledge encompassing broader principles and generalizations that are widely applicable (Hart et al., 2015; Wiek et al., 2012). It is not about abandoning curiosity-driven basic research for the sole purpose of generating new insights, but adequately considering the context and systemic nature of real-world sustainability problems. That implies knowledge creation, transfer, and application mechanisms that include effective feedback loops to adequately evaluate the applicability and usefulness of knowledge. By embracing both practical solutions and foundational knowledge, researchers and institutions can foster sustainable development that addresses immediate challenges while maintaining a robust and diverse knowledge landscape. This of course raises questions about the distribution of research resources among the different goals.

6.3.2 Experiments for Knowledge Generation

Connected to the orientation toward problems and solutions is the assertion that experimental approaches appear especially purposeful for creating knowledge for wicked problems (Akpo et al., 2015; Batie, 2008; Purcell et al., 2019). Such sustainability transition experiments, or transformational interventions, encompass policy experiments, institutional experiments, governance experiments, household experiments, and alike. Larger institutional settings with more complex or more numerous interventions are often referred to as laboratories, such as living labs or urban laboratories (Evans et al., 2015; Luederitz et al., 2017). Those different approaches have in common, that they are situated in the real world and concern real problems, but yet happen in a setting with previously defined borders and a certain degree of control, which allows for more nuanced knowledge creation and social learning about viable solutions (Evans & Karvonen, 2014; Jernsand, 2019; Luederitz et al., 2017).

Transition experiments or living labs aim at collaborative research and innovation environments that involve real-world settings where new technologies, products, services, and solutions can be tested, validated, and co-created, often in partnership with various stakeholders, including researchers, industry, government, and end-users (Evans et al., 2015; Luederitz et al., 2017). Such experiments or labs provide a platform for application, prototyping, and piloting within authentic contexts, allowing for the development and refinement of innovations under real-world conditions, often involving systems thinking.

To fully harness the potential of such experimental approaches, it appears necessary to implement rigorous evaluation schemes to measure inputs, outcomes, and actual impacts as well as processual features (Luederitz et al., 2017). Controlling for effects that are not within the scope of influence of the experiment is especially demanding as the interventions happen in the real world and are thus subject to countless influencing factors. Challenges of such approaches are further related to high costs in connection to little effects and equitable participation as such real-world interventions can be misused by powerful stakeholders following their own agendas (Evans & Karvonen, 2014; Purcell et al., 2019). Furthermore, the setting of such experiments must be well documented to capture the context of knowledge creation to ensure the transferability of the knowledge to other actors and contexts.

Being aware of the challenges, such experiments, and living labs have the potential to provide opportunities for developing and experimenting with cutting-edge solutions for sustainability problems while engaging numerous different stakeholders, thus promoting inclusivity, yielding novel insights, and enabling knowledge creation and learning. Furthermore, such experimental approaches and learning by doing can be seen as experience-based transfer mechanisms that have a high potential to promote social learning if the relevant stakeholders are adequately involved.[3]

6.3.3 Interdisciplinary and Transdisciplinary Framework

Although there is no unequivocal definition for interdisciplinarity or transdisciplinarity, and both terms are not used coherently in the literature (Polk, 2015; Soini et al., 2018), the principles and methodologies associated with both concepts are deemed highly relevant for creating sustainability knowledge (see for example Abson et al., 2014; Batie, 2008; Kates et al., 2001; Wiek et al., 2012). Here, interdisciplinarity refers to approaches that integrate methods, tools, and insights from multiple distinct disciplines or fields of study, emphasizing the collaboration between experts from different backgrounds to address complex issues or questions that cannot be adequately tackled by a single disciplinary perspective (Abson et al., 2017). Transdisciplinary work also incorporates knowledge and methods of practitioners, users,

[3] See Sect. 6.3.4.

consumers, indigenous groups, and other actors dealing with real-world problems and corresponding solutions, and thus refers to knowledge domains not adequately represented in the academic setting and its disciplines. The goal is to bridge the boundaries between those various approaches and the traditional forms of knowledge production in science and research (Binder et al., 2015; Polk, 2015). Both interdisciplinary and transdisciplinary approaches aim at creating a synthesis of knowledge that transcends disciplinary boundaries, establishing a mutual understanding of different disciplinary ontologies and epistemologies and thus enabling novel insights that go beyond the possibilities of isolated disciplinary approaches (confer Gibbons, 1994; Hart et al., 2015).

In inter- and transdisciplinary approaches, diverse viewpoints and methodologies are combined to create a more comprehensive understanding and potentially innovative solutions to multifaceted problems. This is based on the understanding that knowledge has become more dispersed through the ongoing specialization of various scientific disciplines (Abson et al., 2017). It is thus about including all pertinent knowledge, regardless of its source or discipline while broadening the research scope and enhancing the legitimacy of the created knowledge (Lang et al., 2012). The methods of inter- and transdisciplinary approaches entail mutual learning processes resulting in valuable knowledge relevant to both, science and practice (Binder et al., 2015). The necessity of considering all forms of knowledge, including local and traditional knowledge, also becomes obvious when actors with differing cultural or socio-economic backgrounds cooperate. Numerous examples from collaboration projects in developing countries have shown that the classic approaches to research and development, based on unidirectional transfer focusing on technology and one-to-one transmission of expertise, capacities, and structures, have proven to be insufficient (confer Hauser et al., 2011; Johnson et al., 2009; van Kerkhoff & Lebel, 2006).

The difficulties of such approaches are based on the conceptual distance between different disciplines regarding terminology, methodologies, and systems representations (Abson et al., 2014), while even within established disciplines with clear-cut borders, there are numerous disputes regarding methods, data, and their interpretations (confer Soini et al., 2018; Trencher et al., 2017). Furthermore, difficulties arise when scientists exhibit skepticism regarding the credibility of collaborative research with actors from outside academia, concerning aspects such as reliability, validity, rigor of the methods, and other epistemological and methodological considerations. At the same time practitioners might raise queries about the practical significance, often referred to as salience, of such research endeavors and the resulting insights (Lang et al., 2012). The divergent expectations of scientists, firms, public authorities, and other partners regarding the results of transdisciplinary projects can produce serious tensions (Polk, 2015). Critics of such approaches furthermore fear that the distinction between science and non-science could be blurred if the scientific process is no longer steered exclusively by inner-scientific rules and quality criteria, but is also subject to the motivations and assessments of non-scientists (Scholz, 2017).

Inter- and transdisciplinary approaches necessitate a greater investment of time, require increased financial resources for efficient project management, and must involve the implementation of distinctive quality measures when contrasted with conventional scientific or disciplinary approaches (confer Barron et al., 2017; Blättel-Mink & Kastenholz, 2005; Lang et al., 2012; Wiek et al., 2012). Inter- and transdisciplinary approaches are furthermore often misaligned with established academic structures and reward systems, and require non-scientific skills for effective communication on the side of the scholars, and a certain level of scientific understanding on the side of the practitioners (Rau et al., 2018).

Nonetheless, such approaches are seen as essential for creating sustainability knowledge due to the wicked nature of the underlying real-world problems that require an expansion of knowledge-creation processes beyond disciplinary and institutional boundaries (Blättel-Mink & Kastenholz, 2005; Wehrden et al., 2017).

6.3.4 Engagement of Relevant Stakeholders

Closely linked to the idea of inter- and transdisciplinary approaches is the concept of widely including diverse stakeholders in sustainability-related knowledge processes. The rationale here as well is the fact that the relevant knowledge is widely dispersed in society. Diversity in general is an essential prerequisite for fostering learning and innovation, enabling the creation of novel combinations in the sense of Schumpeter. Wuyts et al. (2005) state that diversity in this context pertains to the number of actors, possessing distinct knowledge or expertise, actively engaging in the learning and innovation process through interaction. Next to the number of participants, diversity resides in the extent to which their knowledge and skills diverge from one another. Over the recent years, the creation of new knowledge in general has increasingly become a collaborative endeavor, as Crescenzi et al. (2016) demonstrate with an analysis of publication and patent data, showing that co-patenting and co-authorship have become the majority, signifying a shift toward larger teams including diverse stakeholders working collectively to advance knowledge. As stated in Sect. 5.2, this holds especially for sustainable innovations, which require a broad range of knowledge vested in diverse stakeholders.

The wide inclusion of stakeholders serves to access their knowledge, with a specific emphasis on their tacit knowledge, which can hardly be transferred without direct involvement. This entails the inclusion of users and consumers in line with van Hippel's arguments for user-driven innovations (Hippel, 2006), which can also be understood as a means for enhancing democratic aspects of innovation processes (Grundel & Dahlström, 2016). Another argument for including users and consumers refers to the uptake and ownership and subsequently the success of sustainable innovations, which can be enhanced by integrating relevant stakeholders into the corresponding knowledge processes from the beginning (confer Akpo et al., 2015). It can further improve the social acceptance of innovations, especially in controversial fields such as genetic engineering (see for example Ervin et al., 2010). Including stakeholders also helps to prevent the misuse of technology and the development of unsuitable solutions, as demonstrated by Heiskanen and Lovio (2010) with an example from the area of housing energy innovations. It is thus essential to perceive stakeholders affected by desired changes not merely as part of the problem but as integral to the solution (Clark et al., 2016; Urmetzer et al., 2018). More fundamentally, the inclusion of all relevant stakeholders seems pivotal since sustainable innovations have a strong normative aspect and thus the values and corresponding knowledge of the affected parts of society must be considered. This is a point where such approaches differ from conventional scientific approaches, as they require consensus, or at least exchange regarding the intended results (confer Batie, 2008).

Notions such as co-creation, co-design, or co-production emphasize the idea of broadly including diverse stakeholders (confer Trencher et al., 2014). These concepts encompass a continuum of different approaches. They range from the involvement of stakeholders from the very beginning in the identification of problems and research questions and the elaboration of study designs to involvement in data acquisition and analysis, knowledge transfer, and the application of results. Although there are various definitions and spheres connected to these concepts, they generally involve collaborating with diverse societal actors to bring about sustainable change in a specific location, region, or societal sub-sector (Moser, 2016). Roux et al. (2006) argue that such approaches are suitable for generating sustainability knowledge as they understand knowledge as a dynamic "process of relating", requiring the negotiation of meaning among partners, rather than a static thing that can be easily transferred. These approaches hence place value on the tacit dimension of knowledge and have proven more successful than conventional push-and-pull strategies for knowledge creation and transfer (Roux et al., 2006).

The idea can also be found in other models that emphasize participation, such as open science and open innovation (Smarts et al., 2019), whereby open science can be seen as an umbrella term, embracing a wide range of beliefs regarding the evolution of knowledge generation and sharing, which can be summarized in five different schools of thought: the infrastructure school which focuses on the technological framework; the public school emphasizing accessibility in knowledge creation; the measurement school which explores alternative methods of impact assessment; the democratic school which is concerned with equitable access to knowledge; and the pragmatic school that emphasizes collaborative research (Fecher & Friesike, 2014).

The inclusion of a wide range of different actors is a demanding, resource-intensive, and time-consuming task (Crescenzi et al., 2016; Hart et al., 2015). Its success depends on the effective management of each stage, from joint problem formulation and co-design of research to collaborative implementation, analysis, and interpretation of the result involving all parties (Akpo et al., 2015). The co-creation of knowledge depends on the mutual comprehension of the involved actors, which can be considerably demanding if their knowledge is based on different epistemologies and rooted in vastly different experiences (Rydin, 2007). Achieving the goal of stakeholder inclusion can be accomplished through the use of boundary organizations as outlined by Batie (2008), and the practice of boundary work, which occurs at the intersection between experts and practitioners (Cash et al., 2003). Furthermore, engaging in participatory approaches does not inherently reduce the cognitive gaps between stakeholders, nor does it ensure that the agreed-upon solution strategies are founded upon the most suitable knowledge (Urmetzer et al., 2018).

Inclusive approaches have limitations and are subject to trade-offs. For one thing, such approaches are limited in the capacity to include participants. This poses certain restrictions as the issue of sustainability concerns all of humanity, but not every interested person or organization can be included in the corresponding innovation networks. It is thus the question of how to decide whom to include, and how to balance inclusion and rising costs of coordination within such networks. Another issue is the existence of power asymmetries within such networks. An example is the question of whether to include strong incumbents of unsustainable technologies: Including them might be necessary and relevant due to their expertise and potential market impact, but on the other hand might be counterproductive due to their reluctance against change (confer McCauley & Stephens, 2012). More generally, co-creation approaches could be misused by organized interests and powerful actors for their agendas (in line with the aforementioned challenges in transition experiments), especially in times of rising populist tendencies in politics (Smarts et al., 2019). On the other hand, proponents see co-creation approaches as appropriate means to produce "socially robust" knowledge, i.e. knowledge that has been rigorously tested, validated, and accepted by a broad and diverse community of experts, stakeholders, and the general public, ensuring that it is not biased, incomplete, or limited in its applicability (confer Abson et al., 2017; Klenk & Hickey, 2012; Wiek et al., 2012). However, this can lead to the same tensions as with transdisciplinary approaches between usability, profitability, and efficiency on the one hand and scientific rigor and credibility on the other hand (Trencher et al., 2017).

References

Abson, D. J., von Wehrden, H., Baumgärtner, S., Fischer, J., Hanspach, J., Härdtle, W., et al. (2014). Ecosystem services as a boundary object for sustainability. *Ecological Economics, 103*, 29–37.

Abson, D. J., Fischer, J., Leventon, J., Newig, J., Schomerus, T., Vilsmaier, U., et al. (2017). Leverage points for sustainability transformation. *Ambio, 46*(1), 30–39.

Akpo, E., Crane, T. A., Vissoh, P. V., & Tossou, R. C. (2015). Co-production of Knowledge in Multi-stakeholder Processes: Analyzing Joint Experimentation as Social Learning. *Journal of Agricultural Education and Extension, 21*(4), 369–388. https://www.scopus.com/inward/record.uri?eid=2-s2.0-84938966306&doi=10.1080%2f1389224X.2014.939201&partnerID=40&md5=be43d9e514c5e6d1be9f094f87437c32

Ayele, S., Duncan, A., Larbi, A., & Khanh, T. T. (2012). Enhancing innovation in livestock value chains through networks: Lessons from fodder innovation case studies in developing countries. *Science and Public Policy, 39*(3), 333–346. https://www.scopus.com/inward/record.uri?eid=2-s2.0-84871418935&doi=10.1093%2fscipol%2fscs022&partnerID=40&md5=70c8d0d2b31bc3c7c0ea76b2f67398ec

Barron, N. J., Kuller, M., Yasmin, T., Castonguay, A. C., Copa, V., Duncan-Horner, E., et al. (2017). Towards water sensitive cities in Asia: An interdisciplinary journey. *Water Science and Technology, 76*(5), 1150–1157.

Batie, S. S. (2008). Wicked problems and applied economics. *American Journal of Agricultural Economics, 90*(5), 1176–1191.

Battistella, C., de Toni, A. F., & Pillon, R. (2016). Inter-organisational technology/knowledge transfer: A framework from critical literature review. *The Journal of Technology Transfer, 41*(5), 1195–1234.

Bekkers, R., & Bodas Freitas, I. M. (2008). Analysing knowledge transfer channels between universities and industry: To what degree do sectors also matter? *Research Policy, 37*(10), 1837–1853.

Binder, C. R., Absenger-Helmli, I., & Schilling, T. (2015). The reality of transdisciplinarity: A framework-based self-reflection from science and practice leaders. *Sustainability Science, 10*(4), 545–562.

Blättel-Mink, B., & Kastenholz, H. (2005). Transdisciplinarity in sustainability research: Diffusion conditions of an institutional innovation. *International Journal of Sustainable Development and World Ecology, 12*(1), 1–12. https://www.scopus.com/inward/record.uri?eid=2-s2.0-19544392116&doi=10.1080%2f13504500509469613&partnerID=40&md5=159c2c52e2bf79753a44222ff4b57faf

Cash, D. W., Clark, W. C., Alcock, F., Dickson, N. M., Eckley, N., Guston, D. H., et al. (2003). Knowledge systems for sustainable development. *Proceedings of the National Academy of Sciences of the United States of America, 100*(14), 8086–8091.

Chalmers, A. F. (2013). *What is this thing called science?* (4th ed.). McGraw-Hill Education.

Clark, W. C., van Kerkhoff, L., Lebel, L., & Gallopin, G. C. (2016). Crafting usable knowledge for sustainable development. *Proceedings of the National Academy of Sciences of the United States of America, 113*(17), 4570–4578.

Cohen, W. M., & Levinthal, D. A. (1990). Absorptive capacity: A new perspective on learning and innovation. *Administrative Science Quarterly, 35*(1), 128.

Corsten, H., Gössinger, R., Müller-Seitz, G., & Schneider, H. (2016). *Grundlagen des Technologie- und Innovationsmanagements.* Verlag Franz Vahlen GmbH.

Crescenzi, R., Nathan, M., & Rodríguez-Pose, A. (2016). Do inventors talk to strangers? On proximity and collaborative knowledge creation. *Research Policy, 45*(1), 177–194.

Dosi, G. (1982). Technological paradigms and technological trajectories. *Research Policy, 11*(3), 147–162.

Easterby-Smith, M., Lyles, M. A., & Tsang, E. W. K. (2008). Inter-Organizational Knowledge Transfer: Current Themes and Future Prospects. *Journal of Management Studies, 45*(4), 677–690.

Ervin, D. E., Glenna, L. L., & Jussaume, Jr., Raymond A. (2010). Are biotechnology and sustainable agriculture compatible? *Renewable Agriculture and Food Systems, 25*(2, SI), 143–157.

Evans, J., Jones, R., Karvonen, A., Millard, L., & Wendler, J. (2015). Living labs and co-production: University campuses as platforms for sustainability science. *Current Opinion in Environmental Sustainability, 16*, 1–6.

Evans, J., & Karvonen, A. (2014). 'Give me a laboratory and i will lower your carbon footprint!'—Urban laboratories and the governance of low-carbon futures. *International Journal of Urban and Regional Research, 38*(2), 413–430.

Fazey, I., Evely, A. C., Reed, M. R., Stringer, L. C., Kruijsen, J., & White, P. e. a. (2013). Knowledge exchange: A review and research agenda for environmental management. *Environmental Conservation, 40*(1), 19–36.

Fecher, B., & Friesike, S. (2014). Open science: One term, five schools of thought. In S. Bartling & S. Friesike (Eds.), *Opening science* (pp. 17–47). Springer International Publishing.

Foray, D. (2004). *Economics of knowledge.* MIT Press.

Fritsch, M., & Schwirten, C. (1999). Enterprise-university co-operation and the role of public research institutions in regional innovation systems. *Industry and Innovation, 6*(1), 69–83.

Galunic, D. C., & Rodan, S. (1998). Resource recombinations in the firm: Knowledge structures and the potential for schumpeterian innovation. *Strategic Management Journal, 19*(12), 1193–1201.

Gibbons, M. (1994). *The new production of knowledge: The dynamics of science and research in contemporary societies.* Sage Publ.

Gorman, M. E. (2002). Types of knowledge and their roles in technology transfer. *Journal of Technology Transfer, 27*, 219–231.

Gottschalk-Mazouz, N. (2007). Was ist Wissen? In S. Ammon, C. Heineke, & K. Selbmann (Eds.), *Wissen in Bewegung. Dominanz, Synergien und Emanzipation in den Praxen der 'Wissensgesellschaft'* (pp. 21–40). Velbrück Wissenschaft.

Grant, R. M. (1996). Toward a knowledge-based theory of the firm. *Strategic Management Journal, 17*, 109–122.

Grundel, I., & Dahlström, M. (2016). A quadruple and quintuple Helix approach to regional innovation systems in the transformation to a forestry-based bioeconomy. *Journal of the Knowledge Economy, 7*(4), 963–983.

Grunwald, A. (2007). Working towards sustainable development in the face of uncertainty and incomplete knowledge. *Journal of Environmental Policy & Planning, 9*(3–4), 245–262.

Hart, D. D., Bell, K. P., Lindenfeld, L. A., Jain, S., Johnson, T. R., Ranco, D., & McGill, B. (2015). Strengthening the role of universities in addressing sustainability challenges: The Mitchell center for sustainability solutions as an institutional experiment. *Ecology and Society, 20*(2).

Hauser, M., Loiskandl, W., & Wurzinger, M. (2011). Innovation systems research sustainable natural resource use in least developed countries. *GAIA—Ecological Perspectives for Science and Society, 20*(1), 70–72.

Heiskanen, E., & Lovio, R. (2010). User-producer interaction in housing energy innovations. *Journal of Industrial Ecology, 14*(1), 91–102. https://www.scopus.com/inward/record.uri?eid=2-s2.0-77954364479&doi=10.1111%2fj.1530-9290.2009.00196.x&partnerID=40&md5=5b64f38d46c4b0269aaf7db8739544a4

von Hippel, E. (1994). "Sticky information" and the locus of problem solving: Implications for innovation. *Management Science, 40*(4), 429–439.

von Hippel, E. (2006). *Democratizing innovation*. The MIT Press.

Jacobson, N., Butterill, D., & Goering, P. (2003). Development of a framework for knowledge translation: Understanding user context. *Journal of Health Services Research & Policy, 8*(2), 94–99.

Jasanoff, S. (Ed.). (2004). *International library of sociology. States of knowledge: The co-production of science and social order*. Routledge.

Jensen, M. B., Johnson, B., Lorenz, E., & Lundvall, B. Å. (2007). Forms of knowledge and modes of innovation. *Research Policy, 36*(5), 680–693.

Jernsand, E. M. (2019). Student living labs as innovation arenas for sustainable tourism. *Tourism Recreation Research, 44*(3, SI), 337–347.

Johnson, B., Müller, J., Gregersen, B., & Orozco, J. (2009). Pitfalls and opportunities in knowledge sharing: experiences from a research capacity building project in Central America. *International Journal of Technological Learning, Innovation and Development, 2*(4), 250–273. https://www.scopus.com/inward/record.uri?eid=2-s2.0-84897056348&doi=10.1504%2fIJTLID.2009.026817&partnerID=40&md5=25eb04d759600d092a235e1d3622ccd1

Kates, R. W., Clark, W. C., Corell, R., Hall, J. M., Jaeger, C. C., Lowe, I., et al. (2001). Sustainability science. *Science, 292*(5517), 641–642.

Kirat, T., & Lung, Y. (1999). Innovation and proximity. *European Urban and Regional Studies, 6*(1), 27–38.

Klenk, N. L., & Hickey, G. M. (2012). Improving the social robustness of research networks for sustainable natural resource management: Results of a Delphi study in Canada. *Science and Public Policy, 39*(3), 357–372. https://www.scopus.com/inward/record.uri?eid=2-s2.0-84871442822&doi=10.1093%2fscipol%2fscs024&partnerID=40&md5=bb6ba96108e54d21c582dd44da47aaaf

Lang, D. J., Wiek, A., Bergmann, M., Stauffacher, M., Martens, P., Moll, P., et al. (2012). Transdisciplinary research in sustainability science: Practice, principles, and challenges. *Sustainability Science, 7*(S1), 25–43.

Luederitz, C., Schäpke, N., Wiek, A., Lang, D. J., Bergmann, M., Bos, J. J., et al. (2017). Learning through evaluation – A tentative evaluative scheme for sustainability transition experiments. *Journal of Cleaner Production, 169*, 61–76.

Luks, F., & Siebenhüner, B. (2007). Transdisciplinarity for social learning? The contribution of the German socio-ecological research initiative to sustainability governance. *Ecological Economics, 63*(2–3), 418–426.

McCauley, S. M., & Stephens, J. C. (2012). Green energy clusters and socio-technical transitions: Analysis of a sustainable energy cluster for regional economic development in Central Massachusetts, USA. *Sustainability Science, 7*(2), 213–225.

Miller, T. R., Wiek, A., Sarewitz, D., Robinson, J., Olsson, L., Kriebel, D., & Loorbach, D. (2014). The future of sustainability science: A solutions-oriented research agenda. *Sustainability Science, 9*(2), 239–246.

Morone, P., & Taylor, T. (2004). Knowledge diffusion dynamics and network properties of face-to-face interactions. *Journal of Evolutionary Economics, 14*(3), 327–351.

Moser, S. C. (2016). Can science on transformation transform science? Lessons from co-design. *Current Opinion in Environmental Sustainability, 20*, 106–115.

Nowotny, H., Scott, P., & Gibbons, M. (2001). *Re-thinking science: Knowledge and the public in an age of uncertainty*. Sage Publication.

OECD. (2015a). *Frascati manual 2015: Guidelines for collecting and reporting data on research and experimental development*. OECD Publishing.

Perry, B., & May, T. (2010). Urban knowledge exchange: Devilish dichotomies and active intermediation. *International Journal of Knowledge-Based Development, 1*(1–2), 6–24. https://www.scopus.com/inward/record.uri?eid=2-s2.0-77954427226&doi=10.1504%2fIJKBD.2010.032583&partnerID=40&md5=9210609f89314385e92ac4c149d31962

Polanyi, M. (1966). *The tacit dimension*. Doubleday.

Polk, M. (2015). Transdisciplinary co-production: Designing and testing a transdisciplinary research framework for societal problem solving. *Futures, 65*, 110–122.

Purcell, W. M., Henriksen, H., & Spengler, J. D. (2019). Universities as the engine of transformational sustainability toward delivering the sustainable development goals. *International Journal of Sustainability in Higher Education, 20*(8), 1343–1357.

Rau, H., Goggins, G., & Fahy, F. (2018). From invisibility to impact: Recognising the scientific and societal relevance of interdisciplinary sustainability research. *Research Policy, 47*(1), 266–276.

Rosenberg, N. (1982). *Inside the black box: Technology and economics*. Cambridge Univ. Press.

Roux, D. J., Rogers, K. H., Biggs, H. C., Ashton, P. J., & Sergeant, A. (2006). Bridging the science-management divide: Moving from unidirectional knowledge transfer to knowledge interfacing and sharing. *Ecology and Society, 11*(1). http://www.ecologyandsociety.org/vol11/iss1/art4/

Rydin, Y. (2007). Re-examining the role of knowledge within planning theory. *Planning Theory, 6*(1), 52–68.

Scholz, R. W. (2017). The normative dimension in transdisciplinarity, transition management, and transformation sciences: New roles of science and universities in sustainable transitioning. *Sustainability, 9*(6).

Schumpeter, J. A. (1997). *Theorie der wirtschaftlichen Entwicklung: Eine Untersuchung über Unternehmergewinn, Kapital, Kredit, Zins und den Konjunkturzyklus* (Neunte Auflage, unveränderter Nachdruck der 1934 erschienen vierten Auflage). *ProQuest Ebook Central*. Duncker & Humblot.

Shannon, C. E. (1948). A mathematical theory of communication. *Bell System Technical Journal, 27*(3), 379–423.

Smarts, P., Holmes, S., Lettice, F., Pitts, F. H., Zwiegelaar, J. B., Schwartz, G., & Evans, S. (2019). Open Science and Open Innovation in a socio-political context: knowledge production for societal impact in an age of post-truth populism. *R&D Management, 49*(3, SI), 279–297.

Soini, K., Jurgilevich, A., Pietikäinen, J., & Korhonen-Kurki, K. (2018). Universities responding to the call for sustainability: A typology of sustainability centres. *Journal of Cleaner Production, 170*, 1423–1432.

Spielman, D. J., Ekboir, J., & Davis, K. (2009). The art and science of innovation systems inquiry: Applications to Sub-Saharan African agriculture. *Technology in Society, 31*(4), 399–405.

Stephens, J. C., Hernandez, M. E., Román, M., Graham, A. C., & Scholz, R. W. (2008). Higher education as a change agent for sustainability in different cultures and contexts. *International Journal of Sustainability in Higher Education, 9*(3), 317–338.

Szulanski, G. (2000). The process of knowledge transfer: A diachronic analysis of stickiness. *Organizational Behavior and Human Decision Processes, 82*(1), 9–27.

Trencher, G., Yarime, M., McCormick, K. B., Doll, C. N. H., & Kraines, S. B. (2014). Beyond the third mission: Exploring the emerging university function of co-creation for sustainability. *Science and Public Policy, 41*(2), 151–179.

Trencher, G., Nagao, M., Chen, C., Ichiki, K., Sadayoshi, T., Kinai, M., et al. (2017). Implementing sustainability co-creation between universities and society: A typology-based understanding. *Sustainability, 9*(4), 594.

Tsoukas, H., & Vladimirou, E. (2001). What is organizational knowledge? *Journal of Management Studies, 38*(7), 973–993.

Urmetzer, S., Schlaile, M., Bogner, K., Mueller, M., & Pyka, A. (2018). Exploring the dedicated knowledge base of a transformation towards a sustainable bioeconomy. *Sustainability, 10*(6), 1694.

van Horne, C., & Dutot, V. (2017). Challenges in technology transfer: an actor perspective in a quadruple helix environment. *Journal of Technology Transfer, 42*(2, SI), 285–301.

van Kerkhoff, L. (2014). Knowledge governance for sustainable development: A review. *Challenges in Sustainability, 1*(2).

van Kerkhoff, L., & Lebel, L. (2006). Linking knowledge and action for sustainable development. *Annual Review of Environment and Resources, 31*(1), 445–477.

Weber, E. P., & Khademian, A. M. (2008). Wicked problems, knowledge challenges, and collaborative capacity builders in network settings. *Public Administration Review, 68*(2), 334–349.

Wehrden, H. von, Luederitz, C., Leventon, J., & Russell, S. (2017). Methodological challenges in sustainability science: A call for method plurality, procedural rigor and longitudinal research. *Challenges in Sustainability, 5*(1).

Wiek, A., Ness, B., Schweizer-Ries, P., Brand, F. S., & Farioli, F. (2012). From complex systems analysis to transformational change: A comparative appraisal of sustainability science projects. *Sustainability Science, 7*(S1), 5–24.

Wuyts, S., Colombo, M. G., Dutta, S., & Nooteboom, B. (2005). Empirical tests of optimal cognitive distance. *Journal of Economic Behavior & Organization, 58*(2), 277–302.

Chapter 7
Proximity

7.1 Role of Proximity for Knowledge Processes and Innovation

As depicted in the previous chapters, the knowledge relevant for sustainable innovations is complex and widely dispersed. Its creation and transfer are facilitated by inter- and transdisciplinary approaches, based on the broad involvement of stakeholders and the use of experiments and problem- and solution-oriented methods. The corresponding innovation systems include diverse actors from business, government, academia, and civil society. Furthermore, it should be recognized that most innovations aimed at sustainability only succeed because they involve various stakeholders, knowledge domains, and regulatory authorities right from the outset. Consequently, innovation networks that connect these diverse actors are often an indispensable prerequisite. An actor attempting to draft sustainable innovations in isolation is unlikely to succeed, as this approach would lack the essential complementary knowledge elements. The body of knowledge relevant for sustainable innovations emerges from a collaborative learning process among various stakeholders. It seems unlikely that individual actors possess the capability to solve the intricate challenges associated with developing technologies and social innovations that gain acceptance and widespread adoption, ultimately facilitating the transformation of production and consumption systems toward sustainability.

However, the literature depicts abundant examples of challenges that arise when diverse agents collaborate in innovation networks (confer Klenk & Hickey, 2012; McCauley & Stephens, 2012; Polk, 2015; Pyka & Nelson, 2018). Therefore, to gain a more comprehensive understanding of the dynamics of learning and knowledge transfer within sustainability-oriented innovation networks, as well as the factors that facilitate or impede them, it is advantageous to conduct a thorough investigation of the relationships among the network participants. A powerful analytical framework for this purpose is the concept of proximity, which is rooted in economic geography where it is applied to study various issues such as inter-organizational collaboration,

U. Wilke, *Towards Sustainable Innovations*, Economic Complexity and Evolution,
https://doi.org/10.1007/978-3-032-31024-8_7

regional development processes, or the emergence of innovations (Crescenzi et al., 2016; Knoben & Oerlemans, 2006). It is furthermore used for analyzing various other economic phenomena beyond the innovation context, including land use, labor mobility, and mergers and acquisitions (for a more detailed overview, see Balland et al., 2015). Proximity helps to understand interactive learning and innovations, as both processes are characterized by uncertainty and both require effective mechanisms to solve the coordination problem occurring when two or more participants interact to exchange complementary pieces of knowledge (Boschma, 2005; Torre & Gilly, 2000).

7.2 Theoretical Foundation of the Concept of Proximity

Johann Heinrich von Thünen (1826) and Alfred Marshall (1920) were among the first who prominently introduced the concept of space into economic analysis, demonstrating the relevance and implications of proximity in its basic spatial meaning (Capello, 2014). Later, the French School of Proximity extended the concept to enable a more thorough analysis of the territorial and institutional aspects of regional development and innovation by introducing non-spatial proximity dimensions (Carrincazeaux et al., 2008). Prominent works in this regard include Torre and Gilly (2000) and Kirat and Lung (1999).

While today the differentiation between the spatial and the non-spatial dimensions of proximity is widely applied, there are different approaches for subdividing the non-spatial part, depending on the context and the objective of analysis (Knoben & Oerlemans, 2006). There is ambiguity in the definition and use of those different proximity dimensions, as well as a considerable overlap (Heringa et al., 2014). One source of ambiguity is the fact that proximity is used for examinations on two different analytical levels, a dyadic one, concerning the exchange between two or more separate units, and a general one (Knoben & Oerlemans, 2006). In other words, the notion of proximity can be utilized for examining networks at the firm level as well as for conducting research with regions as the unit of analysis (Moreno & Miguélez, 2012).

Boschma (2005) convincingly presents a proximity concept with five dimensions shaping knowledge exchange and innovations, with the five dimensions being geographical, organizational, social, institutional, and cognitive proximity. Each dimension will be scrutinized in the following chapters. Boschma (2005) shows how each dimension can facilitate knowledge exchange, but can also have adverse effects because of lock-ins. Consequently, excessive proximity, just as insufficient proximity, can be detrimental to interactive learning and innovation. This U-shaped relation between proximity and innovation is however questioned by some authors and their findings (see for example Heringa et al., 2014).

7.2.1 Geographical Proximity

The concept of geographic proximity is rooted in the works of Johann Heinrich von Thünen, who, in his 1826 published treatise *The Isolated State* (Thünen, 1826), examined patterns of agricultural land use. Further seminal investigations in this field were done by Alfred Marshalls (1920) in his work on industrial districts,[1] which have been widely discussed ever since, not only in economic geography (Capello, 2014; Werker et al., 2019). Considerations of the physical nearness of agents can today be found in various analyses, models, and approaches dealing with a range of different topics, from knowledge spillovers to cluster effects to regional innovation systems.

In brief, geographical proximity refers to the spatial distance between two actors, either in absolute terms, measured as linear distance, or in relative terms, evaluated as travel time, costs of physically meeting, co-location in the same territorial unit, or alike (Ponds et al., 2007). As many institutions such as rules, laws, and policies have a geographically defined territorial validity, meaning they are place-specific, it can easily happen that arguments regarding geographical proximity are mixed up with arguments referring to institutional proximity (Mattes, 2012). This is in line with the reasoning of Gertler (2003), who states that crucial for transferring tacit knowledge is complementarity on an institutional level, not mere physical nearness. That means that decisive is not the fact that two agents are spatially close, but the institutional context they share. Werker et al. (2019) consequently suggest that geographical proximity entails two different aspects, one being pure physical proximity referring to the actual spatial distance between two actors, and the other aspect being systemic proximity referring to the commonality of economic, political, institutional, and cultural influences that equally affect two actors.

Following the differentiation of Boschma (2005), it, however, seems more appropriate to distinguish between geographical and institutional proximity, for a number of reasons. First, different institutions are effective at different geographical scales. Some informal institutions, such as traditions and habits, are narrowly localized while other formal institutions, such as laws and regulations, rather work on the level of nation-states or have even supranational or international validity (compare Boschma, 2005). Furthermore, the existence of national borders can institutionally separate two physically close actors. Also, a decoupling of institutional and geographical proximity can occur when individuals or organizations relocate, carrying specific institutions like norms, habits, traditions, or codes of conduct with them to another locality.

Geographical proximity in a purely spatial sense can foster knowledge creation, learning, and innovation by facilitating face-to-face contact and causing low costs of direct interaction (Fritsch & Schwirten, 1999). Face-to-face interactions encompass several characteristics conducive to knowledge exchange (Storper & Venables, 2004). It is an effective means of communication as it offers swift feedback in high frequency, including visual cues from body language. It can furthermore help resolve incentive-related challenges by fostering trust and strengthening relationships, as it simplifies

---

[1] His book *Principles of Economics* was first published in 1890.

the detection of lying, diminishes anonymity and thereby promotes the adoption of shared values (Storper & Venables, 2004). In this regard, geographical proximity is especially conducive to the transfer of tacit knowledge (confer Knoben & Oerlemans, 2006; Ponds et al., 2007). Lower transaction costs of direct contact enable the sharing of uncodified, implicit knowledge, up to the point of personnel working on-site at the partner's premises. The social character of collaborative projects underscores the significance of easy communication and interaction among partners for achieving success (Hansen, 2015). On the other hand, too much geographical proximity can lead to a lack of openness, with an exclusive focus on spatially close partners resulting in missing out on new sources of knowledge and new competencies, just because they are situated further away (Boschma, 2005).

In light of the ongoing digitization and having the experiences of the COVID-19 Pandemic in mind, the question arises whether modern information and communication technologies (ICT) can replace face-to-face contacts. Current research on this topic suggests that ICT must rather be seen as complementary to direct face-to-face contact (Ceci et al., 2021). However, the relationship seems to be complex, as ICT might be a critical technology with high added value, especially in long-distance collaborations after a shared understanding was established during initial direct contacts (compare Dubois, 2019). In combination with other proximity dimensions such as cognitive proximity, ICT can reduce the importance of geographical proximity (Ievoli et al., 2019), while in cases with generally low levels of proximities, ICT might even be harmful when used to overcome long-distances in collaborative projects (Knoben & Oerlemans, 2006).

7.2.2 Cognitive Proximity

Knowledge exhibits a cumulative nature, which implies that an agent must possess a certain knowledge base to be able to acquire new knowledge. In the absence of this cognitive foundation, new information cannot be processed meaningfully and hence does not become new knowledge. Cognitive proximity pertains to the relationship between two or more agents engaged in the exchange or co-creation of new knowledge. To effectively communicate, comprehend, and interpret the information they exchange, these agents require a shared cognitive foundation, encompassing common vocabulary and fundamental understandings (Boschma, 2005). Cognitive proximity can thus be understood as a commonality between different agents in perceiving, interpreting, comprehending, and assessing the surrounding world. In this view, divergence in how people perceive and understand the world stems from their individual cognitive development shaped through interactions with their physical and social surroundings. Consequently, people possess unique perspectives and knowledge of the world, influenced by various factors such as national, regional, and organizational cultures, customs and habits, social norms and values, educational experiences, technologies, and market dynamics (Wuyts et al., 2005).

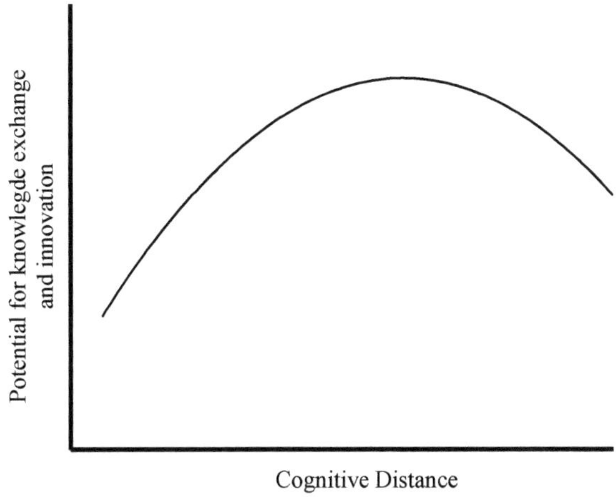

Fig. 7.1 Relation between cognitive distance and knowledge exchange/innovation

Cognitive proximity is closely related to the concept of absorptive capacity, and can be seen as a prerequisite for interactive learning processes (Mattes, 2012). The necessity for cognitive alignment between two agents intensifies with the complexity and subject specificity of the knowledge they intend to exchange. However, when the knowledge bases of two agents are almost identical, the potential for mutual learning diminishes as the reservoir of new input from the counterpart lessens. Therefore, an optimal cognitive distance (or proximity) between two agents appears to exist, allowing for an ideal level of mutual learning. This suggests an inverted U-shaped relationship between cognitive distance and innovative performance (Nooteboom et al., 2007; Wuyts et al., 2005), as depicted in Fig. 7.1. Too much cognitive proximity is associated with missing complementarities between the knowledge bases of partners and subsequently leaves little space for the recombination of existing knowledge items (Boschma, 2005). Too little cognitive proximity obstructs productive knowledge exchange as there is limited or even no mutual understanding.

A lack of cognitive proximity can constitute knowledge boundaries, which arise if actors with different specializations lack common cognitive ground for collaborating, a situation that seems more likely if actors from different institutional spheres (academia, industry, government, civil society) or with different disciplinary background collaborate (Valkering et al., 2013). This illustrates a further issue, namely the relation between cognitive proximity and institutional proximity. Actors from a similar institutional or disciplinary context might depict a high degree of shared knowledge and understandings, forming what is in the literature known as a community of practice or epistemological community, with a high level of cognitive proximity allowing for effective knowledge exchange despite large spatial distances (Knoben & Oerlemans, 2006; Morone & Taylor, 2004; Roux et al., 2006).

7.2.3 Institutional Proximity

Institutional proximity concerns the framework of rules and constraints that significantly influence the exchange between two actors (confer Hansen, 2014). It entails two aspects. On the one hand, it refers to the overarching institutional framework under which two agents cooperate, entailing formal institutions such as laws and regulations, as well as informal institutions such as norms, traditions, and social codes of conduct. Second, it refers to the internal institutional logic of actors comprising elements such as incentive structures, organizational purpose, legal form, hierarchical system, corporate culture, and alike (confer Boschma, 2005; Ponds et al., 2007).

Institutional proximity thus refers to similarities regarding the institutional frame and the internal institutional working mechanisms of the two actors. It can facilitate knowledge exchange due to the existence of commonly applied logic of action (Ponds et al., 2007; Strambach, 2017). For example, two universities within the same jurisdiction will rather easily agree on the terms and modes of collaboration and hence easily exchange information and knowledge. In contrast, unequal partners such as a large multinational company cooperating with a small NGO will most likely face different, more severe challenges in agreeing on specific terms for exchanging knowledge. This becomes even more crucial when considering cross-country collaboration that spans various languages and legislations. Another example that illustrates the importance of institutional proximity is the transfer of corporate structures or research capacities from one socio-economic or cultural context to a significantly different one. Such endeavors hardly work without comprehensive adaptations, since much of knowledge is localized, problem-specific, and embedded in day-to-day practice that are shaped by the institutional framework (confer Johnson et al., 2009; Strambach, 2017).

Whereas institutional proximity can facilitate learning and innovation through social cohesion and shared approaches for problem-solving, too much institutional proximity can be detrimental as it can create lock-ins that are unfavorable for experimenting and trying new methods and solution strategies (Boschma, 2005). Those lock-ins can be created by inward-looking actors that strongly rely on established norms and solutions strategies, preventing institutional adaptation and the experimentation with new approaches, and thus avoiding the build-up of new institutional structures. Too little institutional proximity on the other hand is hindering knowledge exchange as it is associated with higher levels of uncertainty regarding the motives and codes of conduct of other actors. This uncertainty also refers to the application of formal rules and informal norms that shape the collaboration between two partners. Acquaintance with a trusted set of formal rules and regulations such as laws and enforcement mechanisms, but also with informal rules such as norms of reciprocity, significantly improves the collaboration between two partners, even if they have no prior experience working together (Boschma, 2005).

7.2.4 *Social Proximity*

Social proximity refers to social ties between individuals on the micro level of cooperating organizations, entailing trust based on kinship, friendship, mutual sympathy, or previous working experiences (Boschma, 2005). The underlying idea goes back to Granovetter (1985) and his argument that most economic interactions are embedded in networks of social relations. Social proximity facilitates knowledge exchange and innovations by providing clarity regarding the motivations of cooperating partners and reducing the risk of falling for opportunistic behavior. It can provide efficient informal mechanisms based on social relations, thus reducing transaction costs and establishing reciprocity (confer Balland, Boschma, & Frenken, 2022). Such informal contacts based on trust and personal contacts can replace inefficient formal arrangements. While a lack of social proximity can result in mistrust and overly complicated formal transaction mechanisms and thus negatively affect knowledge exchange, too much social proximity might lead to the underestimation of opportunisms and the exclusion of actors with whom no prior experience exists, leading to a lock-in preventing access to new ideas and complementary knowledge of new contacts (Boschma, 2005).

The extent of social proximity between two actors depends on the relationships between the individuals of each actor. It is determined by the degree to which the individuals know each other, how emotionally close they are, whether they have feelings of obligation toward each other, and of course the extent of trust between them (confer Hansen, 2015; Huber, 2012). The role of trust in collaborative innovation processes and interactive learning is discussed by various authors, underscoring the importance of trust for facilitating exchange and cooperation (see for example Dovey, 2009; Hardwick et al., 2013; Velenturf & Jensen, 2016). For knowledge exchange, trust concerns both sides of a transmission process. The sender must be trusted to provide valuable, meaningful, salient, and accurate information, while the receiver must be trusted not to misuse the received information. Since learning and the (co-)creation of knowledge involve costs and therefore require a certain commitment as well as the investment of resources, trust in the sense of expecting a positive, beneficial outcome is a prerequisite. Especially when actors from different areas or institutional spheres cooperate, the partners' motives, discretion, incentives, and constraints are likely to not be fully congruent, which increases the importance of trust for bridging gaps and fostering exchange.

7.2.5 *Organizational Proximity*

Organizational proximity refers to the degree to which collaboration between two entities is structured within an organizational framework (Boschma, 2005). It ranges from a very low degree of proximity characterized by spontaneous, unstructured collaborations with no formal ties, to high proximity given by well-defined hierarchical structures in cases in which two departments within the same organization, or two companies under the same corporate umbrella cooperate. Between these extremes lie various intermediary settings that may involve loosely connected networks founded on cooperative agreements or consortia composed of independent entities collaborating on a funded project. The concept of organizational proximity primarily revolves around issues of control and authority, as well as the corresponding capacity to influence economic activities and deter opportunism (Hansen, 2015; Mattes, 2012). The interdependence of two actors in terms of economic or financial ties significantly influences this matter (Kirat & Lung, 1999).

The transfer or co-creation of knowledge is in many cases connected to some degree of uncertainty regarding the appropriability and utilization of this knowledge (Hennart, 1993). Hence the need for control mechanisms arises, that allow counteracting opportunistic behavior and safeguarding appropriate returns on investment. Transaction cost economics provide insights into the various governance forms applicable to such situations, including markets, hierarchies, and hybrid structures. These diverse forms exhibit distinct incentive structures and employ different mechanisms for enforcement and penalization (Williamson, 1989). These different formal arrangements for collaborating can be understood as different degrees of organizational proximity, which thus follows a similar working mechanism as social proximity via establishing clarity and alignment regarding the partners' goals and incentives and reducing the risk of mischievous behavior. While organizational proximity can be conducive to knowledge exchange, too much proximity can lead to excessive bureaucracy and a lack of flexibility hampering learning and innovations by excluding new (external) sources of knowledge (Boschma, 2005).

Informal, purely voluntary collaborations, characterized by the absence of concrete obligations or mutual dependencies in terms of resources, allow a high degree of flexibility regarding the objectives of a collaboration, the commitment of resources, or the involvement of additional partners. However, this flexibility can also be a disadvantage, as partners can easily and unilaterally end their engagement. Furthermore, the lack of any formal commitments and corresponding mechanisms to enforce them can lead partners to ruthlessly act out of pure self-interest, possibly misusing the information provided by the partners and thus diminishing the basis for cooperation. Contractual arrangements or legal ties provide means for control and penalization but can be cumbersome to establish and are connected to high transaction costs. Strict formal requirements, for example, established by the legal department or procurement office of a large company, can induce costs that might even hinder collaboration or deter potential partners.

7.3 Empirical Measurement Approaches

Numerous authors from different fields such as economic geography, management sciences, or innovation studies have published empirical research on proximity and its role regarding knowledge processes and innovations. Although there is a shared understanding regarding the significance of proximity for knowledge-intensive collaborations, the practical difficulty lies in how to operationalize, untangle, and weigh the different dimensions of proximities, which often coexist and intersect (Crescenzi et al., 2016). One approach is the use of econometric analyses for empirically examining the role of proximity. A widespread approach in this regard is the investigation of patent data, as done for example by Aldieri et al. (2019), Aldieri et al. (2020), Sun and Han (2022), and Ardito et al. (2019). Other scholars use data from surveys and questionnaires, such as Ghassim (2018), Huber (2012), Aguiléra et al. (2012), Heringa et al. (2014), Royo-Vela and Mazandarani (2022), and Capone and Lazzeretti (2018). Bibliometric analyses are further widespread approaches, as conducted by Cunningham and Werker (2012), Werker et al. (2019), Ponds et al. (2007), and Hardeman et al. (2015). There are furthermore quantitative studies using other input, such as datasets of funded research projects (Balland, 2012; Janssen & Abbasiharofteh, 2022), or a mixture of different sources, such as Lopolito et al. (2022) using a combination of questionnaire data and official databases, or Cappellano and Makkonen (2020), who analyze academic articles in combination with employment statistics.

Tables 7.1, 7.2, 7.3, 7.4, and 7.5 provide an overview of various examples of indicators being used for measuring the different proximity dimensions. As can be seen, there is a considerable variety of items and variables. The empirical studies also exhibit quite some variation in their findings regarding the relevance of the different proximity dimensions, which fits the finding of Capone and Lazzeretti (2018), that many empirical studies agree on the relevance of geographical proximity but arrive at conflicting conclusions regarding the role and precise influence of the other proximity dimensions.

This issue is reflected in the criticisms of empirical approaches for measuring proximity: The influence that different measurement approaches and operationalizations might have on the derived conclusions makes the comparison of different studies challenging (Hansen, 2015). Further criticism concerns the data being used for investigating the inter-organizational knowledge processes and the occurrence of innovations. Patents and co-publications might not be the best proxies for such examinations, as they are subject to some limitations. Not all innovations can be patented, as is the case for most non-technical, service, or process innovations, and not all technological novelties that could be patented actually are (Crescenzi et al., 2016; Mazzanti, 2018). This is especially relevant in the context of sustainable innovations, which frequently possess systemic and non-technological attributes. Moreover, the participation of entities primarily driven by non-profit motives, such as civil society organizations, academic institutions, or government bodies, further diminishes the likeliness that project outcomes and innovations are protected by patents or other

Table 7.1 Examples of geographic proximity indicators in empirical studies

Author(s)	Indicators for geographic proximity
Aguiléra et al. (2012)	Spatial separation according to five categories: ultra-local (less than 5 km), local (5 to 50 km), regional (50 to 250 km), national (more than 250 km, but within country borders), international (outside country borders)
Ardito et al. (2019)	Physical distance based on inventors' addresses
Heringa et al. (2014)	The inverse of the geodesic distance measured at the city level
Huber (2012)	Located inside or outside of the analyzed cluster
Capone and Lazzeretti (2018)	Co-location at the municipality level
Ponds et al. (2007)	Collaboration between two different NUTS 3* regions
Werker et al. (2019)	Physical distance based on latitude and longitude data of addresses; affiliation with NUTS region (all levels)
Cunningham and Werker (2012)	Great circle distance; affiliation with NUTS region (all levels)
Hardeman et al. (2015)	The inverse of the distance in kilometers separating two organizations; affiliation with the same country
Balland (2012)	Classification according to three classes of distance: same country, same NUTS 1 region, same NUTS 2 region
Sun and Han (2022)	Dichotomic classification based on whether provinces are adjacent or not

* NUTS refers to the Nomenclature of Territorial Units for Statistics of the European Union, with three different levels: NUTS 1—major socio-economic regions, NUTS 2—basic regions, and NUTS 3—small regions

property rights. As for publications, they cannot reflect interactive learning occurring in inter-organizational collaboration, nor the creation of tacit knowledge or knowledge that is primarily of a practical nature and hence not publishable in scientific papers.

7.4 A Systematic Literature Review of Proximity and Sustainable Innovations

In contrast to the extensive scholarly research on the significance of proximity in the context of purely economic innovations, as exemplified by Balland et al. (2022), there has been limited exploration of this topic in the field of sustainable innovations. As illustrated in the previous chapters, there are numerous disparities

Table 7.2 Examples of cognitive proximity indicators in empirical studies

Author(s)	Indicators for cognitive proximity
Ghassim (2018)	Share of personnel with a bachelor's degree or technical certificate
Aguiléra et al. (2012)	Presence of a common culture, code, or language; Compatibility of technological equipment
Ardito et al. (2019)	Similarity between partners in terms of technological knowledge, measured as the extent of holding patents in the same technological class
Heringa et al. (2014)	Differences in technical terms and jargon used; differences in specialized instruments, software; common domain (specific field); common activity (management, policymaking, research, maintenance, operations, and other)
Huber (2012)	Common technical language; similarity of the way of thinking about the technology or product; similarity in terms of work-related technical details/facts; similarity in terms of work-related know-how
Capone and Lazzeretti (2018)	Classification of firms according to main activity; classification of firms concerning its scientific domain (ICT, physics, chemistry, restoration, diagnostics, environment, conservation, optoelectronics, 3D visualization, etc.)
Werker et al. (2019)	Research profiles of organizations according to science categories of Web of Science
Cunningham and Werker (2012)	Research profiles of organizations according to science categories of Web of Science
Hardeman et al. (2015)	Cosine of the overlap in journals in which any two organizations published articles in a specific period
Balland (2012)	Classification of firms according to four classes: infrastructure segment, hardware segment, software segment, applications and services segment
Cappellano and Makkonen (2020)	Published academic articles using Web of Science; employment data from official statistical authorities

between these two categories of innovations, arising from their distinct target dimensions (economic as opposed to economic, social, and ecological). These differences also translate into differences regarding the necessary knowledge bases, associated knowledge processes, and the composition of corresponding innovation networks. To gain insights into the intricacies of such sustainability-oriented innovation networks and to understand the peculiarities regarding the knowledge processes within these networks, a systematic literature review was conducted, with the aim of synthesizing the findings of papers analyzing the role of proximity dimensions in this regard. The methodology of the review is described in Sect. 7.4.1. The literature sample forming the basis of the review is described in Sect. 7.4.2. Section 7.4.3 presents the findings of the literature review, which are complemented by insights from additional sources from relevant literature. The findings are then summarized and interpreted in Sect. 7.4.4. The work presented in Sect. 7.4 is to a considerable extent based on Wilke and Pyka (2024a).

Table 7.3 Examples of institutional proximity indicators in empirical studies

Author(s)	Indicators for institutional proximity
Ghassim (2018)	Similarity regarding rules and laws; similarity regarding norms and values
Aguiléra et al. (2012)	Affiliation to the same parent group or the same business sector
Capone and Lazzeretti (2018)	Classification of organizations using four different types: research centers, institutions, firms, and universities
Ponds et al. (2007)	Classification of organizations using four different types: academic organization, company, governmental/ non-profit-making organization
Hardeman et al. (2015)	Classification of organizations using four different types: academic organization, company, governmental/ non-profit-making organization
Balland (2012)	Classification of organizations using four different types: academic organization, company, governmental/ non-profit-making organization
Royo-Vela and Mazandarani (2022)	Adherence to laws and regulations; similarity regarding cultural norms; similarity regarding values; similarity regarding habits and routines

Table 7.4 Examples of social proximity indicators in empirical studies

Author(s)	Indicators for social proximity
Aguiléra et al. (2012)	Previous acquaintance with partner organization; duration of the previous relationship with partner organization; trust
Heringa et al. (2014)	Efforts put into cooperation; trust; gender differences; age differences; duration of acquaintance; frequency of contacts; existence of private relationship
Huber (2012)	Previous acquaintance with partner organization; emotional closeness; feeling of personal obligation
Capone and Lazzeretti (2018)	Measurement of network closure by using geodesic distance 2 (having one partner organization in common)
Hardeman et al. (2015)	The number of prior ties measured as the log of the number of co-publications in a specific period
Balland (2012)	Measurement of network closure by using geodesic distance 2 (having one partner organization in common)
Royo-Vela and Mazandarani (2022)	Friendship between partners; trust; previous acquaintance with partner organization; previous working experience; similar level of reputation

Table 7.5 Examples of organizational proximity indicators in empirical studies

Author(s)	Indicators for organizational proximity
Ghassim (2018)	Number of non-local external sources of knowledge from five different domains: suppliers of equipment, customers, universities or research institutes, competitors, NGOs or public authorities
Aguiléra et al. (2012)	Convergence of methods of organization
Heringa et al. (2014)	Similarity regarding adapting to new circumstances; similarity regarding strictness of planning and financial management; similarity regarding freedom to initiate relations outside own organization; similarity regarding preferring to stick to procedures over achieving results; similarity regarding importance attached to protecting intellectual property; classification of organizations using four different types: business, government, academia, NGO
Werker et al. (2019)	Classification of organizations using two different types: academic organization, non-academic organization
Hardeman et al. (2015)	Affiliation to the same overarching hierarchical meta-structure
Balland (2012)	Affiliation to the same corporate group
Royo-Vela and Mazandarani (2022)	Similarity regarding organizational culture; similarity regarding organizational structure; similarity regarding inter-organizational relationship; using similar technology

7.4.1 Methodology

The methodology of the systematic literature review is informed by the approach outlined by Tranfield et al. (2003) and Palmatier et al. (2018). The first step was the systematic search for papers and the subsequent selection process, as depicted in Fig. 7.2. The initial paper selection was done by performing two searches: one in the Web of Science database and the other in the Scopus database. A comprehensive search term was employed containing the keywords "proximity," "sustainab*," "innovat*," and "knowledge", whereby the last two words were included as two alternative options, in conjunction with the first two words. The resulting search queries were "TITLE-ABS-KEY(proximity AND sustainab* AND (innovat* OR knowledge))" for Scopus, and "TS = (proximity AND sustainab* AND (innovat* OR knowledge))" for the database Web of Science. The two searches produced a substantial volume of publications. Following the merger of the two sets of results and the removal of duplicate entries, 585 publications were left. Subsequently, the next step entailed reviewing the abstracts of these publications to determine their eligibility for inclusion in the systematic review. The selection process adhered to the following inclusion criteria: (1) the publication must address the topic of sustainable innovations; (2) the publication must explore the emergence of these innovations rooted in knowledge processes; and (3) the publication must either examine the proximity among the involved actors or employ proximity as a framework for analyzing the relationships among these actors.

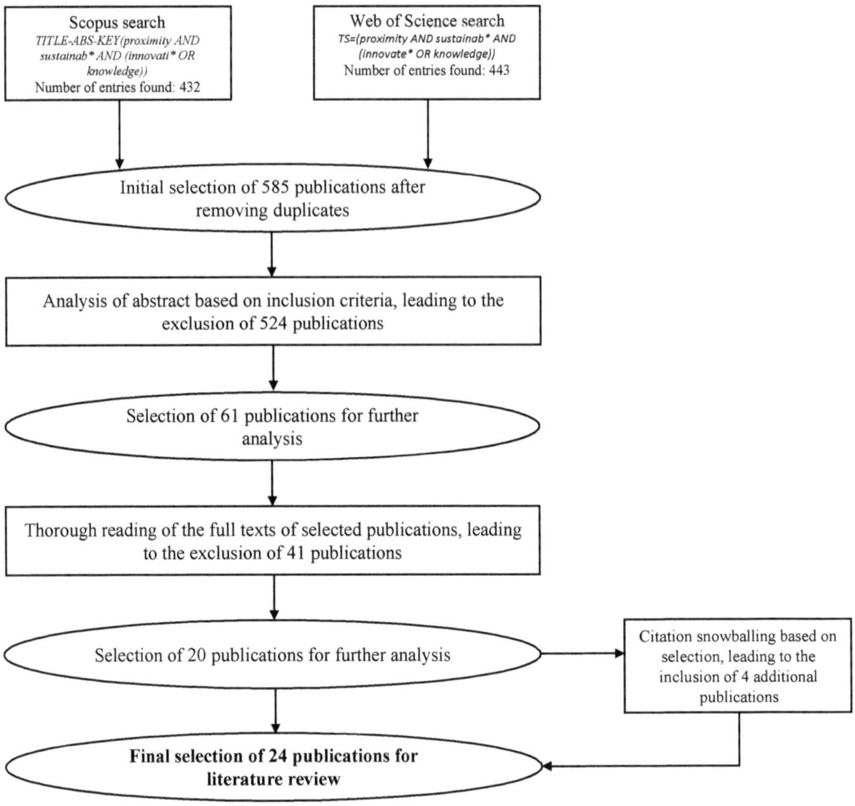

Fig. 7.2 Literature selection process. *Note* Image taken from Wilke and Pyka (2024a). CC BY 4.0. No changes were made

Consequently, publications that investigate other sustainability-related economic processes involving multiple stakeholders were excluded. That encompasses publications concerning proximity within supply chains, the spatial attributes of the flow of goods, materials, or energy, site selection for facilities or business establishments, proximity in contexts unrelated to innovation such as distribution matters, and the utilization of proximity as a concept for designing urban infrastructure topology in pursuit of sustainability objectives. Publications that delve into the spatial diffusion patterns of sustainable innovations, including the dissemination of green energy technologies, were excluded as well, as the focus lies on the emergence of innovations rather than their subsequent widespread adoption. Additionally, publications investigating network formation were excluded unless they specifically address the knowledge flows within these networks.

Following the analysis of the abstracts, a substantial portion of publications (514) was excluded. Additionally, 10 papers were excluded due to their language, most of which were in French. The notable prevalence of French-language publications on this topic can likely be attributed to the French school of proximity, which made significant early contributions to this strand of the innovation discourse.[2]

Next step was an in-depth analysis of the full texts of the remaining publications, resulting in the exclusion of further 41 publications based on the previously outlined inclusion criteria. Among the remaining 20 publications, citation snowballing, both backward and forward, revealed additional relevant publications, leading to the inclusion of 4 additional papers. Since the number of relevant papers identified through this method was high in comparison to the initial systematic database search, different modifications to the original search string were tested. However, these adjustments yielded no significant improvements, and instead, they substantially increased the number of irrelevant publications in the search results. Consequently, the final selection comprises 24 publications that form the basis of the systematic literature review, the findings of which are detailed in the following chapter.

Before presenting the findings, the inherent limitations of this systematic literature review should be noted. First, any systematic review bears the risk of omitting a pertinent paper, a challenge that was supposedly mitigated by employing broad search terms and conducting a comprehensive citation snowballing process to identify relevant references. Another aspect to consider is the methodological diversity found among the scrutinized papers, which can be perceived as a strength, as it provides a diverse array of perspectives on proximity from various angles. Nevertheless, comparing this multitude of approaches brings with it the challenge of dealing with differing definitions, operationalizations, and measurement methods, resulting in a certain level of conceptual ambiguity and slight variations in the precise interpretations of the underlying concepts.

7.4.2 Description of the Literature Sample

Table 7.6 provides an overview of the papers in the final sample, presenting information regarding the methodologies employed in the articles, the categories of innovations under scrutiny, and the proximity dimensions considered. As can be seen, the sample depicts a high degree of methodological diversity, with the majority of papers being empirical research approaches (Table 7.6).

Several papers are econometric studies. Some are based on analyzing patent data, such as Aldieri et al. (2019), Aldieri et al. (2020), Ardito et al. (2019), and Sun and Han (2022). The other econometric studies are based on interviews (Hansen, 2015), data on funded projects (Janssen & Abbasiharofteh, 2022), or a combination of different sources (Lopolito et al., 2022). Four papers in the sample employ case study approaches, namely Addy and Dubé (2018), Ievoli et al. (2019), Dubois (2019), and Velenturf (2016). Two of the papers apply network analysis, namely Qiang et al. (2021) and Shi et al. (2022), while an additional four papers utilize various qualitative and quantitative empirical methods (Bloise, 2020; Ghassim, 2018; Hansen,

[2] See Sect. 7.2.

Table 7.6 Papers included in the systematic review

Publication	Type of paper	Type of innovation	Proximity dimensions
Addy and Dubé (2018)	Case study approach	Social innovations	Geographical, cognitive, institutional, organizational, social
Aldieri et al. (2019)	Econometric analysis (patent data)	Environmental innovations	Technological (cognitive)
Aldieri et al. (2020)	Econometric analysis (patent data)	Environmental innovations	Technological (cognitive)
Ardito et al. (2019)	Econometric analysis (patent data)	Green innovations	Geographical, technological (cognitive)
Bloise (2020)	Qualitative empirical analysis (interviews)	Ecological process innovations	Geographical
Coenen et al. (2010)	Conceptual paper	Innovations for sustainability transitions	Geographical, cognitive, institutional, organizational, social
Delgadillo et al. (2021)	Conceptual paper	Innovations for sustainable product-service systems	Geographical, organizational
Dubois (2019)	Case study approach	Social and organizational innovations	Geographical, cognitive, institutional, organizational, social
Ghassim (2018)	Quantitative empirical analysis (survey data)	Eco-efficient process and product innovations, social sustainability practices	Organizational, institutional proximity (formal and Informal), Cognitive (science-related and engineering-related)
Hansen (2014)	Qualitative empirical analysis (interviews)	Sustainable product innovations	Geographical, cognitive, institutional, organizational, social
Hansen (2015)	Econometric analysis (interviews)	Sustainable product innovations	Geographical, cognitive, institutional, organizational, social
Hansen and Coenen (2015)	Literature review	Innovations for sustainability transitions	Geographical, cognitive, institutional, organizational, social
Ievoli et al. (2019)	Case study approach	Innovations for sustainable rural development	Cognitive, institutional, organizational, social
Janssen and Abbasiharofteh (2022)	Econometric (R&D project database)	Innovations for sustainability	Geographical, cognitive

(continued)

Table 7.6 (continued)

Publication	Type of paper	Type of innovation	Proximity dimensions
Lopolito et al. (2022)	Econometric analysis (questionnaire, Google Maps, databases)	Innovations for sustainability transitions	Geographical, cognitive, institutional, organizational, social
Omobhude and Chen (2019)	Literature review	Sustainable technological innovations	Geographical, cognitive, institutional, organizational, social
Qiang et al. (2021)	Network analysis	Green innovations	Geographical, cognitive
Raven et al. (2012)	Conceptual paper	Innovations for sustainability transitions	Geographical, cognitive, institutional, organizational, social
Royo-Vela and Mazandarani (2022)	Quantitative empirical analysis (survey data)	Non-technological innovations for sustainability	Geographical, cognitive, institutional, organizational, social
Shi et al. (2022)	Network analysis	Green innovations	Geographical, institutional
Sun and Han (2022)	Econometric analysis (patent data)	Green innovations	Geographical, technological (cognitive), institutional
Tani et al. (2021)	Agent-based modeling	Innovations for sustainability transitions	Geographical, cognitive, institutional, organizational, social
Velenturf (2016)	Case study approach	Biowaste-to-resource innovations	Geographical, cognitive, institutional, organizational, social
Velenturf and Jensen (2016)	Conceptual paper	Innovations for industrial sustainability	Geographical, cognitive, institutional, organizational, social

Note Table taken from Wilke and Pyka (2024a). CC BY 4.0. No changes were made

2014; Royo-Vela & Mazandarani, 2022). Tani et al. (2021) present an agent-based model designed to scrutinize the evolutionary dynamics of sustainability transition niches. They conduct a comparative analysis, examining the development of innovation niches with a focus on geographical proximity alongside other niches that are centered on relational proximity (encompassing cognitive, organizational, social, and institutional aspects).

The literature sample of the systematic review further includes two literature reviews. Hansen and Coenen (2015) conducted a comprehensive review of the literature concerning geographical aspects of sustainability transitions, examining not only the emergence of innovations but also further related processes. They draw insights from the proximity literature to suggest potential refinements of current approaches and recommend avenues for further research. Omobhude and Chen

(2019) offer a literature review that focuses on technological developments and knowledge spillovers. Their review delves into the proximity literature, with a particular emphasis on defining proximity and the methods employed to measure it. They translate their findings into the context of sustainable technology development.

There are furthermore four conceptual papers. Coenen et al. (2010) explore the topic of strategic niche management, a concept concerned with governance strategies for niches encompassing economic, political, technological, and social dimensions. These niches serve as testing grounds for sustainability innovations. The authors amalgamate insights from the niche management literature with those from the proximity literature, culminating in a refined analytical framework for examining niches and their dynamic nature. This framework is subsequently applied in a brief case study. The second conceptual paper, authored by Delgadillo et al. (2021), revolves around sustainable product-service systems, which are integrated combinations of products and services offered by the same company. Their framework, developed through a literature review and two exploratory case studies, sheds light on the role of geographical and organizational proximity in driving territorial sustainability transitions. In the third conceptual paper, Raven et al. (2012) present a spatially oriented multi-level perspective (MLP). The MLP framework, traditionally used for analyzing dynamics in socio-technical systems and sustainability transitions, is expanded by incorporating proximity dimensions. The authors illustrate the enhanced analytical capacity of this extended MLP through an empirical example. In the fourth conceptual paper, Velenturf and Jensen (2016) discuss the industrial symbiosis approach. This approach centers on material flows between firms, striving for sustainability by minimizing waste and fostering resource efficiency through innovations and network development. They propose integrating industrial symbiosis thinking with insights from economic geography on proximity to deepen our comprehension of innovative industrial networks.

Over half of the papers in the sample investigate all five proximity dimensions. Seven papers explore combinations of two or more proximity dimensions, while three papers specifically focus on just one dimension, being geographical proximity in one case (Bloise, 2020) and technological proximity in two cases (Aldieri et al., 2019, 2020). Technological and cognitive proximity both refer to the skills, expertise, and knowledge that characterize a firm's operations and which are thus relevant for knowledge exchange and the development of innovations. Hence, both terms can be treated as synonymous.

Every paper included in the analysis has been published in a peer-reviewed journal. Figure 7.3 illustrates the publication years of these articles. The majority of the papers have been published in recent years, with approximately 70% of them appearing since 2018. This suggests that scholars have recently intensified their attention on this research area, which is likely to result in an increasing number of papers in the coming years.

The papers included in the systematic review examine the emergence of sustainable innovations across various industries and socioeconomic contexts, including agriculture, the food industry, the construction sector, the minerals industry, the cleantech sector, energy production, environmental technologies for waste recycling

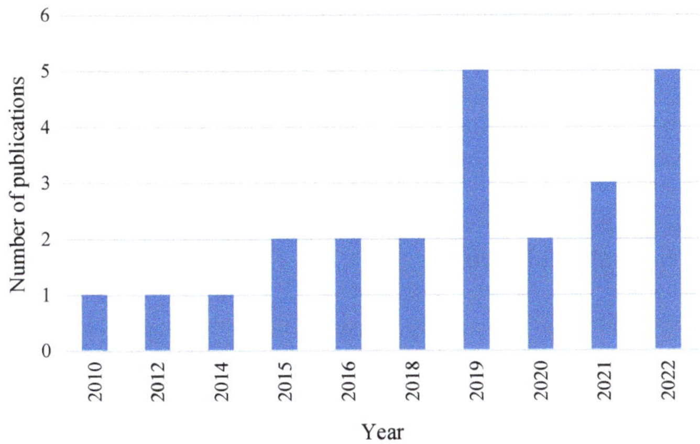

Fig. 7.3 Publication years of the reviewed papers. *Note* Image taken from Wilke and Pyka (2024a). CC BY 4.0. No changes were made

and water treatment, as well as specialized domains like biofuel production and low-carbon technologies. Furthermore, the review encompasses innovations aimed at systematically addressing sustainability challenges, often involving combinations of private sector involvement, new technologies, novel ways of providing public goods, and institutional change. All papers address collaborative efforts among multiple actors engaged in the generation and sharing of knowledge. These innovation networks are situated in middle- and high-income countries, spanning North America, Europe, and China. The contexts range from rural areas to specialized firm clusters. Although the papers depict a large thematic diversity, they all have a common denominator, namely the pursuit of innovations that not only create economic value but also deliver social or environmental benefits, or in many cases, both.

7.4.3 Findings of the Review Extended by Additional Sources

The systematic examination of the literature sample shows that all proximity dimensions are relevant for analyzing sustainable innovations and the associated knowledge processes. All dimensions can have a positive effect on knowledge co-creation and the creation of innovations (Addy & Dubé, 2018; Velenturf & Jensen, 2016). In this regard, conventional innovations and sustainable innovations show a certain degree of congruence. The review further shows that apart from an analysis of each proximity dimension separately, the interdependencies between the different dimensions need to be considered as well. For instance, Hansen (2014) notes a positive impact of geographical proximity on social proximity. That serves as a rationale for firms seeking collaborations with physically close partners, particularly when these partners exhibit low institutional proximity or possess highly dissimilar knowledge bases (low cognitive proximity). Dubois (2019) makes a similar argument, emphasizing that in the absence of geographical proximity, cognitive proximity assumes greater significance. The remainder of the chapter first presents the findings for each proximity dimension one by one and then describes insights regarding the interconnectedness of the different dimensions.

7.4.3.1 Geographical Proximity

There are mixed findings concerning the significance of geographical proximity for sustainable innovations. Sun and Han (2022) as well as Shi et al. (2022) observe the positive and significant impacts of geographical proximity on cooperative networks that foster green innovations. Similarly, Ardito et al. (2019), in their examination of family-owned firms in networks engaged in R&D collaborations for green innovations, reach a similar conclusion. They assert that a substantial geographical distance between these firms diminishes the innovation value within such networks. Proximity in this regard enhances communication and interaction, thereby boosting the efficiency of information exchange. Delgadillo et al. (2021) regard geographical proximity as a crucial catalyst for interactive learning. Proximity in space facilitates easier face-to-face interactions, fostering the exchange of tacit knowledge. Hansen (2014) analyzes firms in the cleantech sector who seek partners for collaborative innovation projects. He finds that such firms emphasize geographical proximity for knowledge exchange and access to complementary technologies.

Regarding sustainability-oriented knowledge processes, geographical proximity is relevant for several different issues. For one thing, problem- and solution-oriented approaches for knowledge creation and transfer often possess a spatial dimension, since numerous sustainability challenges have a local dimension, such as traffic congestion, local environmental problems, or regional economic decline. The corresponding solutions to these challenges need to be tailored to the specific requirements and framework conditions of that locality (compare Beaurain & Dermine-Brullot, 2022). Furthermore, experimental methods, such as urban laboratories, regularly have a narrow geographical focus as well (compare Evans & Karvonen, 2014). On the other hand, that does not automatically imply that all stakeholders involved in the innovation networks dealing with those sustainability challenges need to be situated in the same locality as the problem, nor do they have to be within the reach of an experimental approach that addresses that problem. In this regard, Bloise (2020) sees a positive influence of geographical proximity on the emergence of sustainable innovations but states that geographical proximity does not seem to be a prerequisite for effective knowledge exchange. A similar finding is described by Velenturf (2016), who states that collaborations are less dependent on geographical proximity than expected, as the numerous instances of successful knowledge exchange across large distances show.

A contrasting view is presented by Tani et al. (2021) showing through their agent-based model, that networks relying on relational bonds via cognitive, social, institutional, and organizational proximity outperform those networks solely focused on close geographic proximity. This phenomenon is attributed to the presence of a limited number of specialized agents possessing the capability to make significant contributions to complex and challenging sustainability innovations. These rare agents are geographically dispersed, resulting in actor constellations characterized by low geographic proximity. This perspective is supported by Janssen and Abbasiharofteh (2022), who argue that addressing the wicked problem of sustainability necessitates the collaboration of world-class top innovators who are limited in number and spread around the globe. In summary, while geographical proximity can greatly facilitate knowledge exchange and co-creation in the context of sustainable innovations, it is not a prerequisite, and an exclusive focus on partners nearby may even diminish the innovative capacity of a network by excluding highly relevant knowledge sources from afar.

7.4.3.2 Cognitive Proximity

Aldieri et al. (2019) utilize technological vectors to represent cognitive and technological proximity based on the industrial domains of companies in innovation networks. They discover a hindering effect associated with close cognitive proximity, highlighting that knowledge transfer across diverse industrial sectors is considerably more favorable for fostering environmental innovations. In line with this, Ardito et al. (2019) reach a similar conclusion, emphasizing the beneficial impact of family-owned businesses on green innovation networks, which however is notably diminished when these firms are technologically close. Hansen (2014) argues in the same direction, demonstrating that cleantech companies seeking new knowledge or technologies for collaborative innovations tend to seek partners with low to moderate cognitive proximity. These choices are influenced by beneficial complementarities of sector-specific knowledge bases and different problem-solving strategies.

In contrast, Ghassim (2018), who distinguishes between cognitive proximity in engineering-related and science-related domains, identifies a positive impact on collaborative endeavors within the minerals industry. This positive influence results in enhanced process and product innovations. Firms with a higher proportion of personnel holding university degrees or technical school qualifications are better equipped to access knowledge from external sources, including research institutes, highly specialized firms, or non-governmental organizations (NGOs). Lopolito et al. (2022) also recognize the significance of cognitive proximity as a key driver for knowledge-based networking. Furthermore, Janssen and Abbasiharofteh (2022) observe that actors involved in R&D projects focused on sustainability issues tend to exhibit relatively high levels of cognitive proximity, especially when compared to R&D projects in other subject areas.

A possible explanation for these seemingly conflicting findings may lie in the previously mentioned inverted U-shaped relationship between cognitive proximity and innovation. In this regard, pinpointing the precise inflection points for a specific exchange between two actors appears very difficult. This complexity is further aggravated by the potential influence of other proximity dimensions on the optimal level of cognitive proximity. Dubois (2019) for instance observes that in scenarios characterized by low geographical proximity among actors, cognitive proximity assumes greater significance. Specifically, the alignment of shared perspectives on the importance of sustainable innovations, essentially a common goal, emerges as a crucial factor in establishing knowledge exchange and collaboration across large distances. A similar insight is found by Ievoli et al. (2019), who argue that in long-distance collaborations facilitated by modern ICT (as a substitute for regular physical interactions), cognitive proximity takes on heightened importance. More broadly, cognitive proximity, defined as a shared understanding of the sustainability implications of intended innovations, appears to play a pivotal role in fostering collaboration among diverse actors (Coenen et al., 2010). However, finding the optimal level of cognitive proximity for maximizing the potential for knowledge exchange and innovation appears extraordinarily challenging.

7.4.3.3 Institutional Proximity

Lopolito et al. (2022) identify institutional proximity as a significant catalyst within sustainability-oriented innovation networks, although its significance fluctuates across different phases of a collaboration. Similarly, Dubois (2019) highlights the evolving relevance of institutional proximity. With repeated interactions, actors increasingly rely on institutional proximity in the form of a "tacitly agreed code of conduct" (Dubois, 2019, p. 775).

Ghassim (2018) differentiates between formal and informal institutional proximity, where the former encompasses rules and laws, and the latter encompasses norms and values. He finds that formal institutional proximity facilitates sustainable process and product innovations, while informal institutional proximity positively influences social innovations. Hansen (2014) describes varying levels of institutional proximity in the context of accessing complementary technology and acquiring new knowledge. On the one hand, institutional proximity appears to compensate for a lack of cognitive proximity. On the other hand, collaborations between firms and partners from distinct institutional realms such as academia, state institutions, or NGOs appear particularly conducive to innovations, likely due to complementary knowledge bases, working practices, and incentive structures.

The importance of institutional proximity becomes obvious regarding the aspect of involving a wide range of different stakeholders in knowledge production and transfer, as this implies the inclusion of a wide variety of different actors with different objectives and varying understandings of sustainability (Beaurain & Dermine-Brullot, 2022). The different institutional realms to which they belong (academia, industry, government, and civil society) have distinctive sets of rules, traditions, incentive structures, codes of conduct, and alike, potentially making knowledge exchange demanding. Furthermore, sustainable innovations must fit into the place-specific institutional context in which they are intended to induce change toward sustainability (Strambach, 2017). Even institutional innovations aimed at increasing sustainability, however disruptive, must fit into the existing institutional framework and find connections to it. It otherwise appears highly unlikely that such innovations will diffuse and find widespread application (unless in times of revolutionary upheavals). This institutional fit is also reflected in the composition of the corresponding innovation networks and the associated institutional proximity regarding the rules, norms, and regulations under which the network members operate.

7.4.3.4 Social Proximity

In the context of sustainability transitions, Coenen et al. (2010) emphasize the important role of trust among participants within innovation networks focused on radically new technologies. Lopolito et al. (2022) similarly regard social proximity as a catalyst for networking activities in niche development. According to Dubois (2019), social proximity gains particular significance when formalized cooperation methods are lacking or when institutional proximity is low. Hansen (2014) states that when firms are in search of partners to acquire new knowledge and technologies, they often prioritize a strong degree of social proximity. This preference stems from the fact that a high level of social proximity can help overcome challenges arising from low cognitive proximity. Collaborating with a partner who shares a limited common knowledge base demands more time and resources to avoid misunderstandings and establish mutual comprehension. Furthermore, one partner's competencies and expertise may not be entirely verifiable by the other, and trust plays a crucial role in mitigating these issues. A similar situation occurs with low geographical proximity. Social proximity facilitates knowledge exchange when partners find it difficult to meet regularly due to high costs or time constraints caused by long travel distances. Conversely, geographical proximity can aid in building trust by enabling regular face-to-face interactions, as highlighted by Delgadillo et al. (2021).

In addition to prior collaborative experience, Velenturf (2016) identifies another source of trust concerning sustainable innovations: a shared belief in the imperative need for a shift toward sustainability. This form of trust, rooted in cognition, closely resembles the insight discussed by Dubois (2019) regarding the importance of a shared objective among stakeholders. More generally, trust is seen as a vital component in knowledge processes and interactive learning that involve close interaction of partners (see Easterby-Smith et al., 2008; Roux et al., 2006), and hence plays an important role in sustainability-oriented multi-actor networks consisting of different actors with diverging objectives and modes of decision-making (compare McCauley & Stephens, 2012). Universities and other higher education institutions (HEI) can play a pivotal role in such networks. Due to their perceived neutrality, they are often seen as trusted partners, providing a safe ground for collaboration between potentially competing firms as well as with other actors with differing interests, such as civil society organizations or special interest groups.

7.4.3.5 Organizational Proximity

According to Delgadillo et al. (2021), organizational proximity plays a pivotal role in the interactions between cooperating entities, as the sharing of strategies and organizational structures significantly enhances coordination among them. In a similar vein, Dubois (2019) observes that over repeated interactions, partners tend to develop more or less formalized modes of cooperation, which in turn enhance organizational proximity. Such routine-based forms of collaboration allow for effective exchange despite large distances or low cognitive proximity. Ghassim (2018) reports a positive relationship between organizational proximity and social innovations in collaborations involving distant participants. Hansen (2014) finds that partnerships aiming to combine complementary technologies or acquire new knowledge often feature low organizational proximity. This is because it is less probable that the required technology or knowledge can be found within an affiliated company. Consequently, these collaborations frequently involve research institutes and other partners, with whom informal relationships are common. Ievoli et al. (2019) see a robust link between the utilization of ICT by geographically distant actors and the formation of novel network structures, consequently heightening organizational proximity. ICT enables the establishment of mechanisms and agreements for the remote management of economic operations and the exchange of knowledge, and thus effectively diminishes uncertainty and thereby fosters the advancement of innovations.

As stated above, organizational proximity is linked to formal relationships and hence concerns issues of hierarchy, power, and control. Such topics are for several reasons relevant for sustainable innovations. Co-production of knowledge involving a wide variety of different stakeholders will most likely come along with differences regarding the levels of knowledge of these stakeholders (confer Heiskanen & Lovio, 2010). Such knowledge asymmetries can translate into issues of power and thus need to be considered in the analysis of knowledge co-production. More generally, power issues are relevant in almost every innovation network. Furthermore, sustainable innovations with a focus on transformative change necessitate a thorough examination of the foundational power structures that either facilitate or hinder such transformations, and that might be altered by these transformations. These power dynamics, in and of themselves, constitute an integral component of the social dimension of sustainability. This entails delving into the intricate web of relationships, hierarchies, and influence mechanisms that underlie societal systems and have the potential to either support or obstruct the pursuit of sustainability goals.

7.4.3.6 Interdependencies Between the Proximity Dimensions

To better understand the influence of the different proximity dimensions on knowledge creation and transfer, it appears necessary to investigate the interdependencies of the different dimensions. The review reveals two mechanisms governing the interplay among various proximity dimensions. The first mechanism is reinforcement, where closeness in one dimension can catalyze a corresponding increase in another dimension. The second mechanism is a dyadic effect, characterized by either overlap or substitution. In this context, proximity in one dimension can bridge or compensate for distances in another dimension. The first effect corresponds to a finding of Knoben and Oerlemans (2006), who state that the different proximity dimensions can reinforce or attenuate the impact of other dimensions, although an attenuating effect could not be observed in the literature sample. The second effect is described by Boschma (2005), who states that geographical proximity cannot be evaluated in isolation, as other proximity dimensions can act as a substitute, providing an alternative solution to the underlying coordination problem in knowledge exchange and interactive learning.

In their case study, Addy and Dubé (2018) find several instances of reinforcement effects that operate over varying timeframes. In the medium term, formal organizational structures are likely to have a positive impact on both cognitive proximity and social proximity. These structures promote ongoing exchange and offer shared resources, thereby strengthening the connections among actors. Over the long term, organizational proximity can further enhance institutional proximity by fostering shared codes of conduct, norms, and values. Royo-Vela and Mazandarani (2022), who examine the interconnections among non-spatial proximity dimensions, show that organizational proximity has an impact on both institutional proximity and social proximity, and vice versa. However, they did not identify any significant relationship between organizational proximity and cognitive proximity. Additionally, their findings indicate that both social proximity and institutional proximity are influenced by cognitive proximity, and vice versa. In contrast, no relationship was observed between institutional and social proximity. Notably, the study underscores that the most robust association exists between institutional and organizational proximity, with the social dimension demonstrating the weakest quantifiable impact on the other dimensions. Dubois (2019) observes that both social and cognitive proximity can serve as enablers of organizational and institutional proximity, as collaborations initially rooted in trust and mutual understanding evolve into more formalized arrangements characterized by agreed-upon procedures. Several authors, including Delgadillo et al. (2021), Dubois (2019), and Lopolito et al. (2022) state that geographical proximity fosters trust-building, thereby facilitating the development of social proximity. This effect is also described for conventional innovations by Ponds et al. (2007) and Mattes (2012).

Hansen (2015) provides a comprehensive examination of the second effect, which describes the overlap or substitution of different proximity dimensions. However, his analysis is limited to the comparison of spatial and non-spatial proximity dimensions, with no exploration of the interrelationships among different non-spatial dimensions. In his research, Hansen (2015) identifies a substitution effect between social and geographical proximity. He observes that firms tend to cooperate more seamlessly with unfamiliar partners when they are in close spatial proximity, but they prefer the presence of established social connections when partners are situated at a distance. Crescenzi et al. (2016) see the same relation for conventional innovations. Additionally, Hansen (2015) notes an overlap between geographical and institutional proximity, as many institutions are geographically anchored. This observation fits to the statement of Gertler (2003), that the challenges of long-distance collaborations are primarily related to institutional differences. Furthermore, when examining cognitive and geographical proximity, Hansen (2015) identifies a substitution effect, indicating that partners in close spatial proximity often possess different and complementary knowledge bases. Put differently, geographical proximity can help overcome cognitive distances, because close and direct face-to-face interactions can establish mutual understanding as a basis for knowledge exchange (Addy & Dubé, 2018). Huber (2012) finds the same for the area of conventional innovations, stating that geographical proximity fosters collaboration with cognitively distant partners. Dubois (2019) and Ievoli et al. (2019) arrived at the same conclusion concerning sustainable innovations, highlighting the amplified importance of cognitive proximity in long-distance collaborations. This heightened significance arises when personal meetings are less frequent and when face-to-face interactions are replaced by ICT, underscoring the necessity of shared understanding. Regarding organizational and geographical proximity, a strong substitution effect is identified by both Hansen (2015) and Ghassim (2018). Formalized networks prove to be effective in facilitating knowledge exchange with distant partners, resembling the working mechanism of social proximity. Notably, Velenturf (2016) reveals that social and organizational proximity can act as substitutes, although with some limitations. Trust and formal arrangements, to some extent, complement each other and cannot entirely replace one another. Crescenzi et al. (2016) come to a similar conclusion for conventional innovations, stating that both organizational and social proximity reduce transaction costs via similar mechanisms. However, they might exhibit differences in terms of including new members and their knowledge, as hierarchical and formal arrangements might constitute stronger barriers compared to informal social ties.

Figure 7.4 shows graphically the different effects. The strength of the lines symbolizes the number of times each effect was described in the analyzed literature about sustainable innovations.

7.4.4 Discussion

Summing up, geographical proximity is beneficial for fostering sustainable innovations, due to facilitating regular face-to-face interactions and the sharing of tacit knowledge, especially in situations where there is little shared knowledge or trust among participants, and when there are no established formal connections between them. However, geographical proximity is no prerequisite and can even hinder the innovative potential of a network if it excludes distant partners with valuable knowledge.

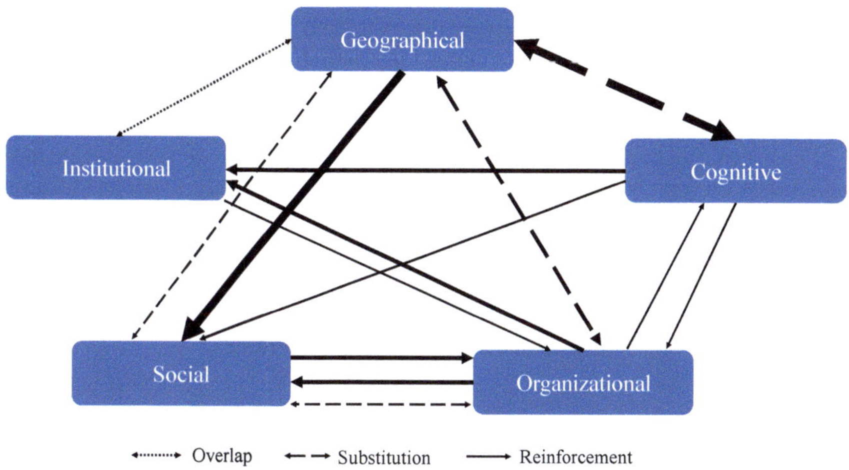

Fig. 7.4 Interdependencies between the different dimensions of proximity

Cognitive proximity stands out as the only dimension of proximity that appears to be essential for effective knowledge exchange. Without a certain level of absorptive capacity and mutual understanding, it is unlikely that two partners can successfully share knowledge or collaboratively generate new insights (compare Boschma, 2005; Huber, 2012). Nevertheless, too much cognitive proximity can reduce the potential for novel combinations of knowledge. In the context of sustainability's social and environmental dimensions, relatively low levels of cognitive proximity seem promising, when the specialized sustainability knowledge from research and civil society partners is combined with the market-oriented economic knowledge of businesses.

The same argument holds for institutional proximity. If there is a shared institutional framework consisting of rules, regulations, and social norms that apply to all partners, this can greatly facilitate the process of cooperation. This principle also extends to the internal institutional arrangements within each participating entity. However, because sustainability-focused innovation networks benefit from including partners from diverse institutional backgrounds (such as business, academia, government, and civil society), having a low level of internal institutional similarity appears more promising than striving for a high level of (internal) institutional proximity.

Both organizational and social proximity can play essential roles in facilitating knowledge exchange and promoting sustainable innovations, particularly in scenarios where institutional, cognitive, or geographical proximity is lacking. Furthermore, these two dimensions can to some degree complement each other, and each has the potential to enhance cognitive proximity.

There are furthermore different interdependencies between the different proximity dimensions. They can be distinguished into a reinforcement effect and a dyadic effect of either substitution or overlap. However, the substitution effect should not be understood in the sense of a perfect interchangeability of two different dimensions.

Furthermore, due to the complexity of the examined processes of knowledge (co-)creation and the development of innovations, which are both dynamic processes that may extend over varying periods, the different effects between the proximity dimensions are likely to vary as well.

Considering all these insights, it does not seem desirable (or even possible) to have high levels across all dimensions of proximity simultaneously when establishing networks for sustainable innovations. As highlighted by Ievoli et al. (2019), the effectiveness of such networks is likely to hinge on achieving a balanced level of proximity in all dimensions, avoiding extremes of excessive strength or weakness in any one dimension. It thus seems necessary to delve deeper into the various combinations of differently pronounced proximity dimensions.

7.5 Refined Analytical Proximity Framework

In the following, a more nuanced analytical framework for examining proximity in its various dimensions is presented, based on the findings from the systematic literature review as well as insights from sustainability science and innovation system theory. Section 7.5.1 presents the theoretical considerations underlying the refinement of the analytical framework, which is then applied in Sect. 7.5.2 to analyze several examples of collaborative innovations from the literature. The insights are summarized and put into perspective in Sect. 7.5.3. The work presented in Sect. 7.5 is to a considerable extent based on Wilke and Pyka (2024b).

7.5.1 Conceptual Considerations

The framework presented here (graphically presented in Fig. 7.5) incorporates a differentiation of two of the five proximity dimensions presented above. One is cognitive proximity, and the other is institutional proximity. Expanding on the earlier mentioned insight regarding the critical importance of three knowledge types for a transformation toward sustainability, cognitive proximity is divided into three distinct sub-dimensions: normative-cognitive, systems-cognitive, and transformative-cognitive proximity. The first sub-dimension refers to the differences and similarities of the network members regarding their understanding of the goal of sustainability. It concerns generally the value-driven meaning of sustainability and associated specific objectives. Systems-cognitive proximity refers to the domain-specific knowledge bases of the partners, including their technical expertise and knowledge about peculiar sub-systems. Transformative-cognitive proximity covers the network members' knowledge regarding solution strategies and transformation pathways that can serve to induce change and achieve specific sustainability goals. This refinement into three separate aspects allows for a more precise examination

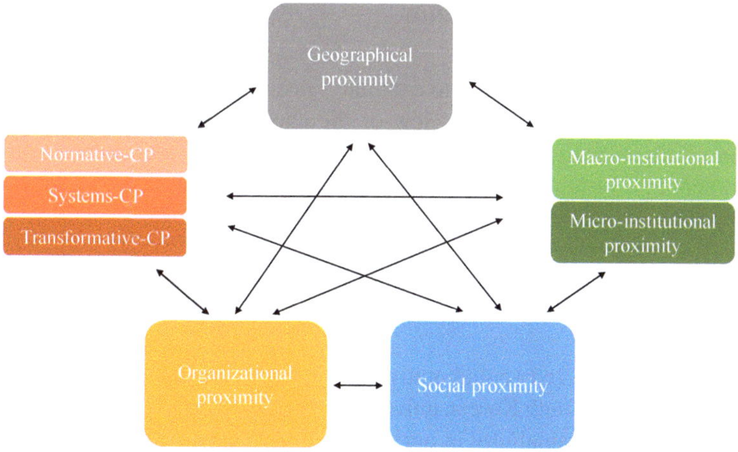

Fig. 7.5 Refined proximity framework. *Note* Image taken from Wilke and Pyka (2024b). CC BY 4.0. No changes were made

of the cognitive proximity dimension and its impact on knowledge exchange and innovation.

The second refinement concerns institutional proximity and consists of a distinction between micro-institutional proximity, which pertains to the internal institutional configurations of the involved actors, and macro-institutional proximity, which relates to the broader institutional context. This distinction carries the idea that macro-institutional proximity is closely tied to geographical proximity, as many institutional aspects, such as rules, regulations, cultural norms, and customs, are inherently related to specific locations. However, there are differences between macro-institutional and geographical proximity. Two actors can be physically close but still exhibit a low level of institutional proximity, as is the case when two actors are near each other but are separated by a border. The difference between the two dimensions also holds in the opposite direction: Two actors can be situated in the same jurisdiction with a similar cultural background and hence within the same institutional framework, but still be spatially far away from each other, as it can be the case in vast regions such as Québec in Canada (compare van Horne & Dutot, 2017) or other sparsely populated regions that extent over a large spatial area.

The other sub-dimension, micro-institutional proximity, takes into account that sustainability-focused innovation networks can involve organizations from diverse institutional backgrounds, encompassing business, government, academia, and civil society. Consequently, they naturally exhibit low levels of proximity in terms of their internal institutional dynamics.

7.5.2 Analysis of Case Studies

Next, the framework is employed to examine selected examples documented in the literature. Table 7.7 gives an overview of the chosen articles, their subjects, and the actor configurations described in those articles. Each paper centers around the development of a sustainable innovation.

7.5.2.1 Transnational Development of a Soil Sensor for Sustainable Agriculture

Baek et al. (2019) analyzed a collaborative design project involving a social enterprise from Myanmar and a South Korean university. The project aimed at developing a soil sensor to enhance sustainability in agriculture. This sensor was intended to enable farmers to measure various soil attributes, optimize input utilization, increase productivity, and consequently contribute to poverty alleviation as a positive economic and

Table 7.7 Selected examples from the literature

Paper	Thematic area	Involved actors
Baek et al. (2019)	Sustainable agriculture; development of a soil sensor for precision farming	South Korean university; Myanmar social enterprise; Myanmar farmers and South Korean farmers indirectly involved
Haas et al. (2016)	Sustainable agriculture; rural development in a low-income country	Nepalese ethical business; Nepalese smallholder farmers; Austrian university; Austrian firm; German governmental development aid organization partly involved
Higuchi and Yamanaka (2017)	Sustainable tourism	Tourism operator; university; consumers (tourists) indirectly involved; all situated in Japan, Hokkaido region
Strambach (2017)	Green buildings sector	German firms; Chinese firms; Chinese government agencies
Valkering et al. (2013)	Sustainable urban neighborhood development	Firms; non-profit organizations; citizens; academic scholars; municipalities; from Belgium, Germany and the Netherlands, with varying degrees of involvement
van Horne and Dutot (2017)	Sustainable innovations in the forest products industry	Firms; academics; government agencies; intermediary organizations; all situated in the Canadian province of Quebec

Note Table taken from Wilke and Pyka (2024b).

social outcome of the innovation. In this international collaboration, the key partners, the Myanmar social enterprise, and the Korean university brought complementary knowledge to the project. Additionally, input from farmers in both countries was sought to address their specific needs, although to a somewhat limited extent. However, the project ultimately did not achieve its intended outcomes, with Baek et al. (2019) attributing this shortfall primarily to disparities in socioeconomic, technological, and cultural factors.

From the perspective of the enhanced proximity framework, low levels of normative-cognitive and transformative-cognitive proximity among the actors become obvious. On the Myanmar side, the soil sensor and its application were viewed as primarily a social innovation, while the South Korean partners regarded it primarily as a technological innovation. The Myanmar partners, and particularly the farmers who were only marginally involved, had differing notions about how to apply the sensor due to variations in farming practices and perspectives. The substantial geographical distance between the partners precluded frequent direct interactions, making it challenging to bridge the cognitive gap, despite the extensive use of ICT.

Moreover, the two countries' distinct socio-economic and institutional contexts (equal to a low level of macro-institutional proximity) also played a significant role. Initially, there were differing interpretations of the expected social impact of the desired innovation and its applications, and these differences could not be reconciled but rather became more pronounced. Additionally, organizational and social proximity were low, hindering the exchange of implicit normative and transformative knowledge, and thus hampering the project's prospect for success.

7.5.2.2 International Cooperation in Organic Agriculture

Haas et al. (2016) present an analysis of a co-innovation case involving multiple stakeholders. This collaborative effort included a community of Nepalese smallholder farmers, a Nepalese ethical business led by a German entrepreneur, an Austrian university, and an Austrian firm. Additionally, government agencies were sporadically involved, albeit to a lesser extent and only at certain stages of the collaboration. Each partner contributed complementary knowledge, expertise, and skills, partially influenced by their distinct institutional backgrounds. This diversity of knowledge resources laid a solid foundation for the development of sustainable innovations.

In the context of the proximity framework, this scenario can be characterized by low levels of systems-cognitive and micro-institutional proximity. At the same time, there were high levels of normative-cognitive and transformative-cognitive proximity, as all partners shared similar perspectives on the environmental and social impacts of their intended innovations, how to measure them, and strategies for achieving change. The presence of established certificates for organic agricultural products also played a significant role in aligning their goals.

Social proximity played a crucial role in facilitating the establishment of this innovation network, as several partners had prior bilateral working relationships.

Despite the considerable physical distance between the Austrian and Nepalese partners, effective knowledge exchange occurred, in part due to the shared cultural background between the German founder of the Nepalese ethical business and the European partners. This cultural commonality can be seen as a situation where one actor brought macro-institutional specific experience to the other partners, creating a setting with moderate macro-institutional proximity and low geographical proximity. The German entrepreneur in Nepal thus played a pivotal role. As the authors put it, "This kind of communication was easier than an intercultural dialog without him acting as a bridge might have been" (Haas et al., 2016, p. 1361).

Furthermore, a degree of organizational proximity emerged when the Nepalese smallholder farmers sought funding from a German development aid organization. This move formalized the ethical business as a marketing partner, which occurred after the innovation network had been established for some time. This additional formalization brought routine to the network's activities and further strengthened their collaboration.

7.5.2.3 Innovations for Sustainable Tourism

Higuchi and Yamanaka (2017) discuss a collaborative process of developing sustainable innovations within the tourism industry. This joint undertaking involved a tour operator and a university and involved a systematic integration of user feedback from tourists. Both partners brought their unique knowledge into the collaboration, indicating a low level of systems-cognitive proximity. In the early stages of their collaboration, the partners faced the challenge of a low level of transformative-cognitive proximity. The university required time to fully grasp the tour operator's business objectives, understand what knowledge would be valuable for sustainable tourism operations, and determine how to effectively engage with users to achieve sustainable outcomes. Conversely, the tour operator needed time to comprehend the university's intentions and appreciate the value and rigorous nature of scientific knowledge. However, despite these initial hurdles, the collaboration progressed smoothly and yielded satisfying outcomes for both parties. This fruitful partnership resulted in several innovations that also received positive feedback from tourists.

Notably, there was no formal organizational structure in place (indicating low organizational proximity), and the two entities had no prior experience working together (representing low initial social proximity). What played a pivotal role in their success was their close geographical proximity and a shared fundamental vision of the desired sustainability impact (demonstrating a medium level of normative-cognitive proximity). The partners maintained frequent interactions, with university members even participating in the tour operator's daily operations. This ongoing interaction helped build trust (gradually increasing levels of social proximity) and allowed the partners to reach a level of cognitive proximity at which they could fruitfully combine their complementary expertise and subsequently develop sustainable innovations.

7.5.2.4 Sino-German Collaboration in the Green Building Sector

Strambach (2017) conducts an analysis of transnational innovation projects in the green building sector involving German and Chinese partners. The study emphasizes the differences between the two countries within this industry. The German green construction sector is depicted as a well-functioning example of an extensive knowledge network, essentially an industry-wide ecosystem, or sectoral innovation system (Malerba, 2002). In this system, diverse actors from across Germany and different institutional backgrounds (with low micro-institutional and geographical proximity) pool their knowledge resources to collaborate on innovation initiatives (with low systems-cognitive proximity). An intermediary organization plays a crucial role in facilitating these collaborative efforts (high organizational proximity) and promoting regular interactions (high social proximity). This collaborative environment fosters high levels of normative-cognitive and transformative-cognitive proximity, which are further reinforced by the existence of a widely recognized voluntary quality certificate for sustainable buildings. The network's success is also reflected in its influence on legislation in the green building sector, implying it is shaping the macro-institutional framework for the entire industry.

Conversely, the examination of German-Chinese cooperation projects, all situated in China with frequent face-to-face interactions on-site, reveals several challenges (Strambach, 2017). These challenges stem from differences in sustainability concepts, associated technologies, and artifacts (low normative-cognitive proximity), as well as differing assessments of cost, time considerations, and subsequent planning approaches (low transformative-cognitive proximity). These differences were attributed to fundamental disparities in the macro-institutional settings of both countries, shaped by distinct institutional trajectories (low macro-institutional proximity).

German firms involved in these projects adopted various strategies to address these challenges. One approach involved transferring knowledge by directly employing Chinese personnel, effectively bridging the macro-institutional gap. Some firms pursuing this strategy relied on Chinese staff with educational backgrounds in Germany (reducing the internal macro-institutional gap within the German firm). Others focused on Chinese personnel with experience in the construction sector in China (minimizing the macro-institutional gap in relations with Chinese partners). The second strategy was to enhance social and organizational proximity by intensifying and formalizing relationships with specific Chinese partners. Those partners were primarily of a similar size and type, indicating a high degree of micro-institutional proximity.

7.5.2.5 Sustainable Urban Development in a Cross-Border Region

Valkering et al. (2013) investigate collective innovation processes aimed at achieving sustainable urban development in a European cross-border region. This region, known as Euregio Meuse-Rhine, spans parts of Belgium, Germany, and the Netherlands and is relatively compact in size, which indicates a high level of geographical proximity. Within this region, multiple communities with distinct official languages, cultures, and institutional settings (low macro-institutional proximity) collaborated as part of a project funded by the European Union (medium level of organizational proximity). A diverse array of stakeholders from business, academia, government, and civil society participated in the funded project, each contributing their unique expertise (indicating a low degree of systems-cognitive proximity).

During the project's preparatory phase, an appropriate level of normative-cognitive proximity was established by formulating a shared overarching objective. This objective was then detailed through the formulation of specific practical challenges and targets. The primary challenges to collaboration were related to low macro-institutional proximity, particularly evident in practical issues such as language barriers. The geographical proximity of actors within the region, which allowed for regular face-to-face meetings, played a crucial role in overcoming these challenges. Furthermore, the project revealed that cross-border cooperation was more successful when actors of similar types or with analogous roles worked together. This finding shows that high micro-institutional proximity could mitigate the challenges arising from low macro-institutional proximity.

7.5.2.6 Sustainable Innovations in the Forest Products Industry

Van Horne and Dutot (2017) present an investigation of sustainable innovations within the forest products industry in the Canadian Province of Quebec. This study involved a range of actors from government, industry, academia, and intermediary organizations. The actor constellation constitutes a situation with a high level of macro-institutional proximity and low geographical proximity, as the actors were dispersed across the expansive region. Following a quadruple helix approach as proposed by Carayannis and Campbell (2010), the authors underscore the significant roles played by all these actors in fostering sustainable innovations. Each participant brought complementary skills, expertise, and knowledge into the innovation system. Simultaneously, the cognitive distance between these actors posed a challenge, illustrating the inverse U-shaped relationship between cognitive proximity and innovation. While the complementarity of their expertise offered opportunities for novel and innovative knowledge combinations, the disparities in their knowledge bases hindered effective knowledge exchange due to a lack of mutual understanding.

A closer examination of the study of van Horne and Dutot (2017) reveals that a substantial part of the problem is linked to low transformative-cognitive proximity. Academic researchers struggled to grasp the industry's issues. They had difficulties understanding what suitable solutions for businesses would entail, while firms and intermediary organizations faced challenges in assimilating the methods and approaches from the universities. The low micro-institutional proximity, stemming from the diverse backgrounds of the actors, is considered a prerequisite for successful sustainability innovations but also presents significant challenges. Differences in time horizons, goals, values, motivations, and problem-solving approaches complicate collaborative efforts. Many innovation projects grapple with tensions between the pursuit of scientific excellence and the practical applicability of solutions. A promising strategy to address these challenges seems to be the direct engagement of university personnel within firms (van Horne & Dutot, 2017). By directly working on-site, the partners could increase geographical proximity (and, to some extent, social and organizational proximity) to compensate for the lack of cognitive proximity and thus facilitate the transfer of implicit knowledge.

7.5.3 Discussion

Table 7.8 provides an overview of the initial levels of the five proximity dimensions for the analyzed cases from the literature. Among these examples, the collaborative project examined by Baek et al. (2019), which yielded results below expectations, stands out as the only one characterized by low to medium levels in all proximity dimensions. In contrast, the remaining examples exhibit high levels of proximity in at least two dimensions and a medium level in at least one more dimension. This confirms the finding that high levels of proximity in all dimensions do not appear to be necessary or advantageous for knowledge creation, transfer, and sustainable innovations.

Cognitive proximity to a certain degree again appears as sort of a prerequisite for successful knowledge exchange. At the same time, sustainable innovations require the integration of interdisciplinary and transdisciplinary knowledge from a diverse range of stakeholders, with an inclusive approach to knowledge processes. This is evident in the examples found in the literature. Most cases indicate low levels in both systems-cognitive and micro-institutional proximity. In essence, creating sustainable innovations with multifaceted objectives, such as generating positive social and environmental impacts alongside economic advantages, demands a broad understanding of diverse sub-systems and is mirrored in the innovation networks that encompass a variety of actors from the business world, academia, government, and civil society. Nevertheless, all of these networks require a common cognitive ground for effective communication and collaboration.

Upon closer examination of cognitive proximity, it becomes evident that normative-cognitive proximity plays a pivotal role. Shared perspectives on the sustainability implications of proposed innovations appear to hold significant importance. This particular aspect seems to be almost a prerequisite for fostering knowledge exchange and innovation, and it correlates with the relevance of problem-solving and solution-oriented approaches in knowledge generation. The importance of a collective understanding concerning normative sustainability objectives within innovation networks has been previously acknowledged by researchers such as Coenen et al. (2010), Akpo et al. (2015), Bünger and Schiller (2022), and Bisseleua et al. (2018). It aligns with similar observations made by other authors such as Wiek et al. (2012) and Abson et al. (2017), who stress the importance of explicitly incorporating norms and

Table 7.8 Initial levels of the different proximity dimensions

	Analyzed examples from the literature					
Proximity dimension	Baek et al. (2019)	Haas et al. (2016)	Higuchi and Yamanaka (2017)	Strambach (2017)	Valkering et al. (2013)	van Horne and Dutot (2017)
Geographical	Low	Low	High	High	High	Low
Normative-cognitive	Low	High	Medium	Low	High	High
Systems-cognitive	Medium	Low	Low	Medium	Low	Low
Transformative-cognitive	Low	High	Low	Low	Medium	Low
Macro-institutional	Low	Medium	High	Low	Low	High
Micro-institutional	Medium	Low	Low	Medium	Low	Low
Social	Low	High	Low	Medium	Low	Medium
Organizational	Low	Medium	Low	High	Medium	Medium

Note Table taken from Wilke and Pyka (2024b). CC BY 4.0. No changes were made

values into the processes of co-creating and transferring sustainability knowledge. When normative-cognitive proximity is initially low, there appears to be a need for intensive discussions about the desired outcomes right from the earliest stages of collaboration.

Transformative-cognitive proximity emerges as another crucial dimension, closely tied to the concentration on specific problems and potentially viable solutions. It revolves around the mechanisms that render a novelty economically feasible while at the same time promising social and environmental benefits, thus constituting a sustainable innovation. This domain seems to encompass sector-specific knowledge, as various entities, such as businesses, academic institutions, civil society organizations, and government agencies, possess distinct knowledge pertaining to sustainability transformations and their perspectives on the necessary knowledge for devising such strategies. A rigorous scientific understanding of an issue generated by a university, for instance, may have limited relevance to a corporation and its market-driven practices. The transformative-cognitive sub-dimension also appears to be linked to the normative-cognitive sub-dimension, as the latter serves as a prerequisite for the former. In the absence of normative-cognitive proximity, transformative-cognitive proximity is unlikely to exist. This is plausible because stakeholders require a shared comprehension of the common objective before they can agree on how to collaboratively attain it.

The analyzed examples from the literature provide further evidence that social and organizational proximity can serve as significant enablers of an open and efficient knowledge exchange. Both dimensions work via similar mechanisms by diminishing the risk of opportunistic behavior. Trust in this regard plays a crucial role and appears as an effective lubricant for the collaboration of diverse stakeholders. Formalized organizational structures help to routinize cooperation and foster exchange.

The distinction between micro- and macro-institutional proximity proves to be insightful. Macro-institutional proximity emerges as a significant structural factor that shapes knowledge processes by providing a framework of established rules, norms, and values. Insufficient macro-institutional proximity can present serious obstacles to knowledge exchange, often manifesting as divergent understandings of concepts or even language barriers, which are interconnected with various facets of cognitive proximity. In certain cases, micro-institutional proximity can partially compensate for the absence of macro-institutional proximity. For example, two similar organizations, such as two firms of comparable type and size from the same industry, overcome macro-institutional borders more easily when cooperating, due to similar constraints, incentives, and structures for organizing day-to-day operations.

As depicted in Sect. 7.4, the proximity literature describes different interdependencies between the different proximity dimensions, namely reinforcement, substitution, and overlap effects. Based on the findings of the case studies and the refinement of the analytical framework, those effects can be further detailed. The overlap between the geographical and institutional dimensions appears to be primarily relevant regarding the macro-institutional sub-dimension, and even then, its relevance is limited. This overlap does not apply uniformly across all regions, as exemplified by the province of Quebec in the case of van Horne and Dutot (2017). Moreover, this overlap can be canceled out by individuals who carry aspects of a macro-institutional background from one location to another, as demonstrated by the entrepreneur in the example provided by Haas et al. (2016).

Furthermore, there seems to be a close link between the micro-institutional proximity dimension and the systems-cognitive and to some extent the transformative-cognitive proximity dimensions. This link, which appears as a substitution effect, is caused by the fact that organizations from the same institutional spheres tend to have strong similarities regarding specific knowledge bases, constituted by shared vocabulary, technical understanding, mental models, solution approaches, and the like.

7.6 Summary

The connection between proximity and knowledge in the context of sustainable innovations is complex and multifaceted. Each of the five proximity dimensions can impact knowledge exchange and creation among partners within an innovation network. There are various combinations of both high and low levels of the different proximity dimensions, with interdependencies affecting the influence of the different dimensions. Moreover, the levels of certain dimensions may evolve over time, underscoring the importance of recognizing proximity as a dynamic concept (confer Balland et al., 2015, 2022). Regarding the different combinations, having a high level in all proximity dimensions appears neither likely nor particularly conducive to fostering sustainable innovations, much like a very low level in all dimensions.

A refined analytical framework provides further insights into the working mechanisms of each proximity dimension and its assigned sub-dimensions. For this refined framework and following the findings regarding the relevant knowledge types, the cognitive dimension is divided into a systems-cognitive, a normative-cognitive, and a transformative-cognitive dimension. The institutional dimension is divided into a macro-institutional and a micro-institutional dimension, taking into account the differences between various actor groups and the influence of the overarching institutional framework conditions.

An analysis of examples from the literature with this refined framework (see Fig. 7.6) provides further indications of the working mechanisms of the proximity dimensions. As mentioned before, geographical proximity is beneficial for sustainable innovations as it enables face-to-face interactions and sharing of tacit knowledge, especially in low-trust situations with no established connections or situations with low cognitive proximity. However, it can hinder innovation when it leads to the exclusion of valuable but distant partners. Cognitive proximity is essential for effective knowledge exchange, but too much of it may limit novel knowledge combinations. Many examples of sustainable innovations in the literature show low levels of systems-cognitive proximity, stemming from network structures that involve a wide variety of different actors. In essence, achieving multifaceted sustainable innovations requires a broad system understanding that is dispersed among diverse actors from various sectors. However, effective communication and collaboration still necessitate a shared cognitive foundation within these networks. Especially normative-cognitive and transformative-cognitive proximity appear to play a decisive role in this regard, forming the basis via a shared normative objective and ideas of how to reach them. Macro-institutional proximity is closely linked to geographical proximity and shapes knowledge processes through established rules and values. Micro-institutional proximity appears linked to cognitive proximity and facilitates knowledge exchange by providing shared internal rules, incentives, solution strategies, and codes of conduct. It can to some extent compensate for macro-institutional proximity. Social and organizational proximity can serve as strong facilitators enabling efficient knowledge exchange by reducing risk, uncertainty, and opportunistic behavior.

Considering the understanding of sustainable innovations as transformative, system-wide changes that go beyond incremental technological novelties, and taking into account the diverse composition of the associated innovation networks with actors from different institutional domains (e.g., business, academia, government, and civil society), it is no surprise to find low levels of systems-cognitive proximity and low micro-institutional proximity. Effective mechanisms for addressing the challenges that arise from these low levels can be provided by either high social, high

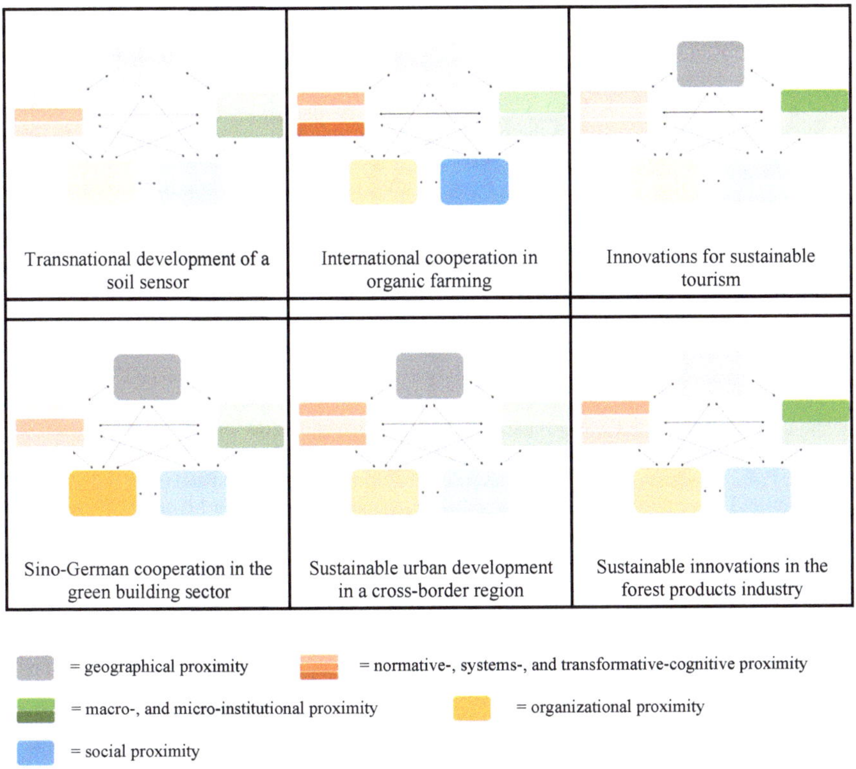

Fig. 7.6 Levels of the different proximity dimensions. *Note* Image taken from Wilke and Pyka (2024b). CC BY 4.0. No changes were made

organizational, high geographical, or high macro-institutional proximity (which is often linked to geographical proximity), or a combination thereof.

References

Abson, D. J., Fischer, J., Leventon, J., Newig, J., Schomerus, T., Vilsmaier, U., et al. (2017). Leverage points for sustainability transformation. *Ambio, 46*(1), 30–39.

Addy, N., & Dubé, L. (2018). Addressing complex societal problems: Enabling multiple dimensions of proximity to sustain partnerships for collective impact in Quebec. *Sustainability, 10*(4), 980.

Aguiléra, A., Lethiais, V., & Rallet, A. (2012). Spatial and non-spatial proximities in inter-firm relations: An empirical analysis. *Industry and Innovation, 19*(3), 187–202.

Akpo, E., Crane, T. A., Vissoh, P. V., & Tossou, R. C. (2015). Co-production of knowledge in multi-stakeholder processes: Analyzing joint experimentation as social learning. *Journal of Agricultural Education and Extension, 21*(4), 369–388. https://www.scopus.com/inward/record.uri?eid=2-s2.0-84938966306&doi=10.1080%2f1389224X.2014.939201&partnerID=40&md5=be43d9e514c5e6d1be9f094f87437c32.

Aldieri, L., Ioppolo, G., Vinci, C. P., & Yigitcanlar, T. (2019). Waste recycling patents and environmental innovations: An economic analysis of policy instruments in the USA, Japan and Europe. *Waste Management, 95*, 612–619.
Aldieri, L., Kotsemir, M., & Vinci, C. P. (2020). The role of environmental innovation through the technological proximity in the implementation of the sustainable development. *Business Strategy and the Environment, 29*(2), 493–502.
Ardito, L., Petruzzelli, A. M., Pascucci, F., & Peruffo, E. (2019). Inter-firm R&D collaborations and green innovation value: The role of family firms' involvement and the moderating effects of proximity dimensions. *Business Strategy and the Environment, 28*(1), 185–197.
Baek, J. S., Kim, S., & Harimoto, T. (2019). The effect of cultural differences on a distant collaboration for social innovation: A case study of designing for precision farming in Myanmar and South Korea. *Design and Culture, 11*(1, SI), 37–58.
Balland, P.-A. (2012). Proximity and the evolution of collaboration networks: Evidence from research and development projects within the global navigation satellite system (GNSS) industry. *Regional Studies, 46*(6), 741–756.
Balland, P.-A., Boschma, R., & Frenken, K. (2015). Proximity and innovation: From statics to dynamics. *Regional Studies, 49*(6), 907–920.
Balland, P.-A., Boschma, R., & Frenken, K. (2022). Proximity, innovation and networks: a concise review and some next steps. In A. Torre & D. Gallaud (Eds.), *Edward Elgar books. Handbook of proximity relations* (pp. 70–80). Edward Elgar Publishing.
Beaurain, C., & Dermine-Brullot, S. (2022). Industrial and territorial ecology: What types of proximity at work? In A. Torre & D. Gallaud (Eds.), *Edward Elgar books. Handbook of proximity relations* (pp. 384–396). Edward Elgar Publishing.
Bisseleua, D., Idrissou, L., Olurotimi, P., Ogunniyi, A., Mignouna, D., & Bamire, S. A. (2018). Multi-stakeholder process strengthens agricultural innovations and sustainable livelihoods of farmers in Southern Nigeria. *Journal of Agricultural Education and Extension, 24*(1), 29–49. https://www.scopus.com/inward/record.uri?eid=2-s2.0-85032832587&doi=10.1080%2f1389224X.2017.1392992&partnerID=40&md5=69d64c77313db12a24a15288c7d891a9
Bloise, C. (2020). Collaboration in a circular economy learning from the farmers to reduce food waste. *Journal of Enterprise Information Management, 33*(4, SI), 769–789.
Boschma, R. (2005). Proximity and innovation: A critical assessment. *Regional Studies, 39*(1), 61–74.
Bünger, A., & Schiller, D. (2022). Identification and characterization of potential change agents among agri-food producers: Regime, niche and hybrid actors. *Sustainability Science, 17*(6), 2187–2201.
Capello, R. (2014). Proximity and regional innovation processes: Is there space for new reflections? In A. Torre & F. Wallet (Eds.), *New horizons in regional science. Regional development and proximity relations* (pp. 163–194). Edward Elgar.
Capone, F., & Lazzeretti, L. (2018). The different roles of proximity in multiple informal network relationships: Evidence from the cluster of high technology applied to cultural goods in Tuscany. *Industry and Innovation, 25*(9), 897–917.
Cappellano, F., & Makkonen, T. (2020). The proximity Puzzle in cross-border regions. *Planning Practice & Research, 35*(3), 283–301.
Carayannis, E., & Campbell, D. (2010). Triple helix, Quadruple helix and Quintuple helix and how do Knowledge, Innovation and the Environment relate to Each other? a proposed framework for a trans-disciplinary analysis of sustainable development and social ecology. *International Journal of Social Ecology and Sustainable Development, 1*(1), 41–69. https://www.scopus.com/inward/record.uri?eid=2-s2.0-84864553399&doi=10.4018%2fjsesd.2010010105&partnerID=40&md5=5eb73922347c6a295357cd738c1d388d
Carrincazeaux, C., Lung, Y., & Vicente, J. (2008). The scientific trajectory of the french school of proximity: Interaction- and institution-based approaches to regional innovation systems. *European Planning Studies, 16*(5), 617–628.

Ceci, F., Lazoi, M., Lezzi, M., & Mohammad, H. (2021). Fostering knowledge sharing in the innovation process: Information and communication technology—Based versus face-to-face relationships. *Knowledge and Process Management, 28*(3), 302–316.
Coenen, L., Raven, R., & Verbong, G. (2010). Local niche experimentation in energy transitions: A theoretical and empirical exploration of proximity advantages and disadvantages. *Technology in Society, 32*(4), 295–302.
Crescenzi, R., Nathan, M., & Rodríguez-Pose, A. (2016). Do inventors talk to strangers? On proximity and collaborative knowledge creation. *Research Policy, 45*(1), 177–194.
Cunningham, S. W., & Werker, C. (2012). Proximity and collaboration in European nanotechnology. *Papers in Regional Science, 91*(4), 723–742.
Delgadillo, E., Reyes, T., & Baumgartner, R. J. (2021). Towards territorial product-service systems: A framework linking resources, networks and value creation. *Sustainable Production and Consumption, 28*, 1297–1313.
Dovey, K. (2009). The role of trust in innovation. *The Learning Organization, 16*(4), 311–325.
Dubois, A. (2019). Translocal practices and proximities in short quality food chains at the periphery: the case of North Swedish farmers. *Agriculture and Human Values, 36*(4, SI), 763–778.
Easterby-Smith, M., Lyles, M. A., & Tsang, E. W. K. (2008). Inter-organizational knowledge transfer: Current themes and future prospects. *Journal of Management Studies, 45*(4), 677–690.
Evans, J., & Karvonen, A. (2014). 'Give me a laboratory and I will lower your carbon footprint!'—Urban laboratories and the governance of low-carbon futures. *International Journal of Urban and Regional Research, 38*(2), 413–430.
Fritsch, M., & Schwirten, C. (1999). Enterprise-University Co-operation and the role of public research institutions in regional innovation systems. *Industry and Innovation, 6*(1), 69–83.
Gertler, M. S. (2003). Tacit knowledge and the economic geography of context, or The undefinable tacitness of being (there). *Journal of Economic Geography, 3*(1), 75–99.
Ghassim, B. (2018). Sustainability-oriented innovation in the minerals industry: An empirical study on the effect of non-geographical proximity dimensions. *Sustainability, 10*(2), 282.
Granovetter, M. (1985). Economic action and social structure: the problem of embeddedness. *American Journal of Sociology, 91*(3), 481–510.
Haas, R., Meixner, O., & Petz, M. (2016). Enabling community-powered co-innovation by connecting rural stakeholders with global knowledge brokers A case study from Nepal. *British Food Journal, 118*(6), 1350–1369.
Hansen, T. (2014). Juggling with proximity and distance: Collaborative innovation projects in the Danish cleantech industry. *Economic Geography, 90*(4), 375–402.
Hansen, T. (2015). Substitution or overlap? The relations between geographical and non-spatial proximity dimensions in collaborative innovation projects. *Regional Studies, 49*(10), 1672–1684.
Hansen, T., & Coenen, L. (2015). The geography of sustainability transitions: Review, synthesis and reflections on an emergent research field. *Environmental Innovation and Societal Transitions, 17*, 92–109.
Hardeman, S., Frenken, K., Nomaler, Ö., & ter Wal, A. L. J. (2015). Characterizing and comparing innovation systems by different 'modes' of knowledge production: A proximity approach. *Science and Public Policy, 42*(4), 530–548.
Hardwick, J., Anderson, A. R., & Cruickshank, D. (2013). Trust formation processes in innovative collaborations. *European Journal of Innovation Management, 16*(1), 4–21.
Heiskanen, E., & Lovio, R. (2010). User-producer interaction in housing energy innovations. *Journal of Industrial Ecology, 14*(1), 91–102. https://www.scopus.com/inward/record.uri?eid=2-s2.0-77954364479&doi=10.1111%2fj.1530-9290.2009.00196.x&partnerID=40&md5=5b64f38d46c4b0269aaf7db8739544a4
Hennart, J.-F. (1993). Explaining the Swollen Middle: Why most transactions are a Mix of "market" and "hierarchy." *Organization Science, 4*(4), 529–547.
Heringa, P. W., Horlings, E., van der Zouwen, M., van den Besselaar, P., & van Vierssen, W. (2014). How do dimensions of proximity relate to the outcomes of collaboration? A survey of

knowledge-intensive networks in the Dutch water sector. *Economics of Innovation and New Technology, 23*(7), 689–716.

Higuchi, Y., & Yamanaka, Y. (2017). Knowledge sharing between academic researchers and tourism practitioners: A Japanese study of the practical value of embeddedness, trust and co-creation. *Journal of Sustainable Tourism, 25*(10), 1456–1473.

Huber, F. (2012). On the role and interrelationship of spatial, social and cognitive proximity: Personal Knowledge relationships of R&D workers in the Cambridge information technology cluster. *Regional Studies, 46*(9), 1169–1182.

Ievoli, C., Belliggiano, A., Marandola, D., Milone, P., & Ventura, F. (2019). Information and communication infrastructures and new business models in rural areas: The case of Molise region in Italy. *European Countryside, 11*(4), 475–496.

Janssen, M. J., & Abbasiharofteh, M. (2022). Boundary spanning R&D collaboration: Key enabling technologies and missions as alleviators of proximity effects? *Technological Forecasting and Social Change, 180.*

Johnson, B., Müller, J., Gregersen, B., & Orozco, J. (2009). Pitfalls and opportunities in knowledge sharing: experiences from a research capacity building project in Central America. *International Journal of Technological Learning, Innovation and Development, 2*(4), 250–273. https://www.scopus.com/inward/record.uri?eid=2-s2.0-84897056348&doi=10.1504%2fIJTLID.2009.026817&partnerID=40&md5=25eb04d759600d092a235e1d3622ccd1

Kirat, T., & Lung, Y. (1999). Innovation and proximity. *European Urban and Regional Studies, 6*(1), 27–38.

Klenk, N. L., & Hickey, G. M. (2012). Improving the social robustness of research networks for sustainable natural resource management: Results of a Delphi study in Canada. *Science and Public Policy, 39*(3), 357–372. https://www.scopus.com/inward/record.uri?eid=2-s2.0-84871442822&doi=10.1093%2fscipol%2fscs024&partnerID=40&md5=bb6ba96108e54d21c582dd44da47aaaf

Knoben, J., & Oerlemans, L. (2006). Proximity and inter-organizational collaboration: A literature review. *International Journal of Management Reviews, 8*(2), 71–89.

Lopolito, A., Falcone, P. M., & Sica, E. (2022). The role of proximity in sustainability transitions: A technological niche evolution analysis. *Research Policy, 51*(3).

Malerba, F. (2002). Sectoral systems of innovation and production. *Research Policy, 31*(2), 247–264.

Marshall, A. (1920). *Principles of economics* (8th ed.). Macmillan.

Mattes, J. (2012). Dimensions of proximity and knowledge bases: Innovation between spatial and non-spatial factors. *Regional Studies, 46*(8), 1085–1099.

Mazzanti, M. (2018). Eco-innovation and sustainability: Dynamic trends, geography and policies. *Journal of Environmental Planning and Management, 61*(11), 1851–1860. https://www.scopus.com/inward/record.uri?eid=2-s2.0-85055419592&doi=10.1080%2f09640568.2018.1486290&partnerID=40&md5=14f8556d894a42be04285f021df037b8

McCauley, S. M., & Stephens, J. C. (2012). Green energy clusters and socio-technical transitions: Analysis of a sustainable energy cluster for regional economic development in Central Massachusetts, USA. *Sustainability Science, 7*(2), 213–225.

Moreno, R., & Miguélez, E. (2012). A relational approach to the geography of innovation: A typology of regions. *Journal of Economic Surveys, 26*(3), 492–516.

Morone, P., & Taylor, T. (2004). Knowledge diffusion dynamics and network properties of face-to-face interactions. *Journal of Evolutionary Economics, 14*(3), 327–351.

Nooteboom, B., van Haverbeke, W., Duysters, G., Gilsing, V., & van den Oord, A. (2007). Optimal cognitive distance and absorptive capacity. *Research Policy, 36*(7), 1016–1034.

Omobhude, C., & Chen, S.-H. (2019). The roles and measurements of proximity in sustained technology development: A literature review. *Sustainability, 11*(1).

Palmatier, R. W., Houston, M. B., & Hulland, J. (2018). Review articles: Purpose, process, and structure. *Journal of the Academy of Marketing Science, 46*(1), 1–5.

Polk, M. (2015). Transdisciplinary co-production: Designing and testing a transdisciplinary research framework for societal problem solving. *Futures, 65*, 110–122.

Ponds, R., van Oort, F., & Frenken, K. (2007). The geographical and institutional proximity of research collaboration. *Papers in Regional Science, 86*(3), 423–443.

Pyka, A., & Nelson, R. R. (2018). Schumpeterian competition and industrial dynamics. In R. R. Nelson, G. Dosi, C. E. Helfat, A. Pyka, S. G. Winter, P. P. Saviotti, et al. (Eds.), *Modern evolutionary economics. An overview* (pp. 104–128). Cambridge University Press.

Qiang, G., Cao, D., Wu, G., Zhao, X., & Zuo, J. (2021). Dynamics of collaborative networks for green building projects: Case study of Shanghai. *Journal of Management in Engineering, 37*(3).

Raven, R., Schot, J., & Berkhout, F. (2012). Space and scale in socio-technical transitions. *Environmental Innovation and Societal Transitions, 4*, 63–78.

Roux, D. J., Rogers, K. H., Biggs, H. C., Ashton, P. J., & Sergeant, A. (2006). Bridging the science-management divide: Moving from unidirectional knowledge transfer to knowledge interfacing and sharing. *Ecology and Society, 11*(1). http://www.ecologyandsociety.org/vol11/iss1/art4/

Royo-Vela, M., & Mazandarani, M.-R. (2022). Are non-special dimensions of proximity in local clusters related? An analysis of 99 European clusters. *Sustainability, 14*(20).

Shi, X., Huang, X., & Liu, H. (2022). Research on the structural features and influence mechanism of the low-carbon technology cooperation network based on temporal exponential random graph model. *Sustainability, 14*(19).

Storper, M., & Venables, A. J. (2004). Buzz: Face-to-face contact and the urban economy. *Journal of Economic Geography, 4*(4), 351–370.

Strambach, S. (2017). Combining knowledge bases in transnational sustainability innovation: Microdynamics and institutional change. *Economic Geography, 93*(5), 500–526. https://www.scopus.com/inward/record.uri?eid=2-s2.0-85030160222&doi=10.1080%2f00130095.2017.1366268&partnerID=40&md5=898772c879f5bad929c4fb7fc96e9b50

Sun, L., & Han, Y. (2022). Spatial correlation network structure and influencing factors of two-stage green innovation efficiency: Evidence from China. *Sustainability, 14*(18).

Tani, A., Lopolito, A., & Morone, P. (2021). Spatial perspectives on niche empowerment: An agent-based model. *Regional Studies, 55*(8), 1341–1353.

Thünen, J. H. von (1826). *Der isolirte Staat in Beziehung auf Landwirthschaft und Nationalökonomie*. Hamburg.

Torre, A., & Gilly, J.-P. (2000). On the analytical dimension of proximity dynamics. *Regional Studies, 34*(2), 169–180.

Tranfield, D., Denyer, D., & Smart, P. (2003). Towards a methodology for developing evidence-informed management knowledge by means of systematic review. *British Journal of Management, 14*(3), 207–222.

Valkering, P., Beumer, C., de Kraker, J., & Ruelle, C. (2013). An analysis of learning interactions in a cross-border network for sustainable urban neighbourhood development. *Journal of Cleaner Production, 49*, 85–94.

van Horne, C., & Dutot, V. (2017). Challenges in technology transfer: an actor perspective in a quadruple helix environment. *Journal of Technology Transfer, 42*(2, SI), 285–301.

Velenturf, A. P. (2016). Promoting industrial symbiosis: Empirical observations of low-carbon innovations in the Humber region, UK. *Journal of Cleaner Production, 128*, 116–130.

Velenturf, A. P., & Jensen, P. D. (2016). Promoting industrial symbiosis: Using the concept of proximity to explore social network development. *Journal of Industrial Ecology, 20*(4), 700–709.

Werker, C., Korzinov, V., & Cunningham, S. (2019). Formation and output of collaborations: The role of proximity in German nanotechnology. *Journal of Evolutionary Economics, 29*(2), 697–719.

Wiek, A., Ness, B., Schweizer-Ries, P., Brand, F. S., & Farioli, F. (2012). From complex systems analysis to transformational change: A comparative appraisal of sustainability science projects. *Sustainability Science, 7*(S1), 5–24.

Wilke, U., & Pyka, A. (2024a). Sustainable innovations, knowledge and the role of proximity: A systematic literature review. *Journal of Economic Surveys, 39*(1), 326–351.

Wilke, U., & Pyka, A. (2024b). Assessing the relevance of different proximity dimensions for knowledge exchange and (co-)creation in sustainability-oriented innovation networks. *Sustainability Science, 19*(4), 1427–1443.
Williamson, O. E. (1989). Transaction cost economics. In *Handbook of Industrial Organization. Handbook of Industrial Organization Volume 1* (Chapter 3, pp. 135–182). Elsevier.
Wuyts, S., Colombo, M. G., Dutta, S., & Nooteboom, B. (2005). Empirical tests of optimal cognitive distance. *Journal of Economic Behavior & Organization, 58*(2), 277–302.

Chapter 8
Conclusion

The study presented here contributes to innovation economics and sustainability science by shedding light on different aspects of knowledge processes occurring in multi-stakeholder networks that bear sustainable innovations. The analysis reveals insight into the relevant knowledge types and peculiarities regarding the associated knowledge processes. The development of a refined proximity framework proves a valuable tool for examining important aspects of actor relationships that shape knowledge (co)-creation and transfer and thus are highly relevant for the emergence of sustainable innovations and thereby help explain their occurrence.

8.1 Proximity in Knowledge Processes for Sustainable Innovations

Humanity faces the wicked problem of sustainability. Its normative nature, the complex interdependencies of its various economic, social, and environmental aspects, global cause-and-effect relations, and a long-time horizon imply no easy solution. The transformation toward sustainability requires fundamental changes in the current consumption and production patterns. Innovations appear as promising means for this purpose. New technologies, social innovations, and radical, systemic novelties can contribute to socially inclusive, resilient economic growth while reducing and ultimately avoiding negative environmental impacts.

Insights from the innovation system approach show that such sustainable innovations are created through the interaction of different actors, with knowledge playing a pivotal role, as the creation and exchange of knowledge lie at the center of every innovation process. Due to the complexity and normative nature of sustainability, the actors in networks bearing sustainable innovations must come from different areas, such as industry, academia, government, and civil society. The inclusion of different types of actors appears necessary for several reasons, which are connected

U. Wilke, *Towards Sustainable Innovations*, Economic Complexity and Evolution,
https://doi.org/10.1007/978-3-032-31024-8_8

to the central role of knowledge. Sustainability science provides insights into which kinds of knowledge are relevant for the transformation toward sustainability, namely normative, systemic, and transformative knowledge. These types of knowledge are widely dispersed among society. Sustainability science furthermore provides insights into the intricacies of the processes related to creating and transferring sustainability-related knowledge. Inter- and transdisciplinary approaches, orientation toward problems and solutions, use of experiments, learning by doing, and engagement of all relevant stakeholders are conducive to the creation, co-creation, and transfer of knowledge relevant for sustainable innovations.

The collaboration of heterogeneous actors from business, academia, government, and civil society is often connected to various challenges. The concept of proximity is useful for understanding such obstacles by providing an instrument for analyzing the framework conditions that influence the flows of knowledge between those actors. The study shows, that each of the five proximity dimensions can positively influence knowledge exchange and innovations in sustainability-oriented innovation networks, each through different mechanisms. The different dimensions furthermore show various interdependencies. They can reinforce each other, overlap, or substitute each other.

The findings regarding the relevant knowledge types and the specific features of the associated knowledge processes serve to refine an analytical proximity framework. This framework was used to analyze examples from the literature, showing that sustainability-focused innovation networks depict different combinations of high and low levels regarding the different proximity dimensions. A frequent combination is on the one hand low levels of systems-cognitive and micro-institutional proximity, and on the other hand high levels in other proximity dimensions. Notably, normative-cognitive proximity, and subsequently transformative-cognitive proximity, play a crucial role in this context. A shared vision regarding the positive outcomes of proposed innovations presumably enhances collaboration. But also, high geographical, macro-institutional, social, or organizational proximity can provide the necessary mechanisms that foster knowledge exchange and thus the creation of sustainable innovations, either by enabling direct face-to-face contact or by reducing uncertainty and the risk of opportunistic behavior.

The low levels of systems-cognitive and micro-institutional proximity are connected to the wide dispersion of sustainable knowledge, the importance of inter- and transdisciplinary approaches, and the broad inclusion of relevant stakeholders in knowledge creation and transfer. Experimental approaches such as living labs, or policy experiments are often linked to issues of geographical proximity. However, the effectiveness of such networks can be reduced if relevant knowledge from actors further away is excluded. Problem- and solution-oriented approaches for knowledge (co-)creation further highlight the necessity to have appropriately high levels of proximity. Partners from different institutional areas, such as higher education institutions, firms, government agencies, and non-profit organizations seek different kinds of knowledge. Firms are interested in economically feasible solutions for their day-to-day operations. Universities strive for scientific findings based on rigorous methods. Government agencies are interested in solutions that fit into the frame of legislation and public governance. Consumers and civil society value the applicability of knowledge and its potential to provide social and environmental benefits. In such cases, organizational, social, and geographic proximity can provide the basis for effective knowledge exchange, especially when there is a focus on specific problems and viable solutions.

8.2 Implications for Innovation Networks and Innovation Policy

The findings of this study offer insight into the actor constellations in sustainability-oriented innovation networks. These insights provide a valuable tool for businesses, government agencies, higher education institutions, and civil society groups when crafting innovation networks. Making a meaningful impact on sustainability goals requires creativity and the combination of diverse and complex knowledge, which is spread among different actor groups in society. This increases the uncertainty of innovation and underscores the necessity for close collaboration and coordination between heterogeneous actors. Taking into account various degrees of the different proximity dimensions is a strategy that, on the one hand, emphasizes the right amount of distance necessary for creativity and finding a new recombination of existing knowledge and thus the development of sustainable novelties. On the other hand, it underscores the importance of not allowing these distances to become too vast to maintain a shared foundation and mutual understanding for (co-)creating and exchanging knowledge. Overcoming greater distances in some proximity dimensions can be facilitated by ensuring closeness in other dimensions. Keeping this in mind when crafting strategies for establishing sustainability-oriented innovation networks has the potential to significantly enhance their overall success.

The refined proximity framework presented in this study and the insights it provides can serve as a valuable tool for identifying potential partners to integrate into existing innovation networks. Using the framework, established networks could evaluate whether the addition of a particular partner would facilitate knowledge exchange and increase the likeliness of innovations, or potentially introduce challenges, due to the new partner's relative proximity to other network members.

The findings of this study can furthermore prove useful for individual actors. Businesses can apply this knowledge to enhance their innovation and network management by strategically selecting partners with optimal levels of proximity to enhance the likelihood of successful collaborative innovation projects. Higher education institutions can identify suitable partners for transferring novel scientific findings into application. Civil society initiatives can utilize these insights to make strategic decisions about introducing their ideas and demands into the right networks. They can decide whether to collaborate with initiatives nearby or at an appropriate distance, or whether to engage businesses, universities, or government agencies in their initiatives.

The findings can furthermore inform innovation policies, enabling more effective promotion of sustainability-oriented innovation networks. One field of application would be the design of funding mechanisms for research and innovation projects. Many funding schemes of agencies such as the European Union (like the Horizon Europe program), or the German Federal Ministry of Education and Research already incorporate considerations about the composition of consortia applying for research funding. They often stipulate the inclusion of actors from different institutional spheres, mainly academia and business or other partners that will translate the findings of funded projects into their daily operations. However, there seems to be potential to further fine-tune the requirements regarding consortia composition. Regarding the importance of cognitive proximity and the high potential of cognitively diverse networks, research policy could consider implementing targeted measures to encourage cognitive diversity in existing partnerships (compare Werker et al., 2019). Especially the inclusion of consumers and civil society actors appears as a measurement that could prove fruitful.

Another area for research policy could be the encouragement of collaborations of regional initiatives with non-local stakeholders. The exchange of best practices between different (regional) projects within the frame of funding schemes is already a widely applied instrument. However, the question remains how effective this exchange is when it merely comes as a requirement in the frame of a funding agreement, and not as an established collaboration based on appropriate levels of proximity. In this regard, policy initiatives appear promising that aim at reducing information asymmetries and enhancing the network members' abilities to search for suitable non-local partners (compare Crescenzi et al., 2016). However, this could collide with the widespread emphasis on spatial clustering. Considering the complex interdependencies of the different proximity dimensions, policy initiatives must go beyond the well-known issue of providing info on potential partners, which should not be understood as down-playing the importance of helping innovative agents in finding partners with complementary knowledge, for example via specialized databases, fairs or brokerage events (see for example Cunningham & Werker, 2012).

Furthermore, political measurements that promote trust building between actors from different institutional spheres, but also between competing firms within the same industry, could help in establishing sustainability-oriented innovation networks by increasing social proximity. A similar approach could be instruments that provide low-threshold mechanisms for establishing loosely formal agreements to increase organizational proximity. Both kinds of instruments could work hand-in-hand due to the similar (and often complementary) working mechanisms of the two proximity dimensions.

8.3 Limitations and Avenues for Further Research

The study presented here has its limitations. One limitation stems from the intricate nature of sustainability, which is a concept that is laden with normative connotations and subject to diverse interpretations. Similarly, the multifaceted nature of knowledge and the systemic and evolutionary aspects of innovations pose challenges for every study examining these topics. As a result, a relatively strong simplification of certain aspects is unavoidable. This could lead to the criticism that the findings are highly descriptive, which is a widespread general criticism about the innovation system approach (Weber & Truffer, 2017). However, the narrow focus on specific aspects of knowledge, sustainability, and innovations appears nonetheless appropriate for deriving valuable insights that help in understanding the systemic and dynamic knowledge processes that lead to the emergence of sustainable innovations.

The methodological approach of this study has its limitations as well. The systematic literature reviews conducted in the course of this study have their restrictions. Like any systematic review, there is always the potential for overlooking a relevant paper, a risk that was mitigated by employing expansive search terms and conducting thorough citation snowballing to identify pertinent references. A further point is the methodological pluralism observed in the analyzed papers in the review regarding proximity and sustainable innovations.[1] It can be seen as an advantage, providing diverse perspectives on the subject from various angles. However, the challenge lies in comparing this multitude of approaches, as it introduces differences in definitions, operationalizations, and measurement methods, and consequently, a certain level of conceptual ambiguity and slight variations in the precise meanings of the underlying concepts.

Another shortcoming concerns the application of the refined proximity framework in Sect. 7.5. It stems from the limited number of literature examples used to draw conclusions regarding the applicability of the framework and the prevalent combinations of various proximity dimensions in sustainability-oriented innovation networks and thus limits the extent to which some of the findings can be generalized (especially regarding the overall prevalence of specific levels of the different proximity dimensions). Nevertheless, incorporating a larger number of examples would have surpassed the intended scope of this study, and the selected cases did provide the ground for comprehensive conclusions. To address this issue, a quantitative approach could represent the next step to assess and validate the findings of this study, investigating the essential criteria concerning combinations of proximity dimensions that enable knowledge exchange and the development of sustainable innovations within multi-actor networks.

Linked to this shortcoming is another limitation: The findings indicate that normative-cognitive proximity, and subsequently, transformative-cognitive proximity, are especially important for the occurrence of sustainable innovations. That means that a shared vision regarding the positive impacts of the intended innovations significantly eases collaboration. However, the findings of the study allow no definite

---

[1] See Sect. 7.4.

assertion regarding whether this alone is adequate for innovation networks to achieve anticipated results. All analyzed examples reporting successful innovations exhibit high levels of proximity in at least two dimensions. Therefore, it may be imperative to also maintain a high level in another proximity dimension.

A detailed inquiry into questions regarding necessary and sufficient levels of the different proximity dimensions should constitute the next steps of a research agenda dealing with this topic. A quantitative approach appears promising in this regard, but also further qualitative in-depth case studies could provide further insights. The in-depth case studies could help better understand the working mechanisms of each proximity dimension while providing additional examples of proximity combinations that allow for effective knowledge exchange. Especially cognitive proximity seems to be worthy of further detailed investigations regarding its cause and effect mechanisms, due to the central role of this dimension. A quantitative investigation, on the other hand, based on a large number of cases, could help to identify the prevalence of the different combinations and whether there exists some kind of proximity threshold or minimal proximity levels that have to be reached to make knowledge exchange and collaborative innovations happen.

Another interesting avenue for further research concerns the question of whether there are differences related to the knowledge type being transferred. For instance, are specific proximity dimensions more conducive to the exchange of tacit knowledge compared to the exchange of codified knowledge? Are there differences between normative, systemic, and transformative knowledge? An argument in this direction is provided by Mattes (2012), who states that strongly codified knowledge generally requires lower levels of proximity compared to more tacit forms of knowledge. Davids and Frenken (2018) argue in a similar direction. They distinguish between analytical, synthetic, and symbolic knowledge, and state that for each of these knowledge types, different proximity dimensions are relatively more or less important. Hence, a closer look at the specific types of knowledge being co-created or transferred could prove to be interesting.

References

Crescenzi, R., Nathan, M., & Rodríguez-Pose, A. (2016). Do inventors talk to strangers? On proximity and collaborative knowledge creation. *Research Policy, 45*(1), 177–194.

Cunningham, S. W., & Werker, C. (2012). Proximity and collaboration in European nanotechnology. *Papers in Regional Science, 91*(4), 723–742.

Davids, M., & Frenken, K. (2018). Proximity, knowledge base and the innovation process: Towards an integrated framework. *Regional Studies, 52*(1), 23–34.

Mattes, J. (2012). Dimensions of proximity and knowledge bases: Innovation between spatial and non-spatial factors. *Regional Studies, 46*(8), 1085–1099.

Weber, K. M., & Truffer, B. (2017). Moving innovation systems research to the next level: Towards an integrative agenda. *Oxford Review of Economic Policy, 33*(1), 101–121.

Werker, C., Korzinov, V., & Cunningham, S. (2019). Formation and output of collaborations: The role of proximity in German nanotechnology. *Journal of Evolutionary Economics, 29*(2), 697–719.

MIX
Papier aus verantwortungsvollen Quellen
Paper from responsible sources
FSC® C105338

If you have any concerns about our products,
you can contact us on
ProductSafety@springernature.com

In case Publisher is established outside the EU,
the EU authorized representative is:
Springer Nature Customer Service Center GmbH
Europaplatz 3, 69115 Heidelberg, Germany

Printed by Libri Plureos GmbH
in Hamburg, Germany